THE KLONDYKERS
THE OILMEN ONSHORE

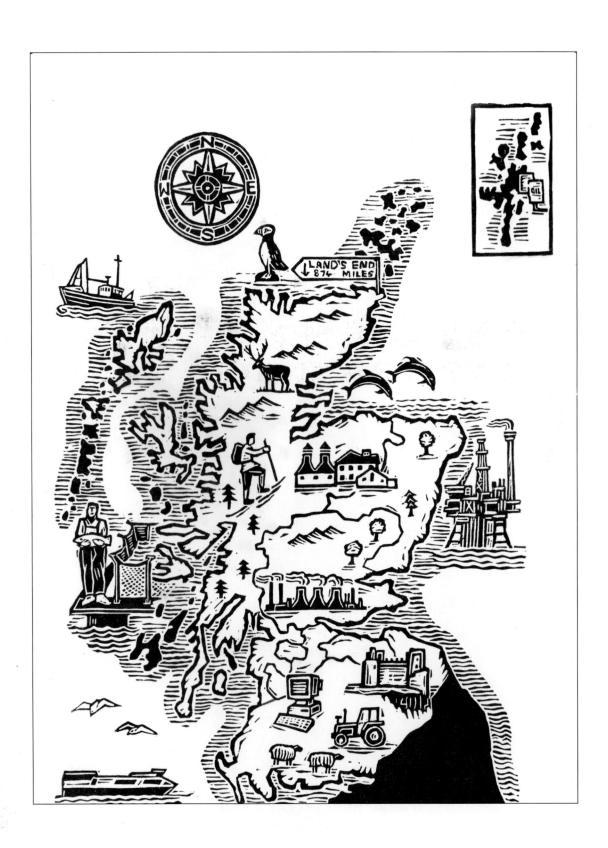

BILL MACKIE

THE KLONDYKERS
THE OILMEN ONSHORE

BIRLINN

Plate 1.

(*Page 2*) Scotland in 1970
on the cusp of the North
Sea oil and gas bonanza
with the discovery of
BP's Forties field.
(*Boxtree Creative*)

First published in 2006 by
Birlinn Limited
West Newington House
10 Newington Road
Edinburgh
EH9 1QS

www.birlinn.co.uk

ISBN 10: 1 84158 359 6
ISBN 13:978 1 84158 359 4

British Library Cataloguing-in-Publication Data
A catalogue record for this book is available
from the British Library

Layout and page make up: Mark Blackadder

Printed and bound by GraphyCems, Spain

Contents

To my understanding and supportive family

Acknowledgements

When I began three years ago researching a book on the history of the North Sea oil and gas industry I intended to cover the whole of this remarkable human and technological endeavour in one volume. However, after spending time at the deserted locations of the former oil fabrication yards in the Highlands, I realised that there were in fact two books, dividing neatly into one on the offshore sector, which became *The Oilmen: The North Sea Tigers*, and another on the onshore developments. I am grateful to a large number of people up and down the coasts of Scotland for opening my eyes to the heroic scale of what has been happening 'on the beach' over the past forty years. I believe it is as romantic a yarn as the hunting and harvesting of fossil fuels out in the dangerous North Sea. The onshore oil people from the yards and communities at Ardersier, Nigg, Kishorn, Amish, Methil and Burntisland – who told the tales and had the pictures to prove them – are too numerous to mention, as are the helpful folk from the bases and terminals at Dundee, Montrose, Aberdeen, Peterhead, Fraserburgh, St Fergus, Orkney and Shetland; they know who they are and I want to thank them all.

For this second book I have unashamedly plundered material from my doctoral thesis. *The impact of North Sea oil on the North East of Scotland – 1969/2000* (University of Aberdeen, 2001), and I am grateful to the politicians, businessmen, industrialists, trade unionists, civil servants, economists and civic leaders who gave generously of their time in the late 1990s for the interviews recorded in the thesis, which I have quoted in *Onshore Oilmen*. Sadly some are now no longer with us but all their contemporary views and opinions about those early frantic and chaotic times are a valuable contribution to the history of the industry in Scotland.

I also want to thank the staff of the National Archives of Scotland in Edinburgh, for permitting me to analyse the sealed papers, letters and memoranda produced by the former Scottish Industry and Scottish Development departments of the Scottish Office, relating to the advent of oil,

THE KLONDYKERS

long before the Freedom of Information legislation opened all doors. The documents, for 1972–75 (ref. Sep. 1: 627/687; Sep. 4: 2473/74/75/76/77, 2487/88, 2521), are records of meetings held by a plethora of specially appointed Government committees and task forces and reveal a fascinating insight into the political thinking and reactions of the day.

The staff of a number of community libraries in Lerwick, Kirkwall, Highland in Inverness, Fraserburgh and Peterhead and the Heritage centres at Methil, Burntisland and Kirkcaldy were also of great assistance in digging out the early information about local events and developments. I also want to thank the public affairs departments of a number of the leading oil companies and contractors who provided the basic details of their various operations.

The first book celebrated the courage of the offshore pioneers. This book is an attempt to give the onshore folk due credit for an equally colossal achievement; quite simply, without their memories there would be no book.

Bill Mackie, Aberdeen, 2006

Picture Credits

Researching this book yielded a large amount of photographs, notably from the oil construction period. One collection now preserved on CD and held by the community at Kishorn is a marvellous photographic record that portrays the development of the Howard Doris yard and the growth of the Ninian Central platform and I am grateful to the people who hold it in trust for allowing me to use some of the pictures. Many of the prints, which had been saved privately, have no copyright markings and the photographers are unknown and I have been unable to credit them.

Another major difficulty is that many of the businesses involved have changed hands several times and there is either doubt about ownership of the images or the photographic records were simply discarded. I would like to thank the following, however, for permission to use their photographs: Orkney and Shetland Museums, Aberdeen City Archives, Aberdeen Harbour Board, Dundee Harbour Board, Fife Council Museums, John Wood Group, Talisman Energy, Total, BiFab, Shell, BP, Van Weminck Studios, Ian Y MacIntyre, Dennis Coutts, Aberdeen Journals Ltd and DC Thomson Ltd.

A special thank-you also goes to Dennis Davidson of Roustabout Publications for rooting out some of the historic pictures from the files of his valuable magazine and to Nigel Martin, who performed the same service from his archives on Sullom Voe. I would never have found the majority of the original images in the book without the tireless research of my good friend and colleague Bert Ovenstone and I am grateful for his work. I also want to congratulate my son-in-law, Allan Montgomery, who contributed all of the new photographs depicting some of the key locations as they are today, and to thank John Doyle, of Boxtree Creative, who designed the distinctive graphics and illustrations.

Preface

From the highway tracking the shoreline of the Cromarty Firth on the eastern seaboard of the Scottish Highlands, more than a score of steel giants, idling in the dappled waters, could be seen gradually emerging through the hazy early morning autumn sunshine: exploration rigs, the frontline hardware in the endless hunt for oil and gas, marooned by a periodic downturn in the cyclical international drilling industry, recalled from scouring the beds of the North Sea and the Atlantic Frontier for the next generation of oil discoveries.

Beyond the 15-mile parade of weatherworn structures, at the gateway to the open sea, two vast deserted oil fabrication yards, once bitter rivals, still confront each other over two firths; on across the face of the mountainous Highlands to Wester Ross, in the shadow of the Applecross Range, overlooking the sea lochs Carron and Kishorn, a great gaping chasm torn out of the hillside was once the birthplace of the largest man-made floating structure on earth; on again, round the rim of Scotland and the islands, at Arnish Point in Lewis in the west, at Ardyne, Portavadie, Hunterston in the south, and across on the east coast at Fife and Methil are abandoned frontier outposts of an industry that flourished and then disappeared within three short decades. Only Burntisland remains active; the others exist as a sobering testament to the ephemeral nature of the oil and gas industry.

There have been other ominous harbingers of an uncertain future. In 1986–87 and 1998–2001 came two seismic shocks that frightened the industry: the great oil-price crashes that brought new exploration and development to a halt, ravaging communities, employment and oil-related businesses and forcing brutal financial changes. All the indications now are that the industry is cannily reinventing itself, braced for a new and very different era. But the deserted yards and the recessions were stark intimations of mortality. They not only gave Scotland an unwelcome foretaste of a world without the uninvited wealth-creating leviathan of the oil and gas industry, they also revealed just how deeply it is embedded in every aspect of daily life –

Plate 2.

'A score of steel giants idling in the dappled waters' – oil rigs stacked in the Cromarty Firth during one of the periodic industry downturns. (*Fitzpatrick Photography*)

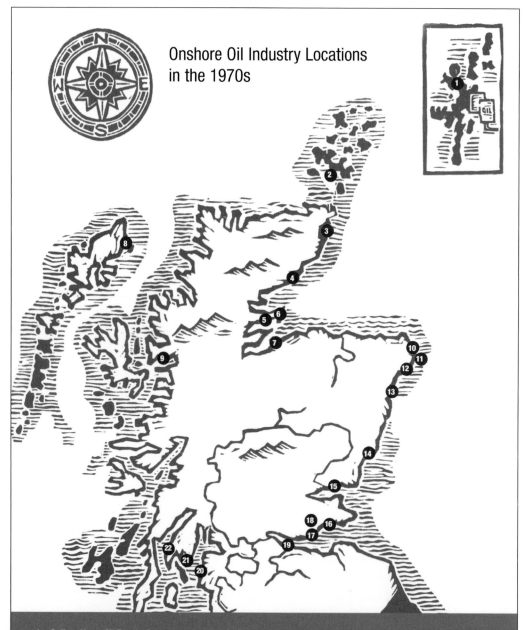

Onshore Oil Industry Locations in the 1970s

1 Sullom Voe – Oil Terminal
2 Flotta – Oil Terminal
3 Wick – Service Base
4 Brora – Service Base
   Pipeline Landing
5 Invergordon – Service &
   Maintenance
6 Nigg – Fabrication Yard
7 Ardersier – Former Fabrication
   Yard

8 Arnish (Stornoway) –
   Fabrication Yard
9 Loch Kishorn –
   Fabrication Yard
10 St Fergus – Gas Terminal
11 Peterhead – Service Base
12 Cruden Bay – Pipeline Landing
13 Aberdeen – Industry Centre
14 Montrose – Service & Training
15 Dundee – Service base

16 Methil (Fife) –
   Fabrication Yard
17 Burntisland (Fife) –
   Sole Fabrication Yard
18 Mossmorran – Gas Processing
   Plants
19 Grangemouth Oil & Gas Refinery
20 Hunterston – Fabrication Yard
21 Ardyne Point – Fabrication Yard
22 Port Avadie – Fabrication Yard

so all-pervasive that after more than thirty years scarcely a family in the oil-related areas now remains uninvolved.

This second of two books on the North Sea industry focuses on the history of the onshore invasion, told through the recollections of the innocent and wholly ignorant, who had to embrace an oil rush that from its beginnings was as thrilling and tumultuous as any nineteenth-century Klondyke.

What happened was far beyond the industrial experience of Scots, let alone the naïve coastal communities. This was instant industry, arriving unsolicited on a gigantic scale. As the pace began to quicken, inexperienced local authorities in the scatter of seaboard mainland and island communities found themselves under huge pressures from two fronts: the powerful international corporations accustomed to control, and national politicians, who were in an undue hurry to reap the financial harvest that would solve the country's economic ills.

This is an account of the business opportunity of the century, hailed as the dawn of a new industrial revolution, yet scorned by so many Scottish entrepreneurs; of a clash of cultures, an unprecedented onslaught on fragile, neglected areas of the Highlands and Islands and all the rest of the communities touched by oil and gas: Shetland and Orkney, Buchan and, at the centre of it all, the city of Aberdeen. Above all, this is the story, in the idiom of the industry, of the people 'on the beach' – among them the women, wives and partners – who made it all possible.

Plate 3.
The 1970s and the heyday
of Scotland's onshore oil
and gas industry.
(*Boxtree Creative*)

The Death of Aul' Torry

1

The elderly woman and her dog stood amidst the rubble and dust outside 9 Fore Close, Old Torry, the cottage that had been her home for twenty-one years. Of the 350 people who had lived in the tiny old fishing village that had become part of Aberdeen, Mrs Charlotte Simpson was the last to leave. She had been one of three objectors at an inquiry into a proposal to raze the houses to the ground and build a service base for the giant international oil company Shell. The council gave her a new house, as well as £3,000 and £150 disturbance allowance. 'But it is not the same. I lived here most of my married life. Now it is gone.'

This sacrificial offering to the oil industry of the settlement at the mouth of the River Dee, in 1974, bears all the hallmarks of classic historical encounters which pit big business against a small community. 'Perhaps the only place where we could have been described as having been steamrollered was Aul' Torry,' admits Lord Kirkhill, a former local councillor. 'The point was that we were certainly going to have to do something about it if we were going to take in the oil.'

Throughout the early onslaught of onshore development the potentially harmful effects on the unique way of life in the North-East were a constant source of concern in the community. In the first major television programme on North Sea oil, *What Price Oil?* (Grampian Television 1973), Professor Kenneth Walton, from the University of Aberdeen's geography department, encapsulated the region's fears: 'What I am more worried about is where people really come into the equation. If we are not very careful we are going to lose the social cohesion that has held the North-East of Scotland together for so long. We can build roads, we can build housing, we can build a gas terminal, we can lay pipe in the North Sea. I don't think we are capable of planning efficiently far ahead on a timescale that will have to be judged in social terms. Otherwise, I think it will be like the notice the wag put up on the outskirts of Seattle, "Will the last person to leave Peterhead please turn out the lights."'

As the planners struggled to find the means of accommodating the

Plate 3.

Defiant to the end – the last resident of the village of Old Torry, Mrs Charlotte Simpson, confronts the giant demolition machine amid the debris of her home. (*Aberdeen Journals Ltd*)

aggressive newcomers, the communities of the North-East and their leaders were fully aware that they were poised on the brink of the unknown. The battle lines were becoming clearer at the opening of the 1970s across the areas where oil was beginning to impinge: the politicians manoeuvring to formulate policies to deal with this unexpected windfall; the businessmen and industrialists threatened by the effects on wages and on labour; the 'closed shop' cartel maintained by the foreign oil companies; the local entrepreneurs urging others to seize the exciting new prospects; the trade union leaders bent on controlling conditions and the flow of work; the environmentalists and conservationists, convinced they had already been victorious in one planning dispute (see Chapter 8), but anxious to forestall any future damage; the academics with social and economic blueprints; and the spiritual leaders concerned about the social and moral impact.

In contrast the incomers – the oil companies, contractors and onshore developers – were largely emollient, swift to reassure and persuade of the bounties, but relentlessly resolved to prevail in their raison d'être: to produce the oil and gas, bring them onshore and release the revenue stream as quickly and with as little opposition as possible. From whatever standpoint, there was also an awareness and acceptance, once the unprecedented scale of the venture was realised, that the daily existence in the oil communities could never be the same again. There is little doubt that three years into the industry's arrival, the social fabric was already straining under the sustained pressure. In some cases, rightly or wrongly, it simply had to give way. No single episode illustrated that more than the demise of Old Torry.

During the early days of exploration in the northern North Sea, Shell Expro had leased a 1-acre plot from Aberdeen Harbour Board in 1965 on an old fish quay on the south bank at the mouth of the River Dee. On the site, accessible at all tides, there was a shed and a crane. The five-year lease was regarded at the time as a multi-million pound gamble. Harbour Board manager Norman Beattie was optimistic. 'If the company are successful in their search from Aberdeen . . . that might influence developers to make use of the port for operations on a larger scale.' Once the company proved the commercial existence of oil in 1971 and larger supply ships came looking for dock space, it was obvious the site was too limiting. They then began considering extending another 3.6 acres into the area occupied by the centuries-old fishing hamlet of Old Torry.

The little settlement, first mentioned in an account of a Viking raid in the twelfth century, was one of the original cluster of communities which eventually formed Aberdeen. With its close-knit families, Old Torry had been noted in the nineteenth century for devising the technique of great-line fishing

Plate 4.

The tiny historic fishing
hamlet of Old Torry (on
the left) at the turn of the
century, rows of sturdy
cottages offset to the
weather and the sea.
(*Aberdeen City Archives*)

on distant water grounds. But the line fishing ended in the 1960s and,
gradually, the lanes of little cottages fell into disrepair as the wider community
spread up the hill to New Torry. The old village, in the 1970s, remained a
warm and friendly place.

Before oil the idea was actually to revitalise the wee community. In a
special council report in 1970, the City Architect proposed restoring the
village using housing grants. Householders applied and began to spend money
improving their homes. One year later, the council abandoned the preservation
plans on the recommendation of their Special (Industrial Development)
Committee, who proposed the site be rezoned for industrial use and allocated
to an oil company. A writer in the *Sunday Times* quoted the campaigning
Progressive Group town councillor, Frank Magee: 'The reason for the village's
death sentence is oil. The damned stuff has simply mesmerised them.'

Shell Expro had actually made the application at the invitation of the
council to expand their Torry base. But the people of Old Torry were
outraged. 'God knows what will become of us,' said one. 'It'll be hard,' said
another. 'Our way of life is at an end.' 'There's only a handful of us. Oil
means money.' One of their ward councillors appeared to be less concerned:
'There is nothing in the area considered worth preserving as buildings,'
claimed Baillie Ellen Williamson. 'We have been taking people out of there.
We are not sacrificing anything.'

Persuaded by Lord Provost John Smith (now Lord Kirkhill), another of
Torry's three Labour representatives, the council chose to rezone the area for
oil development. Smith told them, 'The area is no longer suitable for the best

practice of restoration . . . Industrial activity has outstripped the architects'
plans.' They voted by thirty-one votes to three to apply for a compulsory
purchase order, rezone the village and lease it to Shell. Three objectors
petitioned against the order, triggering a public inquiry. Among them was the
Ailsa Craig Fishing Company. Faced with vacating their premises, they asked
the hearing 'Are we to be removed from our property for something that
might last only ten years?'

A year later in November 1972, despite other petitions, the chairman of
the two-day hearing recommended the order be confirmed, which the Scottish
Secretary duly did in 1973. John Smith recalled twenty years later, 'I started
off having doubts, but I must say I was persuaded by the majority. We just
couldn't get the grants to sustain the housing.' However, it is more likely that
the ultimatum issued by Shell's Aberdeen manager, Fred Chate, was what
swayed the authorities. Chate told the inquiry, 'If facilities at Old Torry are
not made available, we will have to look elsewhere. If Aberdeen cannot
provide the facilities Shell UK need, we will look elsewhere.' He also affirmed
his company's commitment to the industry. 'Exploration will last ten to twenty
years and we have negotiated a thirty-one-year lease for the site.' Seven
months later, as if to reinforce the absolute primacy of the oil industry, the
Harbour Board ordered the fleet of small fishing and pleasure boats to leave
their traditional berths in Torry Basin to make way for service vessels.

The previously unrevealed machinations of the oilmen, politicians and

Plate 6.

Aberdeen Harbour in the
1950s. (*Aberdeen City
Archives*)

officials which resulted in Old Torry being razed to the ground to make way
for Shell are found in the confidential letters, memoranda and minutes in the
closed 1971 files of the Scottish Industry Department (SID) at the Scottish
Office in Edinburgh. They were far more Byzantine than any details made
public. It was also one of the first indications of the kind of commercial and
political leverage that Shell, and eventually other majors such as BP, were
prepared to wield in their new oil 'fiefdoms'.

The affair began earlier, in 1971, when Aberdeen Harbour Board, who
operate the port, were forced to inform BP they would be unable to
accommodate even the company's minimal demands for sizable wharfage and
facilities. The key requirement was the capacity to berth in tidal waters. At
that time, the main commercial docks were both enclosed.

BP told the Department of Trade and Industry (DTI) they also had other
concerns. In a letter to St Andrews House, the DTI said the oil company had
been warned by their local staff about 'certain regulations and practices within
the port of Aberdeen'. In other words, the influence of the powerful harbour
unions. The letter added, 'Another North-East Scottish port authority has
drawn attention to facilities that could be offered by its harbour . . . to meet
BP's prerequisites but is further in sea distance than Aberdeen from the Forties
Field.' The other authority was Dundee, and in May BP decided to locate their
marine base on the Tay (see Chapter 5).

That June the North-East Scotland Development Authority (NESDA) set up the first open encounter between the principal oil contractors and service companies, banks, commercial interests, local authorities and Scottish Office representatives. The intent was to iron out any initial problems involved in absorbing this new and unknown industry. From an account of the meeting by a representative of the SID, it's obvious that the shortcomings of the harbour were perceived as a serious handicap to the oil-related traffic beginning to dominate the port. Maitland Mackie, chairman of NESDA and a prominent local politician and businessman, acknowledged there had been 'disappointment that BP had chosen Dundee'. The SID observer commented, 'Aberdeen City Council appear acutely aware that they have no control of the docks and, along with NESDA, they will probably press for action if they feel more development work should be put in hand.'

John Russell, chief executive of NESDA, followed up with a letter to the Harbour Board. In his reply Norman Beattie, Board manager, detailed the problems they faced, principally the shortage and unavailability of land. He said the oil inquirers had complained that the council's administrative machinery was cumbersome and slow. He also described one particular

Plate 7.

The dock gates that enclosed Aberdeen's inner commercial harbour.
(*Aberdeen Harbour Board*)

situation in Torry where land was being used for housing, although most of the buildings appeared to be substandard. He had asked the town clerk if the land could instead be made available for harbour development. 'If the Harbour Board cannot obtain control, one of the major oil companies, which wishes to develop on a major scale, may be obliged to move to another port. The Corporation are reported as intending to redevelop the whole area for housing. If this is true the consequences in terms of trade will be disastrous.' The company was, of course, Shell, and the land in question, the village of Old Torry. Russell told Beattie he had already written to the town council about Old Torry, while Maitland Mackie had also contacted a powerful civil servant, JH McGuinness, chairman of the Scottish Economic Council, of which the NESDA chairman was also a member. McGuinness agreed to visit Aberdeen in August to talk to the Council and the Harbour Board. He was accompanied by Tom Lister, assistant secretary to the Scottish Development Department. Following the visit, a letter from Lister to Russell encapsulates the Government's view about accommodating the oil companies' demands. He said he was arranging an informal chat with the town clerk about the Torry area. 'This is the Shell area and Shell are the present customers. This is a big factor, because the Department of the Environment, especially in the present climate, are particularly anxious that any improvement schemes put forward should be as hard-headed and as practical as possible and there is no better way of convincing them of this than by having an actual customer lined up ready to use the facilities. It might well be that Shell would be ready to finance them.'

The reason Lister was so anxious to 'chat' to the town clerk, JFV Hunter, was revealed in an interdepartmental memorandum about the meeting between all the parties. It was obvious there was a history of difficulties between the town council and the Harbour Board (although two councillors sat on the Board). Both were embroiled in a legal dispute over fish market rates. Lister told Hunter, 'The Secretary of State has received discouraging reports from NESDA about the arrangements being made to enable Aberdeen Harbour Board to service the oil industry. He regards the matter as one of considerable importance to the country and he is interested to learn in what light the Corporation is regarding it.' A later note showed where the Development Department stood in the dispute. 'Our role is only that of a broker trying to break down barriers in communications and the less said about that the better. The town council in particular is unlikely to react favourably to any impression of breathing down their necks.' The question of conservation had arisen, and Mr Beattie had told the civil servants there were some 'quaint' alleys which some people (not including himself) felt should be

Plate 8.

Old Torry razed to the ground. 'The reason for the village's death sentence is oil. The damned stuff has simply mesmerised them.' (*Aberdeen City Archives*)

preserved. Indeed, he noted having been able to buy up and bulldoze to the ground several other properties of this type near the harbour before they were listed as being of historic or architectural interest.

When the Board and the Town Council officials finally met to decide about Old Torry, with the Scottish Office observers, only the city architect registered his concern at the loss of 'an attractive village preservation scheme'. The council officials agreed that Mr Beattie had a 'good case'. At a private meeting with Shell on 29 September, the council's special (industrial) development committee agreed to use the compulsory purchase procedure to accelerate acquisition, and to drop the previous preservation order; Old Torry would be rezoned for industry.

One of the residents, Mrs Elizabeth Finlayson, has never forgotten those times. 'The Torry people were helpless against the giant oil companies. Gradually the houses were vacated and as each family moved out, for the most part unwillingly, the windows were boarded up, the doors securely padlocked. House after house was emptied until Old Torry resembled a ghost

Plate 9.

The site of the old village
– now a storage area for
the oil and gas industry.
(*Allan Montgomery*)

city.' Old Torry was demolished. The pragmatic view is that the residents were rehoused in, or found, modern homes with all the amenities that many of the dilapidated houses lacked. The nostalgic view is that an historic part of Aberdeen was lost for ever. It could also be said, however, that similar conditions applied to Aberdeen's other historic fishing village, which sits on the north side of the mouth of the Dee. Footdee or Fittie had been home to fishermen for many centuries – just like Old Torry. Similarly, it had been rebuilt in the nineteenth century, and its picturesque squares were designated a conservation area in 1968. Footdee was also marked by the city architect for improvement at the same council meeting in 1970 when the first conservation report on Old Torry was produced. Fittie survived, however, and prospered as a community and as a quaint tourist attraction. According to local historian Diane Morgan, in her book *The Villages of Aberdeen: Footdee* (1993), 'It was generally agreed that conservation measures had come to the Fittie Squares in the nick of time. [But] the sectors of the oil-related industry that required considerable wharfage and storage space were creeping nearer the village.' The razing of Old Torry was 'a dire warning from across the water'. By then a number of silos containing mud from oil drilling were situated at Pocra Quay, just behind Footdee. In 1992, the mud company applied to build 15 more silos, some of them 50 feet high. At a packed public meeting residents unanimously opposed the plan and it was subsequently rejected. Morgan believes that 'Lessons had been learned since the days of the Old Torry clearance, which is now regarded as a panic decision'.

The fact that the council were prepared, in the case of Old Torry, to sever

Plate 10.

Old Torry's neighbour
across the Dee – Footdee
preserved as a living
tourist attraction.
(*Allan Montgomery*)

a centuries-old link with Aberdeen's primary marine industry to make way for the city's newest marine industry was the first and most potent demonstration of the overwhelming power of international oil. Lord Kirkhill now believes the council were 'steamrollered', but at the time he could not see any other option for a city desperate for new industry and jobs. As he told the planning inquiry, 'The prospect for oil generally in the Aberdeen area is a long-term one and tremendous economic advantage would accrue to the city. It is the responsibility of the town council to encourage oil interests in so far as it is consistent with the protection of the environment of the area.' A present-day Conservative councillor, John Porter, takes a similar view: 'There was a price to pay for the huge development in the harbour area when we lost Auld Torry and that was a shame – but it was quid pro quo. We kept Fittie and there were a lot of other things we managed to keep.'

Oil service magnate Sir Ian Wood, whose fishing family originated from the south side of the Dee, concedes that the demolition of Old Torry was a tragedy in one way but believes that in another it was a crucial stage in the development of Aberdeen as an oil base: 'Shell's was the core development. The other companies formed up around it. Without it, there is little doubt that the whole onshore operation would have moved elsewhere.'

Elizabeth Finalyson, now aged ninety-two and a writer of local books, had the last word on the subject in 1992. 'I did not visit Old Torry again until a few weeks ago. It was difficult to believe it had once been home to so many people. The harbour area where our house stood is now occupied by oil tanks and, for the most part, by oil-related business premises. Still, Old Torry lives on in the memories of the older generation – a sacrifice to oil. We shall not forget.'

Cosy Corner

2

Aberdeen: the 'Cosy Corner', a city of 'prim, well-heeled complacency' opting out of the opportunities of expansion, 'full of rich tea planters' elderly spinster daughters living off safe investments', with higher savings than any other Scottish city, a tourist and service town 'stuffed with lawyers, accountants, bankers and insurance agents; this wealth in total contrast to the fact that one third of the workforce were existing on low wages while the city continued to lose its population and export its skills as it had always done.'

This devastating critique of the Granite City in the early 1960s in the authoritative publication *The Economist* was deliberately provocative. Written by a North-East woman, well primed with ammunition by a caucus of concerned insiders, the acerbic article's intent was to galvanise a community with so much to offer from a stupefying torpor that in reality masked a steady economic decline. With remarkable but unconscious prescience, she forecast that within twenty years 'the social services, education and environment of which it is so proud could well become the ideal basis for one of Scotland's new concentrations of population and industry'. No new significant employer had set up in the city since the war, she wrote, because of a notable reluctance to make prospective newcomers welcome, especially by local businessmen who operated a wage rate cartel. The president of Aberdeen Chamber of Commerce, JC Williamson, was quoted as saying in a Grampian Television interview 'Let industry come to the North-East – but not here.'

The trenchant 'Cosy Corner' attack struck a raw nerve and the city hierarchy was suitably outraged, but was the criticism accurate? More than thirty years later, the leaders of the two key local authorities in the 1960s adopted opposing views. Sir Maitland Mackie, former convener of Aberdeenshire County Council, preferred to regard the prevailing economic health of the 1960s as 'stable'. 'We were comfortable then, there were no great hardships and it was possible to make a living. Farming was going through change, fishing was also changing, but society was much more stable.' His civic equivalent, Aberdeen's lord provost at the time, Robert Lennox, a left-wing trade unionist, was of a totally different opinion. 'The area wasn't stable, it was stagnant. Wages were low, and we were in need of new industry and new investment. What we, in fact, subsequently discovered in 1966 [through the Scottish Economic Plan] was that Aberdeen and the North-East were in serious decline. The place was slowly dying.'

Approaching Aberdeen before oil could fairly be likened to entering a forgotten and isolated valley. Stable or stagnant, the regional capital of the North-East was undoubtedly a world unto itself, even throughout the social and cultural revolutions of the 1960s. It owed its evolution more to geography than to bureaucracy, an area for the most part historically secure and traditionally remote, and independent behind the barriers of the Grampian mountain escarpments and the fringing North Sea. The shoulder of Scotland, known as Buchan, was fashioned by land and sea, both equally hard and demanding mistresses. Within this geographical crucible the character of its

Plate 11.

The 'Cosy Corner' – Aberdeen in the 1960s. (*Aberdeen City Archives*)

Plate 12.

Aberdeenshire convener,
Maitland Mackie (right)
listens intently to the
Scottish oil minister, Lord
Polwarth (left).

people has been forged, as H Mackenzie put it in 1953, 'by a constant struggle to wrest a living from a reluctant soil and at times, an even more reluctant sea' (*The Third Statistical Account of Scotland: City of Aberdeen*). It was a Herculean task according to historian James Hunter in an article in the *Scotsman* and, 'Nothing ever accomplished with regard to the offshore oil industry has had about it anything more than the merest fraction of the pioneering effort which in the course of the eighteenth and nineteenth centuries, went into the task of transforming the countryside around Aberdeen into one of the most agriculturally-productive parts of Britain.' Those who chose to seek their living from the sea have always had a similarly arduous but more dangerous existence.

More than twenty years ago, Dr Cuthbert Graham, local historian and journalist, neatly dissected the onion-like nature of the economy of the region, in his *Portrait of Aberdeen and Deeside* (London 1980). 'Peel away the outer skin of oil-related activity and you come on Aberdeen as the third fishing port of the United Kingdom. Underneath that again you uncover the monumental granite industry and a small but vital shipbuilding industry which remains viable . . . Under that again are textiles and papermaking which have been with the city since the eighteenth century. Finally and forever is the land . . . to which Aberdeen is linked by the deepest bonds of all.' Shipbuilding and the textile factories have since perished; granite, which gave the city its distinctive fabric, is long finished, while fishing is caught in a mortal struggle with the European Union. But Graham's point is well made: the oil industry appears to have created a 'skin' that, because of the prosperity it has brought to the region, has camouflaged the true state of the area's indigenous pursuits.

Plate 13.

A sea of fish at Scotland's premier market after the trawling fleet has landed. (*Aberdeen City Archives*)

Just as the influences of land and sea shaped the essence of the area, they also produced a society that is embodied in Aberdeen, the capital city, or, in truth, the regional 'village' centre. Writer Lewis Grassic Gibbon had mixed feelings about it: 'One detests Aberdeen with the detestation of a thwarted lover. It is the one haunting and exasperatingly loveable city in Scotland – its fascination as unescapable as its shining mail.' On the other hand, English poet John Betjeman was delightfully astonished at 'finding so substantial a city of such architectural elegance so far North'.

A native of Aberdeen is more properly a citizen of the North-East, for the urbanisation of many inhabitants is of comparatively recent vintage. Cuthbert Graham again: 'Go to any corner of the province and you will find that reference back to Aberdeen comes as natural as breathing. To a large extent the reverse is also true. Every other city family has its roots either in farm or fishing havens. In this way the key to understanding the North-East lies in appreciating the familial domination by Aberdeen.' The ceaseless darg to harvest a fecundity where none had existed, and the comparative isolation behind natural ramparts, honed a nature that is quintessentially peasant

Scottish in its dour canniness, but is uniquely of the North-East in its sly, dry, often cruel wit, couched in a distinctive tongue of an onomatopoeic colour and richness that stubbornly survives the modern pervasiveness of universal language, and in the idiosyncratic style of its music and ballad. Spoken and written Doric, the work- and love-songs of the 'farm toun chaulmer' and the strathspeys of the ubiquitous fiddle and accordion have been the region's abiding gifts to Scottish culture.

For centuries, the people of the North-East had known of the wider world furth of the two rivers of Dee and Don. As one of Scotland's historic gateways to the Low Countries, to France, to the Baltic and beyond, they knew of it through the export of their sons; sons who fought as mercenaries for foreign kings in the conflicts of Europe and, with the global march of imperial British power, worked as civil servants, soldiers, colonial administrators, tea and rubber planters, missionaries, builders, civil engineers, scientists and investors in the new territories. In all this long history, even after the railways, created by another army of outsiders, had prised open the region to the rest of the world in the 1840s, the North-East maintained a talent to absorb and adapt, remaining, as it always had been, slightly remote. But such isolation, insularity and independence served to preserve intact its communal distinctiveness. An English journalist, G Moorhouse, writing in the *Guardian* in 1969, believed that this enduring spirit had preserved something unique. 'In this great wedge of land is most of Scotland's essence . . . the wild magnificence, the landed richness, the bleakness and the softness, the industrious virtues, the narrow vices, the enterprise and the endemic dependence of Scotland. There may not be another slab of country in the British Isles where you so much discover a nation in microcosm.' That 'nation in microcosm' had been ruled in Aberdeen in modern times by an oligarchy of local business dynasties, with interlocking directorships and lawyers playing a prominent role. Its members are still found on the key organisations that govern the region's life.

Before 1969, when the first oil was found in the North Sea, this compact community was still set apart from the rest of Scotland. LP Hartley's aphorism 'the past is a foreign country' is particularly apt in relation to Aberdeen and the North-East. Archie Robb, former deputy director of social work in Grampian Region (reorganised from the old North-East County Council's structure) remembers it as 'a more gentle time'. 'There were social problems, of course, but they were the kind we could cope with. People's expectations were different. There was a fair degree of poverty. A lot of people were on low wages and there was still some pretty poor housing. I remember it sometimes felt very isolated. A journey south to Edinburgh or Glasgow by car was a three-hour-long adventure. You wouldn't come back the same day. The roads were terrible, although there wasn't the same traffic. Aberdeen seemed so far away from everything.'

Aberdeen had then, in fact, the societal structure of a large rural service town rather than that of a provincial metropolitan centre. Entertainment was predictable if prosaic. There were 347 premises licensed to sell liquor; 126 were public houses, 5 were restaurants and 34 were sizeable hotels. The main hotels were the principal locations for public restaurants. Of the 5 independent restaurants 2 were Chinese and 1 French, the sole concessions to international cuisine. The 19 cinemas of the 1930s golden age, when Aberdonians spent more on film-going than the population of any other area, had been reduced to 13. There were 4 bingo clubs, 1 theatre, 3 gaming clubs, 84 betting shops and 55 registered social clubs. Public dance halls were still in fashion and only one had a regular liquor licence. A trade related to the social scene is the taxi-hire business; the city's taxi population in 1969–70 was 248, deployed mainly for functions. Aberdonians preferred the cheaper public transport system.

As a regional shopping centre, the city retained an old-fashioned Edwardian air. The two principal trading thoroughfares, Union Street and George Street were dominated by a number of sizeable family retail businesses, while the popular ubiquitous Northern Co-operative Society had outlets in all the main housing areas. The Dutch clothing retailer, C&A, was the forerunner of a number of national chain stores (including the first Marks and Spencer north of Edinburgh) who were to totally alter the nature of city-centre shopping.

According to the *Third Statistical Account*, the people of Aberdeen showed little appreciation of the arts: 'Aberdeen is not generally regarded as an important cultural centre, even by its own people. In the past the Aberdonian has been too busy earning his living to devote too much time to creative art.' However, this caricature of a cultural desert was not entirely accurate. The North-East was on the circuit for national ballet, orchestra and opera tour companies. The area had also made a number of important contributions to Scottish culture including the first native portrait painter of note, George Jameson; writers such as Lewis Grassic Gibbon, architects Archibald Simpson and Alexander Ellis, who, with John Smith, gave the city its eponymous granite buildings; and, through the universities, many important scholars, including the father of physics, James Clerk Maxwell, and the 'commonsense' philosopher of the Scottish Enlightenment, Thomas Reid.

The level of crime was relatively low for such a large conurbation. Television journalist and producer Ted Brocklebank claims that 'the Americans who came to Aberdeen straight from the hell-holes of Alaska and

Plate 14.

Crowds on one of the UK's finest shopping thoroughfares – Aberdeen's Union Street in the 1960s. (*Aberdeen Journals Ltd*)

the Gulf couldn't believe the lack of crime and people's trusting natures.' Murders were rare. A comparison with Dundee shows that the Tayside capital was far more violent. Although the most serious offences in Aberdeen were connected with housebreaking, violent assaults involving knives were beginning to cause concern. There were drug offences, but on a minute scale. Alcohol and not opiates was at the root of most criminal activity according to George Souden, who was head of the Criminal Investigation Department of Aberdeen City Police then. 'A lot of our time was spent picking up fishermen who'd got drunk and jumped ship. There were a lot of fights in the dance halls, again mostly involving trawlermen. We had drugs, but not to a massive extent – I remember only one undercover operation to catch a gang selling drugs out of a couple of off-Union Street pubs. Crime was very much contained and we knew where the criminal fraternity hung out. Prostitution, too, was very localised. They operated in the harbour area as they had always done. No incomers. That all changed with oil.'

Apart from the foreign seamen who had used the port for centuries, Aberdeen's experience of non-UK incomers had been restricted to Italian and Polish immigrants who settled between and after the world wars, a small colony of Hong Kong Chinese restaurant owners and workers, a tiny group of Scandinavians and the overseas students attending the University of Aberdeen,

Robert Gordon's Institute of Technology and the city's teaching hospitals and medical school. In 1970, the chief constable's report recorded the presence of 266 'aliens' working in the area. But a relatively new group was becoming significant. Of the aliens, 71 were Americans, 124 Europeans, 44 Asians and 21 Africans. By 1971 the balance had changed: the number of aliens had risen to 418, with 163 Americans, 160 Europeans, 65 Asiatics and 30 Africans. Chief Constable Alexander Morrison noted in his annual report, 'The increase is due in large measure to oil exploration in the North Sea.' Those incomers were the harbingers of enormous changes, but the city and the region was in reality in a parlous economic state.

The area's ailments were first revealed in the main *Scottish Plan* of 1966: declining traditional industries, no prospects of new business, and debilitating migration that concealed chronic unemployment. The accepted standard indicator of economic ill-health were the unemployment figures, but they were virtually nullified by the loss of skilled men – and their families – who were leaving in their hundreds for the car factories and steel plants of the Midlands. So, with a low unemployment rate of 2 per cent the area languished well down the list of Government priorities. The more urgent task was to woo new jobs to the Central Belt, as economist Maxwell Gaskin, a consultant to the Scottish Office, later recalled. 'One could not argue for any significant diversion of resources to an area like the North-East. My recollection is that the region was seen as a potential problem rather than a major immediate one.' The only hope was that the region would benefit from the fashionable planners' 'trickle-down effect', which it was hoped would bring an overspill of work to the peripheral regions. Even if it did, Dundee and Tayside region were the more likely recipients. A reasonably buoyant Dundee had thrived since the war through the political fillip of special Government development area funding. So there was to be no panacea for the North-East, and, not for the first time, the historically remote area was to be left to its own devices. The message for Aberdeen was 'Cold comfort for cosy corner' according to the *Press and Journal*.

This time, however, the *Scottish Plan*'s bleak figures of a previously hidden loss of population revealed the true situation. From 1951 to 1961 35,000 people had left the North-East, 17,000 from Aberdeenshire alone, representing the biggest exodus in the United Kingdom for that period. Since World War I, like the rest of Europe, the country had been experiencing rural depopulation in favour of massive urban growth. The difference in the North-East was that the migratory movement from the hinterland, the traditional supplier of people to the city, was propelling them outside the area, to England and to overseas. An Aberdeen University social survey of young migrants, quoted in the *Plan*, said professional and highly skilled groups were most likely to move, and the most mobile manual workers were the skilled mechanics, fitters and electricians. This was one reason the rapidly expanding oil industry was eventually forced to import skilled workers, ironically from the south. Economist Alex Kemp, who was born in the North-East, said a lot of young bright people left. 'All Aberdeen graduates – apart from those going into teaching or the Church – would leave. It was automatic, we never even thought about doing anything else. The idea was to go where the best opportunities were.' In the 1960s 85 per cent of graduates left Aberdeen, and 54 per cent of professionals migrated.

Kemp, now a highly respected professor of petro-economics, was among the group of Aberdeen academics led by Max Gaskin who carried out the *Scottish Plan's* North-East spin-off survey. Their findings confirmed the region's economy was slowly declining. Nevertheless they were convinced it was not too late to act. Gaskin's plan was to establish stability of employment by creating about 8,000 new jobs by 1976. Between 6,000 and 7,000 would have to be imported, largely from new manufacturing industry. The rest would stem from the demands of this imported activity on existing industries, mainly in the service sector. The anticipated resultant increase in population would be 26,000 people. That was the objective. The difficult part was how to achieve it in an area notoriously incapable of attracting any new work since the war. The only sizeable new industries to arrive had been the American companies, Cleveland Twist Drill to Fraserburgh and Consolidated Pneumatic Tools and Euclid (Great Britain) Ltd to Peterhead. Then, between 1968 and 1971, three other factories were warmly welcomed: Michelin, supplier for tyre manufacture; Willerby's, the tailors; and Mullards, who produced electronic equipment. They provided fewer than 200 jobs, and none of them now exists. 'Distance was the off-putting factor. It was a long way north and communications were not as good as they are now. It was difficult enough to get firms to set up in the Central Belt,' said John Hutton, former director of NESDA, which was formed by the area's councils to implement Gaskin's plan but served for a time as the region's development arm. Hutton, who was charged with wooing new industry north, was only reiterating a recurrent historical criticism of the North-East even to this day.

With a change of government to Conservative in 1970, all the grand *dirigiste* plans were cast aside unrealised, although Gaskin's strategies for new housing and roads would later be utilised by planners trying to accommodate a wholly unexpected industry. So unexpected that there was no hint in Gaskin's report of what had been happening offshore for at least five years previously, including the discovery of commercially viable deposits of oil six months before the survey was published in 1969. Professor Gaskin has since admitted the implications could have been examined, but, as he subsequently explained, 'Exploration in the northern sea had started during the course of the study, but nothing had then been discovered and all was completely speculative. It would have been extremely difficult for us to say anything worthwhile at the time.' Alex Kemp said it had to be remembered the bulk of the study was done in 1967 and 1968. 'There was nobody in authority who talked about oil at that time. Not the Scottish Office where there was a review process. Not the local authority. Not even the *P&J* [*Press and Journal*]. I remember there was a well-known geologist then who said he would drink every barrel of oil that came out of the North Sea. So there was nothing to say at that time.' In defence of the economists, the obsessive commercial secrecy of international oil companies has always been a hallmark of their business practices.

The fact was that as well as the regular visits to Aberdeen and Peterhead by busy little geological survey vessels since 1964, the steady flow of supply vessels, and the increasing squadrons of helicopters operating out of Dyce, an advance guard of oil companies was already firmly implanted in the city. They would ultimately create not a paltry trickle of Gaskin's projected 8,000 new jobs but a flood, and not one industry but an aggregation of many.

The Scottish Klondyke

3

Jimmy Simpson, sales director of the Aberdeen wine and spirit wholesaler Gordon, Graham and Stewart, was working in his small office in an empty warehouse in the harbour area's Regent Road when two Texans walked in. 'The customs people next door had told them to look me up. They were after warehouse space. Somebody had mentioned oil. I did a deal with my employers to rent them the space they needed and then talked the Texans into letting me manage things for them. The next year I hired another floor from my employers and leased it. It didn't take a genius to see that warehouse and office space would be at a premium if this oil boom arrived.' This was the 1960s – and it had arrived.

The enterprising Simpson was the first local entrepreneur to seize the moment. 'Eventually I was able to buy over the whole warehouse. I was just forty and I had made up my mind what I wanted to do with myself. I am just an ordinary guy who was in the right place at the right time.' But there was nothing ordinary about the genial former fairground boxer and miner. From that warehouse, 5 Regent Road, first home for a clutch of the big international oil companies and now legendary in North Sea history, Simpson built a mini-empire that involved hotels, pubs and the entertainment business. Most notably he created the Aberdeen Service Company, now familiar as the multi-million-pound oil service firm ASCO.

Oil fever had begun to grip the city. From the 1960s Shell had a small office in Union Street, and a few hundred yards away, above a Wimpy bar in Bridge Street, BP maintained a presence. Busy oil-related vessels had also been a familiar sight in and out of the docks. But when BP confirmed in 1970 the huge potential of Forties and then Shell proved the giant Brent, the build-up onshore began to emulate the frenzy offshore. This isolated region, lucky to persuade even one new industry to come north, suddenly found itself inundated by the advance scouts of scores of companies clamouring for land or office space.

In a modern parody of the American Klondyke, among their ranks were

Plate 15.

Aberdeen's first oilman – the entrepreneur Jimmy Simpson of Aberdeen Service Company. (*Roustabout Publications*)

the flashy speculators, 'get-rich-quick' entrepreneurs and confidence tricksters preying on a vulnerable remote backwater. Local businessmen marvelled at their audacity. Jimmy Simpson told a story about two flamboyant characters in Stetsons and high-heeled boots who walked into 5 Regent Road one day. They rolled out a detailed map of the harbour with a number of blocks marked out in red. 'They said those warehouses were for sale if I was interested. What they obviously didn't know was that I already had them all.' Another local businessman told a similar tale. 'I was showing some people round land the company owned at East Tullos (where our headquarters are now actually) when a car drove up and some people got out, led by a young fellow who began talking animatedly. I finished my business and walked over. The young man was obviously making a hard sell. I asked him who he was. He said he was Ian Wood and this was his property. I said, "That's a coincidence; my name is Ian Wood and this IS my property."' Sir Ian is now the most successful native-born Scots oilman.

Then there were the blatant attempts to woo strategic council officials. The office of Jack Nicoll, then Director of Tourism and Publicity for the City of Aberdeen, was one of the first stops for these confident, voluble men. 'There was one guy dressed like a city gent, pin stripes and bowler hat,

Plate 16.

Young Aberdeen businessman Ian Wood at the table (right) signing the John Wood Group's first service contract for the Brent field.

(*John Wood Group*)

surrounded by a bevy of pretty secretaries, so-called, who invited me out for an expensive lunch to discuss a huge industrial development. He needed land and he talked in millions. He was obviously a "conman", one of many who thought they were dealing with yokels. I never saw him again.' Jack went on to head Grampian Region's leisure and recreation department.

The build-up onshore was only reflecting what was happening offshore throughout the peak exploration decade of the 1970s. Yet the genetically pessimistic folk of Aberdeen were still slow to grasp what the oncoming onslaught would mean. The most common perception was 'The ile – it winna last.' As late as 1977, when there was a lull in offshore development, political economists at the University of Aberdeen warned, 'A significant part of the employment and income generated from North Sea oil and gas activities is of a temporary nature. Such activity cannot offer a sound base for the regeneration of the Scottish economy.' That view still lingered in the mid-1980s when John Moorehouse arrived as director of public affairs at Shell Expro. 'I used to give regular talks reassuring people the industry would still be prospering well into the next century. We are certainly going to exceed that. But there was that doubt when I arrived, it was still there when I departed in the 1990s, and it will probably still be there even after half a century.'

The local authorities were definitely ignorant of the importance of what was happening a hundred miles from the mouth of the Dee. The first mention appears in the minutes of Aberdeen Town Council on 23 November 1970, when an advisory committee working party reported on 'the discovery of a commercially exploitable source of oil or gas in the North Sea'. The working party had discussed 'possible demands for land and port facilities which might emerge in future' and stated that 'all aspects of the matter are being kept under active review'. This source was, of course, Forties. Councillor James Lamond was city treasurer, and later lord provost and a Labour MP. 'It just didn't make the impact it should have done. You would think as city treasurer I would have had an inkling, but no. Arnold "Bobo" Burns (a Progressive councillor) was the only one and that was just because his brother-in-law, an oil company executive, kept hammering on about it. We actually asked him to give us a talk. But we still didn't realise what was going to hit us.'

The implications of the area's attitude were apparent in a survey of oil companies conducted by University of Aberdeen sociologist Robert Moore in 1980. The firms complained that, 'although they eventually came round', the Aberdeen authorities, business, labour and general public were 'slow to appreciate the benefits of offshore oil and were therefore slow to gear up for it'. Ted Roberts, senior offshore installation manager on Forties, had two assignments at the start of the 1970s. One was to set up the production teams to develop the field, the other was a mission to inform. 'There was such ignorance about us – especially among the councils. They were so suspicious of the "ilies" as they called us. It took a long time to get through that we weren't there to put one over on them.'

Even Maitland Mackie, Aberdeenshire county convener and chairman of NESDA, and indubitably the most perceptive of the local leaders, did not appear capable at first of fully anticipating what was to come. There was no mention of oil in the first edition of his authority's *Northern Light* publication in 1969 – it was still promoting the area for new industry. They finally caught up in the 1971/2 annual report in a startling illustration of the breakneck speed of the onshore development. Mackie said planners were anticipating an approximate population increase of 20,000 people in the following two years. The forecast had then to be revised to 50,000 over three years. Yet NESDA's development officer, John Hutton, recalls they had first recognised the significance of offshore activity in 1970 (when the body was founded) after holding meetings with Jimmy Simpson and oil company managers. Then NESDA exhibited at Oceanex in Great Yarmouth, centre for the southern gas fields. 'I began to realise much more what was needed. People couldn't see the new industry then, it was so scattered. They couldn't accept it could provide many jobs, require more services and that we would be under pressure for land, premises and labour.' Hutton was sent to the oil cities of the United States in 1972 – a seminal pilgrimage. At the Offshore Technology Conference and Exhibition in Houston, where he addressed 300 American businessmen, he was amazed to be inundated with queries about Aberdeen.

Malcolm Bruce, now Liberal Democrat MP for Gordon, arrived in Aberdeen in 1971 to work as research and information officer at NESDA. He considers the authority's early work was vital to the development of the industry and to the region's ability to cope. His recollections reflect the excitement of the era. 'Queues of people waiting outside the office in Union Terrace from 8.30 in the morning to 7.30 at night – including many local businessmen anxious to capitalise on the new opportunities. Certainly we didn't have any money, just a few staff, nor did we have any powers – but we had the "ears" of both councils. We could put the incomers in touch with the right people and act as a filter for information, about local services, planning regulations, financial advice and legal matters. We were constantly assessing the potential, calculating the needs for offices, warehouses and housing, drawing up directories of companies. I remember we were criticised for our forecasts, although we tried to keep them at a conservative level. It is amazing to think now that even those figures – 5,000 jobs, 20 years of oil – were so far out from what actually happened. But there was such a lack of understanding.'

When Malcolm left NESDA in 1975 (he and industrial journalist Ted Strachan later launched the successful oil industry insiders' publication, *Aberdeen Petroleum*) he was replaced by Ian Moir, an Aberdeen graduate with degrees in geography and agricultural economics. 'My principal task was to help incoming businesses find property. It was a super time to be involved because you didn't have to try very hard to find developers. Some very large companies just came wandering in off the street – typical was Chevron. Their guy just came to the front desk and asked to see somebody. Then there was the Norwegian gentleman who said he was the representative for Aker Offshore Contracting. To be honest nobody at the front desk had heard of Aker. I soon discovered they were one of the largest engineering companies in Norway and are now AOC.'

At least three firms called every working day and Ian had to find them a base for research and planning. 'Regent Quay, No. 5, was the first stepping stone for many of them, although there were other property agents involved.

Plate 17.

Regent Quay at Aberdeen Harbour, Warehouse No. 5 was the hub of the new industry.

(*Aberdeen City Archives*)

The oil men wanted to move in quickly and money was really no object. No. 5 should have been preserved in the mid-70s; that was the hub where a lot of major companies had their start.' Pat Allen was a young receptionist at Gordon, Graham and Stewart when Jimmy Simpson seized his opportunity, and she went to work for him in No. 5. 'We had a portacabin [*sic.*] in a warehouse full of barites – drilling mud – and also bats; you could hear my screams up the top of Marischal Street. That was the start of Aberdeen Service Company.' Because of the demand for serviced office suites, two floors of offices were created above the warehousing level. 'There were probably about twenty companies – many of them big names – BP, Schlumberger, Amoco, Vetco, Sedco. There were also two mud companies, Milchem and Imco, as well as Offshore Drilling Supplies, who I eventually went to work for – just an amazing amount. I had a shelf running the length of my portacabin with a phone for each company. It wasn't a switchboard, just individual handsets and I was the receptionist for them all. It was really crazy when you think back on it now. Each company only had one or two people – a lot were still in Yarmouth.'

Jimmy eventually built an enormous business, which moved to Peterhead, before he sold out to Siddlaw Industries. Pat said 'His office in the warehouse was wood-panelled, oil paintings on the wall, drinks cabinet – fabulous antique furniture. Then you came out and you were in the middle of the warehouse again. It was like, bizarre. He was such a character, just as flamboyant as some of the Americans.'

In the 1960s and early 1970s, John Porter, later to serve as a prominent Tory councillor, worked for Lloyds Bowmaker, the corporate and retail finance company. 'I wasn't aware then about the significance of oil. It was somewhere over the horizon, so I didn't really give it much thought. We were seriously misjudging the thing, except for those with a shrewd eye for property who bought one or two bits and did rather well.' Then he got a call to an office in No. 5. 'This was the first American oilman I had ever met. A real culture shock. In the banking business then you were very conservative. This guy had his feet on the desk, boots and hat on. I said to myself, "I don't know what you are wanting but I don't think I can help you here." But I soon realised he was a very shrewd bloke and this was just his style. These people were big and loud; they were relaxed and flexible. The complete opposite to what we were in Aberdeen. We lived in our own little goldfish bowl and it was incestuous. They were looking for a huge credit line for their business, one of the smaller service companies. But they grew into a big company and I did very good business with them.'

Ian Moir had to deal with the local banks. 'One of the main ones at the start was the Bank of Nova Scotia. They had a strong influence – many businesses gravitated to them.' The other was the Clydesdale Bank. Edwin Reid, inspector of branches from Montrose to Shetland, was very much the local face of oil banking. Ian said, 'This company – quite large – came to see me. I suggested some banks but they wanted somebody they could talk to. I told them to try Edwin. A week later, my boss, John Hutton, called me in. "I have just had the Bank of Nova Scotia on the phone and they are not very happy. One of their prominent customers has just moved to the Clydesdale after a reference by you." Edwin played a very important part in smoothing the way for a lot of those businesses.'

Like many collaborations in the oil industry, the Clydesdale banker's introduction to the business was almost casual. 'I had once seriously considered closing the branch at Aberdeen harbour. Business was small because no one lived there.' The same branch became the fastest-growing banking house in Scotland. 'It can all be traced back to a bleak February day in 1971 when a man walked in the door. He was a British diving consultant who wanted sterling travellers cheques immediately. "I am going to Norway from Dyce Airport in about twenty minutes and I'll open an account when I come back." I obliged and he did open an account, but he also introduced a number of oilmen and we never looked back.' The consultant in a hurry was Keith Johnston, who eventually launched a variety of oil-related businesses. 'I became the contact for the Clydesdale and I calculated I put about sixty accounts his way.'

However, the commercial sector were not the only ones to face massive new challenges. By the early 1970s it had become obvious the new Scottish industry had chosen Greater Aberdeen as the launchpad for its assault on the North Sea, and it was also where their onshore employees elected to set up homes. The principal local authorities in the North-East – initially Aberdeenshire County Council (which became Grampian Regional Council and then, in 1996, Aberdeenshire again) and Aberdeen Town Council (Aberdeen District Council) – were faced with either a fortuitous gift or a poisoned chalice; at that point it was unclear which it was to be. But like it or not, they had simply no choice except to embrace the newcomers. The city's lord provost, John Smith, issued an early plea to both the industry and to the people of Aberdeen: 'We must pay attention to preserving the high amenity of the area and ensure there is reasonable balance between the oil producers and a community rich in its own traditions.' In their critical study, *Scotland and Oil* (Edinburgh 1975), A McGregor Hutcheson and Alexander Hogg maintained that the keynote had been massive pressure by the oil industry for immediate decisions and actions: 'The repeating theme has been that of the likely losses to companies if decisions are delayed, of their ability to spend vast sums of money . . . and their expressed readiness to take their custom elsewhere if early action was not forthcoming.'

What faced the small local authorities – and the communities of the Highlands and the Islands – was a juggernaut that in its velocity and irresistible force was unprecedented in Scottish history. No other modern enterprise has made such massive industrial, commercial and social demands on any area in such a short timescale. Only the creation of the planned postwar New Towns can compare. More than thirty years on, the ratcheting-up of statistics still appear as extraordinary as the logistics being rolled out offshore. From 1970 onwards – when ten companies a month were arriving – the region and the city had to solve several basic and urgent problems: placing the new firms, providing service infrastructure and housing, and catering for the new families' needs in educational and social facilities. More homes were also required for local families and for the increase in non-oil support staff such as specially recruited teachers and social workers. The joint authorities had been told by their economic development staff that the oil industry was likely to create 14,000 new jobs on- and offshore in the 1971–76 period. Of these it was calculated only 4,000 would be filled internally, so there would be a need for 10,000 in-migrant workers. This in turn had far-reaching implications for housing and other infrastructure. Just how daunting this was is shown by a comparison of the new construction needed to house the in-migrants: 3,000 to 3,500, compared with 720 in 1972 and 1,355 in 1973. Onshore planners were invariably caught out by the scale and speed of offshore developments, which meant the associated demands for facilities, land, housing and office premises were always underestimated. In October 1971, 56 companies were involved in oil in Aberdeen; by August 1974, the figure was 236; by 1984 there were 600 new companies who created 33,000 new on- and offshore jobs, rising to a pinnacle of 52,000 just before the 1986 recession. There are now 900 oil firms in the area. Of the 340,000 people employed in the industry throughout the UK in 2005, 71 per cent of the direct jobs and 43 per cent of the total were in Scotland and most in the North-East.

Throughout that period from 1971 to 1986 the poptulation rose by more than 30,000 from 438,000. The regional council's excellent *Quarterly Economic Review* revealed the oil industry had more than surpassed the wildest dreams of the economic planners: from 1973, the loss of people remained remarkably steady at 11,000 to 13,000 every year, 2,000 fewer than before. But the total population gain was primarily due to a considerable increase in the annual rate of new oil-industry arrivals, which climbed steeply from 14,000 in 1970, to 20,000 in 1975, and then didn't drop below 17,000

from 1983 onwards – and this despite a coincidental fall in the natural rate of increase. Remarkably, the debilitating postwar drain of people from the North-east had been reversed.

By the 1980s the city had already run the gamut of the cruder excesses of the 'boom-town gold rush' phase. American commentator Al Alvarez describes the scene when oil first arrived in *Offshore: A North Sea Journey* (London, 1987). 'There were rumours . . . that Calvinist Aberdeen was becoming another Klondyke. In reality this meant that for a brief period, men in ten-gallon hats and cowboy boots shivered in the dank hotels, the pubs were crammed with roughnecks and roustabouts. But the American wildcatters moved in, made their lucky strikes and promptly sold out to the major companies.' In *The Oil Rush* (London, 1976), Mervyn Jones and Fay Goodwin saw Aberdeen very differently from *Newsweek*, who had given it the name of 'Sin City'. Their impression was, 'Anyone in search of Beirut or Bangkok is in for a disappointment . . . the fact remains that sin in Aberdeen tends to be discreet and doesn't offend the eye of the respectable citizen.' It was certainly the case in the beginning that the early Americans who discovered, drilled and brought the fields to production – the so-called 'rednecks' or 'good ol' boys', who carried Texas or Louisiana with them in their carpet bags wherever they went – were only too willing to teach the locals how an oil town should 'party'. While bottles of Bourbon, rye, tequila and American beer rubbed shoulders with single malt and gin on the pub shelves, Stetsons on the streets were never really overly prevalent, to the disappointment of visiting journalists.

Aberdeen was totally different from any previous oil province. Outside the United States, where the rise of oil to global importance had begun ninety years

Plate 18.

Line-up at an oil company party – complete with the obligatory Stetson-wearing American. (*Roustabout Publications*)

before, the international oilmen had never had to deal with a long-established Western or European community on the scale Aberdeen represented, with a stable democratic polity and a culture far older than their own. A social worker explained to a gathering of oilmen in Scotland that they would have to think how they treated the 'natives' of the North-East: 'It is vastly more difficult in this country than overseas and I would suggest you take a different approach. You are dealing with different people altogether in Scotland.'

Some of the early arrivals were the tough and rootless who knew nothing of and cared less about the community they had made their temporary home. According to a former police officer, the wildcatters were 'a rough, tough bunch'. George Souden, who was chief superintendent in charge of the Central Division of Grampian Police, recalls, 'They were real cowboys, the drillers. It was just another posting to them. They could have been in Timbuktu. Some were bad people. We were called to this American's house – a Texan. His wife was in a terrible mess. I have never seen anything like it. It turned out he had pistol-whipped her because she had forgotten to do something. He was never charged. His company put him and his wife on the next plane back home. There were quite a few cases of wife beating. The ones who followed later, now, they were a different breed – do anything to help.' What also became obvious from local court cases was that 'offshore oil worker' had replaced 'trawl fisherman' on the charge sheets of the villains of the pub and street brawls.

Television producer Ted Brocklebank, who devised a number of documentaries on the oil industry, remembers asking one American what he thought of Aberdeen. 'He said, "Hey, is that where we are at?" It was just another oil town to him. He had his American company, his American store, his kids went to the American school, he talked on the phone to the guys back in Texas every day. He could have been anywhere.' There were also UK oilmen like that particular Texan. Chris Harvie writes thus of the British oil executive in his critical North Sea history *Fool's Gold* (London 1994): '[His] tolerance was limited. The platforms were grim; Aberdeen an absolute hell-hole – "the armpit of the universe".' These were the 'foreigners who arrived without love' as described by Gabriel García Márquez in *One Hundred Years of Solitude* (London, 1972). In an uncanny foretaste of what many fear will happen after oil, he tells how outsiders took over a small South American settlement to mass-produce bananas, a 'vast avalanche of foreigners' who built their own town, disrupted the community and then abandoned them, leaving empty buildings.

But they weren't all loveless foreigners. One of the remarkable features of the early days was the number of Scots who 'came home' to work offshore after forging careers in foreign oil fields. They are not numbered among those who 'arrived without love'. They included the big driller from Nairn, Jock Munro, one of the discoverers of the Brent Field; Matt Linning, mastermind of the Forties Field; and Mitch Watt, who led the Amoco team to the first oil in the British sector. The latter looked and sounded like a Texan but was born in Glasgow. Diver Keith Johnston had often crossed swords with big Jock offshore. 'He bent my ear a few times. He was a big guy, a real tough guy. He used to roar at the divers, "I don't want you on the deck I want you in the water." But Jock was revered.' Keith also knew Mitch Watt well. 'I became his vice chairman on the North Sea Safety Committee. He had good people round him, two American Indians, brothers. One was nicknamed Running Bear – proper name Bert Hirondelle. He tapped me on the shoulder in a wine shop one time while I was looking at a bottle of Hirondelle wine. 'Drinking the family blood, eh?' His brother was called Mad Dog Who Loves His Horses. They were both drilling managers.'

These were the characters of the Alvarez Klondyke – outlandish people last seen in Aberdeen in the 1900s when Buffalo Bill parked his Wild West Show on the Links – who used to enliven the early social scene. There were other nationalities, French, Norwegian and Dutch, but Jimmy Simpson was a match for them all. Keith Johnston said Jimmy was well known for his taste in motors. 'He told me, "I have never had a Ford", so he flew a Lincoln Continental over from the States.' Pat Allen said, 'Down Regent Road it was, like, oil and fish. There was a harbour café next door to No. 5 where this fantastic combination of people met.' Another American automobile caught Keith's attention in the city's Station Hotel car park. 'That was the first hotel used by oil people because it had the only telex. I saw this big Cadillac with a tax disc stamped Guilford. I knew right away – Occidental. And there he was, J. Paul Getty, just getting into his car. I introduced myself and gave him my card. He had driven all the way up from England, because only three Viscount aircraft a week came out from London.'

Pat Allen remembers those days as one big party and 'a lot of socialising, money was obviously never a concern'. The high-rolling, high-spending 'Hollywood image' was confirmed by the lavish flood of early parties, receptions and launches. 'There wasn't an awful lot to do socially. Myself and my girlfriend, Brenda Bryant – who now runs a personnel agency and also worked at Regent Road – used to apply for late licences and organise "hootenanny nights" at the Dee Motel and the oil guys just loved them. Another friend of mine, Phyllis Thomson, has horrendous memories of those nights when she worked part-time behind the bar. She always says, "It was awful the way the money was just flying over the counter."' Phyllis and her

Plate 19.

A pioneer of the oil and gas industry in Aberdeen, former naval diver, Keith Johnston. (*Roustabout Publications*)

husband Dave ran an Aberdeen accountancy business. 'A lot of the first Americans frequented the motel, it was a real hive. Big Stetsons and fancy boots. They really upset the locals – they were so brash and loud. They just emptied their pockets on the counter but they talked to the staff as if they were nothing. There often used to be trouble. The manageress wasn't very big, but by God, she could handle a six-foot oilman – no problem. But there were one or two very nice ones. It was always my luck to be working on hillbilly nights. I hated it. The Americans were very popular with the local women. Guys with Stetsons and boots and the women hanging off the arm – skirts up to the top of the leg and the makeup. But they gave themselves away when they opened their mouths. There was just so much cash flying about – that sticks in your mind.' As well as the motel, the oil crowd also frequented the old Marcliffe, the Albyn, the Imperial and the Royal. Pat Allen hadn't really realised at the time that they were pioneers. 'Everyone was just flooding into Aberdeen. We were aware it was going to be something quite big and we worked really hard well beyond nine to five, especially if there were tenders going out. And then we would be taken out for a lovely lunch the next day. I always felt that if you did a good job for them and worked hard, it was certainly appreciated and didn't go unnoticed. I don't think my annual salary was fantastically high, but there were an awful lot of perks and bonuses.'

With so much money washing around, Maggie Thomson, who worked in Conoco administration, discovered – to use the modern idiom – there was no such thing as a free lunch. 'One contractor took us down to a local hotel where there was a buffet laid on. I have never seen food or champagne like that in my life. His company paid for that. So I know there were probably a lot of bribes then, but you were never sure. My partner, Stewart, who was in the oil business, says everything they offer you is a bribe, so he accepts nothing.' Maggie knew one man who was arrested for fraud. 'What he did was ethically wrong. He gave company business to a couple of firms he had started.' The case never came to court. 'I remember another time a platform's cinema seats had to be replaced. He devised a modified seat which was accepted at £12.50 each. They were manufactured in one of his chum's garages for £1.50. The tragedy was those companies could easily have succeeded legitimately.'

Keith Johnson has never forgotten a Fourth of July celebration at Kippie Lodge, the oilmen's club outside town. 'They had a big cake in the shape of the USA. Then some guy came up and cut California off – did he get dirty looks. They used to have some great barbecues – one must have been about a hundred yards long. They used to bring the meat in from the States, as if we didn't have food here. The business done there and the deals clinched – at one time the Americans dominated and they didn't want anybody else in.' In fact the club originally had 150 charter members, half Americans and half locals.

Gerard Flecher was the head chef at the Station Hotel when the oil industry began to take off. He was born in Colmar in Alsace. His wife, Mary, said they had only intended to stay in Aberdeen for two years, planning to move on and probably open a restaurant in Edinburgh. 'Then we caught on to the idea that something was happening here.' Gerard agreed: 'All we knew was it was oil-related. We got a lot of trade at the Station. There weren't many restaurants then – mostly hotels; they closed at 9 o'clock and the pubs at 10. So people went home.' Mary: 'Gerard being continental thought this was very strange.' Gerard: 'I think there were only the Athenaeum and Luigi's. And not a lot of continental cuisine.' The husband and wife team were to change all that when they opened their own restaurant, Gerard's.

'Gerard brought French cooking to Aberdeen. We even had to introduce them to wines.' Gerard said, 'From the time we opened there was a great demand and we had to engage more chefs and waiters. The new restaurant had a licence to 11 o'clock. 'That caused a lot of bother, people were coming in after 10 and I would have to ask them before 11 what they were going to drink.' Gerard remembers the first Americans as nice to deal with. 'Money was never a problem as long as they got what they wanted. It all changed after 1986.' Mary said, 'Eventually we were given the signatures of staff able to sign for meals and they spent a lot.' They had from 1,000 to 1,400 sittings a week. Mary said, 'I remember looking around one night, people were wearing evening dress and next to them people with denim; I thought: we have cracked it. We are getting the right mixture.' For the Flechers the downside was, like most other local businesses, trying to keep skilled staff. They couldn't compete with the offshore catering companies who paid more. The couple opened another restaurant but are now retired.

To an English incomer, Pauline Baxter, eating out in Aberdeen was wonderful. 'My husband had an unlimited expense account and we used to go to Fidlers, Mr G's, Ardoe House, Norwood Hall and the Aberdeen Rendezvous – when it was a really posh restaurant – at least once a week. One oil show we were out nine consecutive nights. I had to buy clothes thinking "Now, who did we go out with last night and what did I wear?" Then an article in the local paper about Fidlers said they could charge what they wanted because everything was on expenses. So Shell stopped staff claiming meals there. All my husband's contacts were at Shell, but Ian still went to Fidlers. It was only Shell people who couldn't pay – they very rarely did anyway.'

From the earliest days, for sheer ostentation and display of wealth and power in what became Europe's oil capital, the only show in town has been

Plate 20.

Gerard in his domain – Aberdeen's first bona fide French restaurant, a favourite eating place for the oil crowd.

Plate 21.

The 1989 Offshore Oil and Gas Exhibition at Aberdeen Conference and Exhibition Centre – shop window for the industry.

Offshore Europe, which has a counterpart in Houston, Texas. It has been housed every second year since 1975 in a conference and concert complex at the Bridge of Don, originally a joint venture by Grampian Regional Council, the organising Spearhead Group and the former Scottish Development Agency. Offshore Europe began modestly enough in 1973 in a tented village on the University of Aberdeen campus, with 160 exhibitors and 7,000 visitors, including a delegation from Communist China. The early shows were garish 'hard-sell' public relations contests, but another element was the major international conference on the petroleum sciences and technology, run under the UKOOOA (Offshore Oil Operator's Association) and the Society of Petroleum Engineers. In the early heady days, when oil was $30 a barrel and the revenues were rolling in, the exhibition's after-hours corporate hospitality was legendary. On more than one occasion cruise liners were hired as venues at Aberdeen harbour.

In 1981 the show was nine times larger than the original. By the time the permanent centre was built four years later the 'showbiz razzmatazz' had virtually faded, and the more professional and mature exhibition featured more than 1,100 companies and organisations, attracting 25,000 visitors. At the sixteenth biennial show in 2005 attendance records were broken: there were 1,553 exhibitors and 32,104 visitors from more than 104 different nations. Offshore Europe remains an important showcase for the industry – as well as a tremendous boost to the Aberdeen service economy. Companies spend lavishly on their exhibits: in 2003 one firm was rumoured to have paid £1 million for its stand. Sir Ian Wood describes how he took his father to the 1975 exhibition to show him the company's stand: 'We were trying to make our name and had spent a bit of money. He looked around and said, "What did this cost you?" I told him and he looked at me. "In 1955, I could have built two fishing boats with that. I hope you know what you are doing."' As it turned out, his son did.

The Incomers

4

I was a 31-year-old child bride – it was my second marriage. I thought
we were going to Dubai in the Persian Gulf so I packed my bags and
suitcases with linen and cotton clothes. We arrived in London, where
we waited for three weeks. Then we were told they were going to start
exploring for oil in the North Sea. They were outfitting a rig at
Middlesbrough, so they sent Bill down there and my daughter and me
up to Aberdeen. To me that was somewhere near the Arctic Circle.

Barbara Glidden

Barbara Glidden, a bubbly Southern American, whose husband, Bill,
was an oil geologist, arrived in 1967 and claims to have been the
first American oil wife in Aberdeen. 'To come from a swimming
pool and a three-bedroomed house to a but 'n' ben on the side of the road in
Scotland and have to make a coal fire was a big change in my life.'

Equally ignorant about the North-East of Scotland was another oil wife,
Pauline Baxter, an Englishwoman, who came from Portland in Dorset to
Aberdeen to follow her husband, who worked as a service company engineer
offshore. 'I am ashamed to say now, I didn't even know where it was. We flew
up to have a look around and I can remember the pilot saying, "We have just
crossed the Border between England and Scotland and we will be landing
shortly." I thought, "Where the hell are we going then – how much further is
it going to be?" Now I get annoyed with people when they say they don't
know where Aberdeen is.'

Even while the wildcatters and their like were cutting a swathe through
the city's social life, foreign and non-Scots oil families, who represented a
broad sweep of nationalities, had begun to track their menfolk to the North-
East, bedding down into the community, as more and more companies began
to cluster around the industry's early onshore core. For many the first
experience of what was then the UK's most northerly city was a severe culture
shock. 'Cold and granite', was the impression of the lady from the sultry

savannahs when she and her family arrived by train. 'It was October but it was sunshine when we left London. As we kept going further north, it kept getting greyer and greyer – and more dreich.' She has obviously long since absorbed the native dialect. 'We got out at Aberdeen Joint Station, and stayed in the Station Hotel at £18 a night. That evening we went out to look at Aberdeen and thought, "We are going to be living here?" All you could see were grey buildings, grey streets, grey skies and grey people. It was just absolutely the most depressing place I had ever seen.'

Pauline, from the beautiful balmy Dorset countryside was similarly unimpressed by the overall colour of the Granite City. 'We went down George Street and I thought, "Oh my God, is this it? What have we come to?" I didn't realise that was only George Street and not Union Street. So my first impression was, "It is grey, it is dirty and it is cold."'

Barbara said, 'I came with my daughter with all my linen and cotton and we were freezing to death. I went to C&A's to buy some warm sweaters and cardigans and the lady said, "Oh, are you on holiday?" I said, "Well no, my husband is working in the North Sea." She said, "In the North Sea? Ach, you are having me on." We were the first American family here up until about 1971 or 1972.'

Dundee girls Jean Gaffney and Sheila Robertson had followed American oil operators Conoco from their Tayside base to a new service centre at Kirkhill Industrial Estate, near Dyce airport. Sheila had been reluctant to move to Aberdeen. 'The roads were really bad and there wasn't a dual carriageway. I had only been with Conoco for under two years and I couldn't

Plate 22.

Conoco's Jean Gaffney (centre), on duty on the Murchison platform as chaperone to the company's oil wives.

get redundancy. So I didn't have a choice, but I wasn't looking forward to it. Every Friday we left Kirkhill and headed down to Dundee. That was before we were settled – we were just that glad to be home again.' She said they didn't really talk to Aberdonians. 'They weren't interested. It took a long time to get established and make friends – and they were all in the oil industry.'

A familiar figure on the oil scene – social and otherwise – the kind of character Scots call kenspeckled – was James Primrose Smith, a media cameraman. No matter the cold winds that so exercised the incomers, Jimmy usually sported slacks, open sandals and a vivid Hawaiian shirt – topped occasionally by a bow tie and a monocle. He left a lasting legacy in his beloved oil magazine, *Roustabout*. Founded with his wife, Iris and son Jan, the first industry freesheet is now thirty-three years old and still flourishing, under the control of the present managing director, Dennis Davidson, and his team. Throughout the harum-scarum early years, Jimmy, his camera and his coterie of pressed volunteer writers captured the people and events round the bars and hotels. The periodical also reflected the sometimes controversial views of the incomers about their new life. In one of the 1972 editions, 'The Girls' Guide to the Oil Game', written by the Petroleum Women's Club of Scotland, proffered some trenchant advice from 'veteran' wives to the 'rookies': 'The Petroleum Club has an unwritten code which says, "Don't harp on about how great it was where you came from. You are here now and what you make of it is up to you. Don't blame your new surroundings for all your problems. Most things happen anywhere."' But Aberdeen and the North-East were not just anywhere, and the womenfolk of the new families encountered difficulties in assimilating. Shopping was an example.

In 1971, when Aberdeen's retail turnover was £67 million, a shopping survey revealed the city was lagging behind the rest of the country. 'It has not yet experienced the full effect of changes in consumer taste. Some of the major stores fall somewhat below the standard expected for a city of its size.' The survey foresaw, however, 'increasing prosperity is likely to change consumer tastes and this has already been seen in the recent introduction of new shops stocking different types of goods . . . no doubt given added impetus by the newcomers who bring with them new ideas and fashions.' The retail sector had already responded; the St Nicholas and Bon Accord shopping centres, drawing in the principal chain stores from Union Street, had been planned before oil, and the Trinity Centre followed shortly afterwards; the old, established fashion and department stores had long since succumbed to market forces, leaving only one independent to fight on, while a family-owned furniture company weathered the onslaught of the all-purpose home supply superstores on the edges of the city.

Plate 23.

Jimmy Primrose Smith, founder of the ubiquitous oil magazine, *Roustabout*. (*Roustabout Publications*)

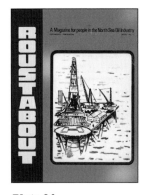

Plate 24.

The first edition of *Roustabout* – the industry's earliest social contact with the people of the North-East.

'In terms of shops, I thought there was nothing up here to start with,' claimed Pauline Baxter. 'The choice was very limited. Markies and Woolworths were the only recognisable stores. What I did like was the late-night shopping on a Thursday. We didn't have that or Sunday opening.' Barbara Glidden found it difficult coming to terms, pre-decimalisation, with pounds, shillings and pence, but it was the lack of familiar provisions that was the real problem. 'I was learning how to cook the food and I was absolutely amazed there were no green vegetables, no spinach, no collards. There was nothing green, except cabbage, never one of my favourites and Brussels sprouts, even worse. I asked this farmer, "What are those growing in the field?" and he said, "They're neeps – what you probably call turnips." "Oh, turnip greens – in America we eat the tops – very nice." So I picked some and cooked them but they had all those prickles and they tasted really bad.' Diving consultant Keith Johnson said the Americans also went for the tops of the rhubarb plant. 'I always remember a guy called Scooter Billups, the buyer for Glomar 3; I had a lot of rhubarb in the garden and when he found out he said, "If you want the goddamned order you are going to have to bring me rhubarb." Local businessman Hamish Barrack found an enterprising way to solve the shopping problems by opening a specialist American food store, which flourished for a number of years.

When Shell's director of public affairs, John Moorehouse, arrived in Aberdeen in 1984 he was asked for his first impressions. 'I said it was wonderful, just like my home county of East Yorkshire with its rural hinterland, and I understood the sense of humour; even some of the words were the same. I felt totally at home. But your fruit and vegetables were absolutely atrocious, they wouldn't be allowed anywhere near the counters of shops in England and the prices were approximately 30 per cent higher. Also if I hadn't been on expenses, I wouldn't have found anywhere I could afford to take my wife out for a meal.' Eventually local stores and restaurants began to meet the demand for international foodstuffs, with the traditional Tex-Mex favourite, chilli, challenging the established Indian curry.

The appearance of the incomers was the cue for an inevitable rise in food prices according to one American wife. 'Meat and fish were particularly expensive. I just don't know how local people were able to manage, while the families from Dutch or British companies were really at a disadvantage because they didn't get overseas cost-of-living allowances.' Americans were exempt from paying either US taxes or taxes in the country in which they were operating.

There were also difficulties with the sometimes impenetrable Doric. Pauline Baxter thought it was a foreign language. 'But I know people didn't understand me either. I went into a baker's shop in Union Street and I wanted to buy a pasty. I didn't know what it was called so I just pointed and said, "I will have one of those." The assistant just smiled and said, "You tell me what you call them and I'll tell you what we call them." Which I thought was very good of her.'

The quest for an appropriate education for their youngsters was an immediate preoccupation of the adopted Aberdonians. Barbara, who had a daughter from her first marriage, found a place at one of the local independent girls' schools. But her fellow expatriates wanted continuity of study so the American School was founded in 1972 to provide US-style education for youngsters predominantly from oil or military families. It had a roll of thirty-six pupils, from kindergarten to senior level, and eight teachers. In 1994 the school at Milltimber, on the western outskirts of Aberdeen, was re-established as the International School of Aberdeen (ISA), private and fee-paying. Approximately 62 per cent of the children are from the United States and Canada, but some twenty-three other nationalities are represented, including British. It is the only school in Scotland to offer the International Baccalaureate Diploma (IB) programme, a globally recognised teaching system developed in France. Some pupils from neighbouring Cults Academy followed sixth-year studies with free scholarships to the IB programme.

The sizeable French oil community also created their own school in 1973, founded by Total Oil, in premises in the grounds of Aberdeen Grammar School. The 160 or so pupils, who wear the same uniform as their hosts, are taught from primary level right up to the Baccalaureate qualifications needed for university entrance in France. During a peak oil development stage Shell's Dutch children attended their own primary school. Kathy Davidson, formerly with the personnel department, was responsible for the school at Causewayend. 'It became too big, so Shell turned one of the houses we had in Kincorth into a school. There were five Dutch teachers, all Shell employees, and about seventy pupils and rising.'

Generally, however, the absorption of oil-family children into the mainstream local educational system has been a considerable feat by the North-East authorities. At one time 2 per cent of Aberdeen's school population were described by the authorities as 'working in two languages'. Obviously there are foreign children with no connection to the oil industry, but, according to the school service English as a Second Language (ESL), at one point 90 per cent of the 620 bilingual pupils had parents working in the North Sea, leavening the rich mix already living in the city. The principal minority languages, for example, are Chinese and Bengali. One factor is that most of the oil families are transient. Aberdeen's higher-education and research establishments account for the rest of the different ethnicities. Since

1972, the ESL system has catered for the children of these incoming families. Numbers fluctuate according to the fortunes of the industry; in 1999, for example, there were 555 children from 67 different countries, who spoke 50 to 60 different mother tongues, studying in 50 city schools.

Apart from education, for the newcomers the principal obstacle was locating a suitable home against a hostile background of soaring prices and rents, and a severe shortage of leased accommodation. Young local first-time buyers were unable to get on the property ladder, and the blame for the outrageous housing lottery that emerged in the 1970s and '80s was placed squarely on the wealthy oil community. The salary- and expenses-rich incomers could pay well over the odds, and they, or more usually their companies, were prepared to do so. It must not be forgotten, however, that the original sellers who launched the price race were generally local people.

One angry American oil wife gave vent to her feelings in *Roustabout*: 'Who is exploiting who? Two years ago the average monthly rent for a furnished two- or three-bedroomed semi-detached was £60. But we didn't complain as we thought the rents were reasonable. When the rents rose to £80 and £90, I thought, well, there is a housing shortage. But during the past year the rents have soared unbelievably – £120 to £170 is an average although the property is exactly the same.' The American oil wife's family had taken a small bungalow, no garage, heated by night storage heaters, with old and inadequate furnishings and only one electric plug in the kitchen. 'Rent £130 a month with a six-month lease. That means that after six months the landlord can raise the rent.' She also described the offer system: a minimum rent was quoted at £120 and then rented to the highest bidder. 'I suppose the landlords figure we are just a bunch of suckers and that they should take us for every penny they can get – while it lasts.'

The Labour MP for Aberdeen North, Bob Hughes, told the Scottish Grand Committee in 1972 'The people in Aberdeen who have benefited are property speculators.' He described a two-roomed house in Footdee, which had been empty for eight and a half years, was without water and light, had damp walls, for sale at offers over £300. 'It sold for £2,375. Two attic rooms were sold for nearly £4,000. These are scandalous values about which the Government should be doing something.'

Barbara Glidden said she encountered a great deal of prejudice towards Americans at first. 'The salaries were bigger, the fishermen were going off on the rigs, housing was just over the moon. You couldn't find any place to live, the service companies were having to pay rent and living allowances for their people.' The former director of planning at Grampian Region, Peter Cockhead, summed up the dilemma: 'Neither the oilmen nor the locals seem to recognise the problem is due to the inadequacy of a system delivering real estate in a community faced with a sudden influx of money and people.' The Gliddens first lived in the Station Hotel but found it too expensive. 'Bill's company didn't pay expenses. Then I found a little cottage to let at Blairs on Deeside, two bedrooms, lounge and kitchen – no washing machine – I washed clothes in the bathtub, leaving them out on the line to drip dry.' They later bought another Deeside cottage, and still live there.

Local woman Maggie Thomson was responsible for housing at Conoco. 'We had about thirty-six company houses – worth about £6 million. Managers, drilling managers, supervisors, all Americans, stayed in them, and they were the best of the houses. We had about forty leased company flats in the city centre as well as houses. I would take them [Conco employees] to where they wanted to live. Personnel looked after dentists, doctors and they nearly all put their children to the American School, which was free. If their washing machine broke down or if any redecoration was needed they had to come through me. When they saw a house they wanted, the solicitor would find out if the bank would pay for it. When it came to selling, the company would pay any loss but the bank would get any gain. Because employees kept wanting bigger ones, I suggested the company shouldn't be buying them. They always had to be gutted, which was totally uneconomical. The company also paid their utilities. Somebody would see a house and we would have to pay well over the odds. So I suggested giving them money to find their own properties and pay their own bills. That is how it changed. When one manager moved into a house in the West End, I had it repainted. Before, these people would have gone to a design studio and spent thousands.'

Maggie found the husbands easier to deal with. 'The wives were quite difficult. One would want her house the same size as the other one because her husband had a more important job. Their houses at home weren't half the size they got over here. The maintenance on one huge house out Deeside was horrific. The man got it because it was lying empty, but there were complaints from other managers. They weren't happy with one bathroom, everybody wanted two. Then it was two bathrooms and a conservatory. The houses just blew my mind at that time.'

The stories of the profligacy of the oil wives with company money are many. One woman, whose huge house had vast cellars, filled them with cheap utility furniture from the 1950s and 1960s. At the end of her husband's tour she persuaded his company to ship the lot out to the States, where she set up a lucrative period furniture store. Another wife fell in love with the original red Post Office telephone boxes. So she had one sent home to America – all half a ton of it.

Shell was another company that purchased property to house their staff. The redoubtable Margaret Mair, one of the original local employees at the company's first office base, in Market Street, said that before the production people arrived the drillers were like gods. 'A lot were Dutch. Some stayed overnight in hotels, but a lot lived in Aberdeen, especially office staff who were in Milltimber – a right little Holland there. The houses were fully furnished right down to the teaspoons.' Her former colleague, Kathy Davidson, who was involved in housing staff, said, 'Some of them weren't so good when the people left – unbelievable. I remember a very high-up guy whose house was scrawled from top to bottom with graffiti and swear words. He must have had a row before he left Shell. We built homes over in Kincorth and nobody wanted to go at first until we moved the Dutch school there. No one was interested in houses in Portlethen. Everybody thought they should get one of the better houses. When they were moved here, they would say, "I am not coming to Aberdeen unless I can pick my house." And at that time Shell were desperate to attract people.' The Kincorth enclave at the south entrance to the city became a sizeable colony of Dutch families. The company has since sold off the properties and now provides loans for house purchase instead.

During the boom years companies also block-booked complete floors of hotel rooms, which could stand empty for indeterminate periods. Maggie Thomson said that when the Conoco were recruiting for platform staff most of the men stayed in the Royal Darroch (later destroyed in a tragic explosion). 'They would come to me on a Monday morning for expenses – £600 or £500 whatever. We had two pool cars they could use. Most of them commuted but there were people with families who were allowed a relocation visit in order to find a house and were put up in a hotel. I hate to say it, but some treated their wives and kids to a weekend – just like a perk.' To an enterprising Aberdonian this level of spending could only mean 'bottomless pockets'. A Grampian Regional Council housing review in the 1970s made the point, however, that the incomers tended to rent: 'The majority of house moves involved either the formation of new local households or the trading up or down of the local population.'

Sheila Robertson and Jean Gaffney were given accommodation by Conoco in a prestigious row of flats at the heart of the wealthy 'purple patch' in the West End. Sheila's flat had a hallway as big as a living room. 'I had two bedrooms, the living-room had three sofas, a dining-room table, six chairs, marble fireplace, a big sideboard and there was still room. My main bedroom had two double beds, two wardrobes and two dressing tables. I was there for a year.' Jean occupied the basement. 'I think it was the maids' quarters – but the accommodation was great. Service flats, we didn't even have to dust. I had come from a council flat in Dundee. Everybody else was married or had partners and they found it easier to settle. But everybody was given the chance of temporary accommodation, paid for three months.' Relocated employees also enjoyed free meals that first year. 'We either got luncheon vouchers or if we bought food we gave them the receipts.'

Sheila said, 'Because we couldn't get on the property ladder at that time, we also had the option of a council house. I was offered accommodation at Blackburn and Portlethen. Jean was told she would only be offered a house if she was pregnant or married.' But again they were given assistance and Sheila was able to buy her first one-bedroom flat. 'I paid £20,000 and my father was horrified. Eighteen years I was there.' Jean stayed in Aberdeen for fifteen years. 'We were building a house, then my husband died so I commuted from Dundee. Then there were huge changes and I thought it was time to move on so I returned home. But that start in Aberdeen is the reason we both own our own houses now.' Sheila is also back in her hometown.

It was totally different for Pauline Baxter when she began to hunt for a house in 1977. 'I went with an American, wife of one of my husband's colleagues. She knew the area. So we drove to Ellon, Kemnay and then Inverurie, where we almost bought a house. But there was no way I could sell our house in Dorset and buy the one in Inverurie. It was so expensive – about twice what we would have paid for a similar house where we had come from.' The Baxters ultimately rented one of the Scottish Special Housing Association's semi-detached houses set aside for oil workers in Portlethen.

Another Conoco evacuee from Dundee is John Brodie. 'I decided to go to Aberdeen because they provided me with 5 per cent of my salary as a moving allowance and the Scottish Special Housing Association got me a house in the Sheddocksley housing estate [where he still lives in retirement]. I was living in a council house in Whitfield, Dundee. They paid for us to come and look. When the wife saw the house she said, "Oh, yes!" We were classed as incoming oil workers, category A. The locals had no chance of a house like this. We had a bathroom, which was quite unheard of where we came from. The local authorities were falling over themselves to attract folk.'

The Gliddens were told originally they would only be in Scotland for about a year before being sent to the Persian Gulf. 'At that time I was going to have my baby and I wanted it born in Aberdeen, which had the most fantastic maternity care. Clarissa was born in January 1969 – the first oil baby.' They had been living in Aberdeen for some time before the production phase began, attracting a fresh influx of fellow countrymen. Barbara discovered there was a definite hierarchy. 'They were production people and, because we were in drilling, I was expected to kowtow to them. I must say I never gave the time of day to my sister Americans. One woman said, "You have been here all this time and never organised a womens' petroleum club? We have got to form one." We used to meet in the Treetops Hotel. Then there was a lady who had a baby – they said it was first-born to the oil industry in Aberdeen and they showered it with gifts. I said I already had the first baby. They told me she was "illegitimate" – born before the WPC.'

In fact, one of the first things the vanguard of Americans did was to repeat the pattern of 'occupation' they follow elsewhere in the world, in the mode of the 'colonial club culture' of the former British Empire. They established their own luxurious club, described earlier by Keith Johnson, with a section for wives who raised money for charities. A diplomatic touch was that Maitland Mackie, whose second wife was an American, was first president of the Petroleum Club at Kippie Lodge. 'They would have these balls and dances, Texas barbecues and all,' said Barbara, 'but it just lost the closeness and friendship we had. You had to get on with these people – your husband's job depended on it.' The women's organisation is still thriving, with forty nationalities represented among their members.

But the Gliddens had already made their own friends: 'Local people, not oil people, and we also attended an Episcopalian Church.' Bill worked on contract to Shell, and they became involved in the company's social life. 'We had a close relationship with some Dutch people and some Scots – particularly myself with the wives. You just became part of the Shell family.' Barbara ultimately felt accepted when she became active in Scottish politics. 'My moment of fame came in 1979 – I was installed as chairman of North Angus and Mearns Conservative and Unionist Association. That was far more interesting than the Womens' Petroleum Club.'

Pauline found it more difficult to make friends in the Portlethen oil colony. 'It was a lovely little house and I liked it, but I knew absolutely no one. We were all different nationalities and different social levels. There were Canadians on one side, people from Milton Keynes the other, and across the road the American who worked with my husband. People from everywhere, but nobody spoke. We were all strangers. I didn't get to know people until I got a dog. Then I started ten-pin bowling – introduced by an American lady – and I got to know more people.' Ian Baxter retired from the oil industry and they are now living in their own house in Old Portlethen. To the Baxters and their grownup children, the North-East is their home. 'I just love all the open spaces, the countryside. You have all the shops now in the city centre and everything you want to do. Ten minutes inland and it is a completely different world.'

Like Barbara Glidden, many incomers from the States fell in love with the rural life. Texan Elmer Atkins, the Aberdeen boss of SEDCO, was one. Ted

Brocklebank, now an MSP, recalls a conversation with him: 'He used to say he thought he had died and wakened up in heaven. "Man, there's deer on the hill outside my house and fish in the river at the end of my garden, and peaceful!"' Another American, who, like his compatriots, was being paid extra for working in Aberdeen, regarded being posted home as a tragedy. 'I lose a fortune, but I also lose a way of life.' Ted Roberts, Yorkshire born and bred, was the Forties Field's first Offshore Installation Manager (OIM). He lived in – and worked – a croft at Cuminestown, in Aberdeenshire. 'It was the kind of life I was brought up to and I was as happy as a pig in muck. My neighbours were great. We used to help each other out as farmers anywhere do. It was nothing for me to bring in the "hairst".' Ted is now living in a village in his native county. But a number of fellow oil people have since chosen to retire to the region, after serving the full thirty-year lifespan of the industry. 'At one time there was quite a colony of BP staff living here in Aboyne and in Banchory,' according to Andy Lawrie, another former Forties OIM. There were, and still are, oil incomers settled round almost all points within a 30- to 40-mile radius of the city. Many, like Lawrie, and his fellow ex-BP OIM Jim Souter, didn't want to leave their adopted homes. 'I am from Glasgow,' said Jim, 'and my wife belongs to Arbroath. She didn't care for Aberdeen at first. Thought the folk were cold and unfriendly. Then she got to know them and now we love it. It's our home.'

The Baxters from Dorset used to go to see *Scotland the What* – the acutely perceptive annual local comedy and musical shows which were well flavoured with Doric. 'We laughed along with everybody else and after living in Findon we understood what they were saying. Our first New Year up here, a friend said to come and 'first foot' them. We didn't know that meant AFTER midnight. Where we came from everybody would see the New Year in and have a quick dram and go to bed. So we turned up before the bells. It wasn't until a long time afterwards somebody told us, "You shouldn't have done that, they will blame all sorts of horrible things on you."'

[5] The Rivals

The rumours were rife in Dundee at the start of 1979: the American company Conoco, one of the main oil service operators in the port, were preparing to pull out, like others had done before them. The company acted swiftly. At a press conference it was announced that twenty-six of the local workforce would indeed be moving up to Aberdeen, but the base at Princess Alexandra Wharf would be retained and staff would be doubled by the arrival of a platform project team.

One year later, with the typical swift brutal logic of an international company, they had all decamped to Dundee's traditional bitter rival some 60 miles further north. By 1991 the other major firm, BP, had also taken their important marine operations the road and the miles from Dundee to Peterhead. The role of the Tayside capital in the North Sea boom was virtually over. Aberdeen had pulled ahead in the old tug-of-war to become Scotland's third city.

The rise and fall of Dundee's riverside harbour as a strategic oil centre has been commonly regarded as a tale of lost opportunities. 'Dundee was the more logical place,' according to one senior oilman. 'But the reason that Aberdeen made it was because Aberdeen showed they wanted our business. Dundee were too disorganised.' That opinion, in fact, may be only partly true. The real reasons for the choices that eventually confirmed the Granite City as the magnetic centre of the industry are more complex.

The comparative fortunes of the two rival cities was very different at the beginning of the 1960s, just before the oil industry suddenly materialised; a succession of economic surveys and plans showed Dundee clearly in the ascendancy. The Toothill Report (1961), sponsored by the Scottish Council (Development) Industry, revealed that unemployment in the Aberdeen and Dundee exchange areas was low and more or less equal. The Tayside figure was a true reflection, but, as we have seen, what the survey didn't show was that the North-East rates concealed a high level of migration. Dundee was prospering while Aberdeen was stagnating. More importantly, the two areas

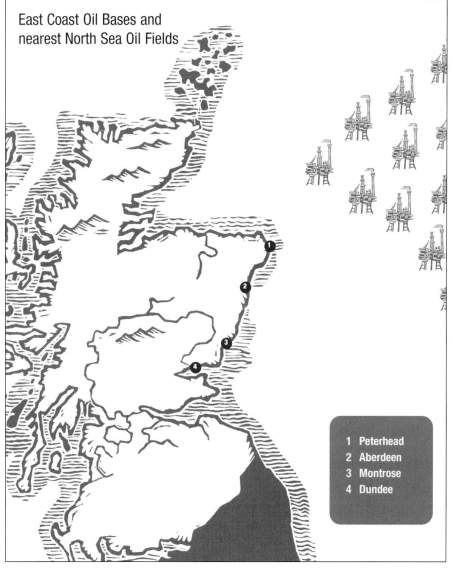

East Coast Oil Bases and
nearest North Sea Oil Fields

1 Peterhead
2 Aberdeen
3 Montrose
4 Dundee

Plate 25.

(*Boxtree Creative*)

had not been on an equal footing since 1945. The Tayside city was continuing
to reap the benefits of Special Development Area status granted when its
heavy industries, principally jute, had begun a sharp slide. New industries,
notably the American companies Timex and National Cash Register, and the
drop in unemployment were a direct result. Aberdeen, with no special status,
had no history of heavy industry, except a small engineering sector and two
shipyards. Instead, the area was dependent on agriculture and fishing, both
shedding labour and in gradual decline. The inquiry could offer no reprieve,
stressing it did not want to prop up industries in decay. Another disturbing
aspect was that, unlike Dundee, the port of Aberdeen, principally dependent
on fishing, was not listed as an important Scottish trading harbour.

Plate 26.

Dundee harbour in the
1960s – recognised as an
important east-coast port.
(*DC Thomson
Publications*)

The next report, launched five years later by Labour's Scottish Secretary, Willie Ross, was the ambitious *Scottish Plan*. It revealed for the first time the true extent of Scotland's migrating hordes, with the North-East the worst affected. But the verdict was remarkably similar to Toothill: the Dundee area, with its postwar successes and skilled labour force, was the most promising of the two cities, and it also had affinities with the Central Belt. This was not the case with the North-East and Aberdeen, which 'had to overcome a natural feeling among industrialists that the area is too remote'. There were no recommendations about Aberdeen's Dyce Airport although Dundee was commended for its ambitions for a full city airport. In the marine sector, however, the *Plan* did recognise the importance to their local economies of Scottish seaports, especially Dundee and Aberdeen.

In typical blunt fashion, the Scottish Secretary made the situation clear at a press conference, in a statement which was to resonate just a few short years later. 'A lot of local authorities could do a great deal more for themselves in being prepared to welcome firms, but you cannot rob the industrialist of the right to choose what he thinks would be the right area.' Asked if Aberdeen's priority were not greater than that of Dundee, he replied that Dundee was more ready for expansion: 'Success leads to success. You can't hold back success.'

So, at the start of 1970 the balance weighed heavily in favour of Dundee emerging as the main service centre for the oil and gas industry. In Aberdeen,

Plate 27.

Once Dundee harbour's
most important commodity
– bales of jute arrive
for the mills.
(*DC Thomson Publications*)

the companies had only established tentative footholds, retaining headquarters
in London, Lowestoft and Great Yarmouth. Both cities by then had equal
development area status. There were other ports in the running: Peterhead,
Montrose, the deep-water wartime anchorage at Invergordon in Easter Ross,
and Shetland, landfall for the East Shetland Basin where Shell had found the
Brent oilfield.

Dundee and Tayside Chamber of Commerce took the lead in the battle for
business. 'We felt the authorities weren't doing enough,' recalls John Aitken
from Perth, the lively Chamber's publications and publicity manager. 'We first
heard about oil in 1971 and gave the membership every encouragement to go
for business. The response was mixed. I suppose some of the traditional jute
companies felt it wouldn't last. There was also a bit of a lack of cooperation.
The port authority tended to do their own thing. But we really were the
pathfinders in what became the Dundee and Angus Oil Venture Group – with
no support financially from anybody.' The chamber was invited by BP
Exploration to Great Yarmouth to talk to their staff and other oil firms. 'They
wanted companies keen to be involved 365 days a week, 24/7, as they now
say. So we were in more or less at the beginning.'

In 1971 Dundee edged ahead: they won the major prize of BP's marine
base after the company had spurned Aberdeen (see Chapter 1). In truth it
came about more by default than good marketing. BP had been concerned
over the lack of 24-hour access to Aberdeen Harbour. They were also

apprehensive about the working practices of the port's dockers. Aberdeen was governed by the National Dock Labour system, which was also operated on Tayside. In view of what was to happen, the company's concerns were hugely ironic. But BP chose Dundee.

John Titterington, the last manager of BP's Dundee base, explained. 'BP moved to Dundee, where the port authority bent over backwards to get them in, because the harbour was very quiet. So they leased a couple of berths at Queen Elizabeth Wharf and some of the warehousing.' As a real sign of commitment when the future of the industry was still uncertain, they signed a lease – later to be re-negotiated for a 21-year term – for the 636-foot wharf. It would have cost them £0.5 million if they had built it from scratch. They also leased land at Stannergate, where the east-coast rail line ran parallel to the riverside. The base's role was to service three supply boats, the BP exploration rig *Sea Quest* and, eventually, the Forties Field, where development was well underway.

The BP decision heralded a period of great optimism on Tayside and the authorities were determined to attract more oilmen. Industry experts told them to ignore the presumption the companies would be 'here today and gone

Plate 28.

Oil supply vessels lie alongside BP's wharf on Dundee's riverside.

tomorrow'. Oil traffic had begun to boom. New exploration groups arrived from the southern gas fields and in the fourth-round award of Government licences for North Sea blocks some new blocks were close to Angus and Fife, which was thought might presage work for the Robb Caledon shipyard in Dundee. William Fitzgerald, lord provost, told the authorities' new co-ordinating oil committee, 'North Sea development is like a gold rush. At the moment there is a lot of nibbling going on. If someone bites, we will hook them.' He said they might be tempted to sterilise land for oil companies 'even if it meant losing other industry'. Already some local businesses were engaged in oil operations. No indication there of a tepid welcome from the leaders of the community.

But by 1972 they began to be concerned. Only one other group had declared an interest in developing new facilities: Robb Caledon and the shipping company, Ocean Inchape, had formed a joint venture, Tayside Offshore Supplies and Services, to service and maintain rigs. Otherwise the 'nibbles' had not become substantial bites. The lord provost complained, 'When Dundee has facilities already available why are the oil companies developing further north?' Dundee's 'Mr Industry', Maurice McManus, was despatched to the London headquarters of the main companies to put their case, and deputations also visited a number of oil-related areas seeking advice. The committee complained to the Scottish Office that other east-coast ports had an unfair financial advantage. The Scottish Office under secretary of state, George Younger, denied this and assured them he would make special efforts to draw the oil industry's attention to what Dundee had to offer.

Meanwhile, the operation at Queen Elizabeth Wharf, under the first manager, Denis Maycock, was building up. The supply-boat fleet expanded from three vessels to thirteen, handling 100 tons more cargo than Dundee's most famous industry, jute. A second oil company joined them in 1973. American Conoco North Sea initially serviced its only exploration rig, Sedco 703, out of Scotland's first custom-built marine facility, the £0.5 million Princess Alexandra Wharf, owned by Dundee Petrosea. They later staffed the base themselves in 1976. Petrosea, formed by Dundee, Perth and London Shipping (DP&L) and an American company, Theiss Petrosea International, supplied offices, services, pipe yard and the stevedores (dockers). Initially the company operated two newly designed supply ships, the Polar 901 and 902. Arch Bell, the Texan manager, said, 'Local industry has taken to the oil business like ducks to water. It strengthens the opinion that it is a wonderful base to operate from.' Conoco's former director of government affairs, Dan McGeachie, who is from Arbroath, worked in Dundee as a journalist and so 'was rather keen on Conoco developing there. In Aberdeen we would have been just one of the mob. We got on well with the Dundee politicians. We had a hyperbaric unit there and a drilling rig, Dundee Kingsnorth.' The hyperbaric unit, used for treating divers for decompression problems, later moved to Aberdeen to become a national centre. The general manager of Dundee Harbour Trust, A Murray Smith, described the development as 'a break-through' following BP. In the two years since the first oil supply ship for BP, the *Lady Camille*, sailed into the port, traffic had grown. Twenty-seven vessels belonging to eleven owners made regular trips offshore for BP, Conoco and Tayside Offshore. And there was a variety of ancillary oil boats keeping the riverside berths busy.

Welsh economist Howard Price was sent to Dundee as manager, from BP's offices in Harlow. 'There was something of a crisis. They were trying to meet the demands of an operation no one really fully appreciated. There was a great sense of excitement. Everybody knew the North Sea was different. It was all about depths of water and weather conditions and taking known technology to its limits. The demands were going to be exceptional – the rewards potentially also exceptional.' Howard moved north in 1975 and Forties oil came ashore later the same year. 'There must have been well over 1,000 men working on each of our four platforms simultaneously and we had to cater for them and supply the materials to drill and to construct.' Like many veterans of the North Sea, the former BP manager has vivid memories of the problems the phenomenal offshore weather caused. 'You could only offload in seas of less than Force 8. The health and safety requirement was limited to wave heights of 20 to 25 feet. Anything over you had to forget and stand off.'

Conoco's first Dundee employee, base manager Jack Livingstone, was a Fife mining engineer who had also worked on land drilling and quarrying operations. 'We had about fourteen or fifteen of a staff in Dundee. BP had ninety-four. We had five rigs going at the time and eight supply boats – but it fluctuated. Very much hand-to-mouth for a while.' They started with a manager and a superintendent who also organised the helicopter flights. 'In exploration that drill has to keep turning. The first rig, Sedco 703, cost $33,000 a day and the bill was $1 million a month. It couldn't move on its own – not like the subsequent Aker rigs – and two boats came with the Sedco.'

Howard Price over at the BP base actually had 120 staff, mostly labourers, and 99 per cent were local: 'At one stage, the Dundee base in pure marine tonnage movement terms was the largest in the world. Not in scale of operation or acreage, Stavanger would have run us close, but they didn't have as many platforms operating.' Howard's deputy, fellow Welshman Dave

Plate 29.

BP base manager in the 1970s, Howard Price.

Thomas, had worked for BP all his life, beginning in refineries. He was the materials and transport superintendent. 'We had twelve supply boats, maximum and we were loading on average about 600 tons of material a day to go to the Forties, plus shipments transferred from Dundee to Lerwick. The food and provisions came through a contracts division in Dyce, Aberdeen. Dundee firms had very few contracts from us; our transport was hired from local companies and it was exceptionally busy – a 24-hour operation.'

Like Jack at Conoco, Howard was also responsible for the helicopters at Aberdeen, until the administration was moved to BP's operation centre. 'I realised we didn't have enough storage space. Dundee is a remarkable city, but it has always had a problem – the road bridge is in the wrong place. Stannergate was used for storing pipe, but it was insufficient really.' The storage area was moved to Longtown Road on the Kingsway ring road. The harbour was used purely as a workshop and for loading vessels. Howard added, 'That meant that all the material had to come through the town although a lot of the material came in by rail.'

Typical North Sea weather was causing constant havoc to the flow of supply boats and Howard came up with a solution. He told BP's marine captain, 'I want a super vessel to meet the demands of more than one platform at the same time.' He said there was one being built in Sweden – called the *Stena Piper*. 'I said I wanted it. She cost more than £5,000 a day, so you were talking big money. Well, they hired this thing.' It came in one Saturday afternoon. 'Shed 16 was very high but I could see this vessel towering over it and I thought, "Good God – what have I done?" She replaced two and a half supply ships at least and could supply two platforms. Of course, now there are much bigger vessels.' Later, *Forties Kiwi*, the BP support ship, which operated out of Grangemouth, was chartered to sit in the field and supply fuel and cargo.

Two of Jack Livingstone's friends were at Aberdeen harbour one day. One said to the other, 'Who's that boat working for?' The other man said, 'That has got to be a Conoco boat – it is well down in the water line.' Jack laughed, 'I am a Fifer and a miserable sod. We had a system to service two platforms and maybe a rig. Every boat did a milk run and it was full when there were enough containers for two thirds of the boat. Every boat sailed loaded with fuel, water and three filled mud tanks.' The supply boats had to carry back waste and scraps from the rigs. 'The scrap that came from the Murchison installation took about three days to offload.' At first there were no containers, just pallets on the decks, covered by tarpaulin. 'The stuff was getting soaked so we needed containers and this guy started hiring them. He turned over a £1 in his first year. Suddenly we had 250 on hire all the time.

That guy sold his business and retired to Jersey!'

Two of Jack's employees were young Dundee girls, Jean Gaffney, who started at the offices on the wharf in 1976 and Sheila Robertson, who joined in 1979. The girls were amazed by the contrast in cultures between Dundee's traditional industries and the newcomers. 'I don't think the rest of Dundee knew we were there,' said Sheila. 'When I applied I didn't know what it was or even where it was, because you always associated the docks with the boat yard.' Jean found the company well established. 'They were setting up the warehouse and I had to help catalogue all the equipment, more a secretarial role. I knew absolutely bugger all. Dundee was going through a spell of unemployment and we never realised how big oil was going to be. It was exciting but anything went and money was no object, compared to the civil service; when you wanted a pen you got a new one – not a refill.'

Sheila arrived when they were planning to move to Aberdeen and, in fact, they did so eighteen months later. 'I think that was when the whole thing was escalating. More and more project people just kept coming in – that was for Murchison.' Jean: 'They were from all parts of the world.' Sheila: 'How we managed to fit them all in I don't know, but they kept coming.' The wages were another source of astonishment for the girls. In Jean's first year she had three pay rises. 'I am earning now what I was earning in the 1980s. My father was dumbfounded. It was more than he had earned in thirty years at Keillers confectionery. Silly money.' Sheila's first pay rise after three months was 20 per cent. 'I went from £40 in my previous job to £60 and then I got this pay rise and I am like, eh? Put it this way, I left Conoco when I got redundancy in 1993, and I was on £24,000. I am on £15,500 now. There is no comparison here in Dundee now.'

Jean believes they were the poor relations in Dundee. 'Once we started to interact with Aberdeen, we began to realise the scale of it. But we worked hard and played hard. Conoco's first oil was produced in the 1970s, the millionth barrel in the 1980s; Sheila remembers: 'First oil, the first million barrels – they kept involving you as part of a team. The word today is empowerment and you were encouraged to say what you wanted.' Jean said she has never experienced anything like it since. 'Dundee was a different culture altogether when I moved back there fourteen years ago. A real shock – the attitude to work. I had ended up buying for Murchison and Hutton – oil-field equipment. You name it – up to three quarters of a million I was able to sign off, and I had no experience. You just grew with it.' Sheila: 'I started off in reception and ended as supervisor in IT – assistant manager. I was moving all the time and that helped your approach to your work.' Jean said, 'You had to be a jack of all trades. It wasn't uncommon to don a pair of coveralls and

``Plate 30.

The Dundee stevedore.

(*DC Thomson Publications*)

help clear out warehouses.' She added, 'Trying to relate it to somebody in my workplace now – they have got no idea. I would hate to think what we would have been doing now if we hadn't joined Conoco.'

For both companies and any of the firms using the harbour, a major barrier was the one BP had tried to avoid when they decided to bypass Aberdeen: the restrictive practices enforced under the dock labour scheme. The dockers enjoyed the sole rights to load and unload vessels at the quaysides. While the Conoco boss found the Aberdeen men just as awkward to deal with, both base managers had a fund of tales about the daily jousts with the stevedores of Tayside whose union, the giant Transport and General Workers, was as powerful and combative as any on Clydeside.

To the Americans who controlled the industry, collective bargaining was anathema. They flatly refused to deal with trade unions offshore, and that is still true of some companies. Onshore, however, there was no choice. 'They had the ball at their feet then,' said Jack ruefully. 'I reckoned there were only two of us making more wages than the porters – and one of them was American. You needed a squad of four but we had to pay for six; one was in the cabin making the chips and another one, I don't know what he did, but only four would come out.'

Howard Price said, 'The dockers, they were – what's the word I can use for them? Their history in Dundee had not been a good one – they had been exploited and obviously there was an attitude of mind. I got on very well with them, but I remember one occasion when they were all on strike, in sympathy with their Aberdeen colleagues. The *Sea Quest* was lying in Aberlady Bay ready to go after refit and maintenance. The rates for drilling then were substantial, £2,000 or £3,000 a day. But she couldn't get supplies from Dundee.' The DP&L chairman called to apologise. 'He said the union chairman and secretary wanted to see me. We talked for ages. Then one said, "Well, we had better go and load that ship." We went out onto the jetty. The wind was howling, it was raining and it was dark. One operated a big overhead crane, the other hitched the chains to the container and on it went to the vessel. Some dockers walked past. A few words were spoken. Off the men went. Next day all my men were back in work. They broke their own strike.'

Jack said he knew the Conoco Americans didn't like the union situation. 'But their attitude was – just spend the money. The dockers weren't going to work overtime one time and that was to put the pressure on because they knew Murchison was starting up and a helluva crowd of stuff had to go out. So we stuck the stuff on lorries, went up north and shipped it out of there. The dockers got wind of this and sent boys up to picket. But the locals sorted that out. They couldn't find anywhere for bed and breakfast.'

BP's deputy manager Dave Thomas spoke about the belligerence of the dockworkers. 'One of the leaders said to me one day, "We have got you by the balls. We could close down the Forties in 24 hours." I said, 'Don't even think

Plate 31.

Dundee's 'own' drilling rig, Dundee Kingsnorth at its moorings in the Tay.

about it. BP are not going to be held to ransom by you. The Government is getting £5 million in royalties from BP. You try that on, in 24 hours they will be setting up in Bergen and ship from over there.' Jack Livingstone said they planned to use a rig to transport material to Murchison. 'We had to park it off Arbroath; because of customs regulations it had to lie four miles outside to be loaded. Either that or the dockers would have to go out on the boat. Working out how to deal with stuff like that wasted your time.'

By 1980, Dundee had still failed to attract any new oil companies and there was ongoing criticism that the area had not made enough of its initial involvement in the oil boom. The authorities were still concerned that everything was now going north to Aberdeen and Peterhead. Nevertheless Dundee's first major tenant, BP, were quick to reassure their hosts they 'had no intention' of joining the stampede up the coast. John Williamson of BP Exploration said his company were pleased and satisfied with the facilities and services.

In 1978, Houlder Offshore, managers of Kingsnorth Drilling, decided to leave for Aberdeen. They were followed by Conoco. Livingstone, who took his staff to what was to become part of the North Sea headquarters, had been asked to produce a logistical exercise to identify the most cost-effective bases to service their oil fields. 'When they came into production they wanted to be where the other oil companies were. I found it was cheaper to work in Dundee but it is six hours, sailing to pass by Aberdeen, a twelve-hour round trip. Boats were costing about £4,500 a day. So it was an extra twelve hours' sail. That was what clinched it: you had to be nearer.'

Plate 32.

A giant jack-up towers over the maintenance base at Prince Charles Wharf, Dundee. (*Dundee Harbour*)

Then, in 1991, it was the turn of BP. John Titterington, who had been sent to Dundee for three years and stayed for eight, had also been asked to assess the viability of remaining. 'We had taken over Britoil and obviously we were looking at our various options. There was the Dundee base, the Britoil base in Aberdeen, Peterhead, and a small base at Holsgarth on Shetland. It was decided to consolidate into one base, run by the oil service company ASCO at Peterhead. All the big exploration was moving into the northern waters from the central basin.' BP's once-busy wharf in Dundee is now occupied by a housing development. John himself commutes round the world's oil fields, still working for BP. 'Dundee is a superb place. I live in Forfar and see no reason to leave – Angus is a great area.'

One oil-related company which had survived was Kestrel Marine, which built small modules and topsides for offshore platforms at Prince Charles Wharf. After the city's shipyard, Robb Caledon, closed, Kestrel took over their premises in 1982 and operated until they shut down in 2000. Kolfor Ltd, founded thirty years ago to manufacture generators for the industry, is now owned by a Swedish group. Worried by the exodus, Dundee's public and private sector leaders decided to take a hand and formed Dundee and Angus Oil Venture Group in 1984 to help, in their own words, 'the struggling oil and gas industry promote itself on the world stage'. The marketing group now represents some fifty members from a wide range of oil-related interests in the area.

As for the oil industry's gradual disenchantment with Dundee, a number of oilmen blamed the unions – and in particular the dockers. 'The biggest problem,' claimed Dan McGeachie 'was industrial relations in the docks, the biggest single factor involved in ditching the Dundee project. Maybe I am overstating this – but it was an important factor.' John Titterington said he had no quarrel with the quality of the Dundee staff. 'If anything is to be said it would be about attitude at times. This union thing.' Former SNP leader and Dundee MP Gordon Wilson admitted the city had a rather difficult labour record. 'It was partly because of conditions in the jute industry. You had people who were exploited and you get that kind of ethic building up. It carried on after the oil had gone.' Dave Thomas, who now lives in Margate in Kent, thinks Dundee generally was hell-bent on industrial suicide. 'It was a shame because it had so much going for it – the port facilities for a start. But they weren't prepared to go on the treadmill of an oil exploration system. Sad for Dundee.'

Joe Savage, secretary of the TGWU 7/32 branch (Dundee), the dockers' union, during the key period, unsurprisingly takes an entirely different view and has contrasting memories of the oil service operation on Tayside. He started work in the docks in 1964, when the city's wharves and small harbour were busy with jute, timber, paper, cement and general goods. He still regards that as real stevedoring. 'On the jute ships you were pulling bales of jute about all day and that was hard graft. With the oil the cargo was pre-slung, all you did was hook on and lift the whole package – there was no tonnage involved, it was just the rate for the job.' It was casual labour then and if the dockers weren't hired they were paid dole money. The National Dock Labour Scheme replaced the dole and guaranteed regular employment with the stipulation that any cargo had to be handled by dockers.

Joe became branch secretary in 1974 just as the oil boats were beginning to arrive. 'We started negotiating about manning and rates with our employers, the Dundee Stevedore Company. Then they talked to BP or Conoco or whoever was bringing stuff in. Sometimes we would meet with the oil people as well as our employers. We just negotiated the rate for the job as we did with jute. The oil companies wanted 24-hour cover and we needed two twelve-hour shifts. After a while that stopped and they just kept a gang on all day and then on standby. We got paid overtime in four-hour blocks if we were called out. If you came out for an hour you were paid for four.'

'When the DP&L took over, if you couldn't come to an agreement with the supervisors you ended up meeting the employers. We had a pretty good relationship with them. All in all it wasn't too bad. We didn't have much trouble. We had strikes, but not over anything significant. It may have been worse in the early days but things started to improve once we got a working relationship with them. We would have a meeting and we would get the problem resolved before it got to anything.' Joe claimed the oil work was nothing like what it used to be. 'I loved working in the docks then. All these different boats with different cargos.'

The biggest industrial dispute at Dundee was not caused by the dockers, who acted in support of offshore workers sacked from a SEDCO drilling rig operated by Dixilyn for Conoco. 'They brought a big shot across from America.' The burly former docker laughed. 'I think he thought he was walking into a Mafia-type situation. He had a couple of heavies and I am sure they were tooled up. But once we spoke to him he relaxed with a big cigar. It turned into a good meeting and they got something resolved with the guys from the rig.'

Joe refuses to accept that the dockers' attitudes were in any way responsible for the oil companies moving. 'They got rid of the dock labour scheme 1989 and then after the national dock strike in 1999, the Conservative Government managed to get rid of dockers all together. BP only moved after that.' He said that now the system was moving towards agency labour.

'Workers are back to being abused like they were in the days of casual labour. As far I am concerned the oil companies got a good service out of Dundee.'

Another perceived weakness in Dundee's suitability as a major oil base was the inadequacies of the Riverside airstrip. The Chamber of Commerce described it as 'the missing link' in the city's hopes of entering the top league of oil focal points. It was one of the reasons Houlder Offshore, who managed Kingsnorth Drilling, decided to leave the city in 1978. Ed Edwards, the operations manager, told the media, 'In many ways Dundee has been ideal for our purpose but anyone flying from London has to land at Aberdeen or Edinburgh and then travel by car or rail to Dundee. In this sort of weather that can be hazardous.' He added prophetically, 'Unless something is done to provide better communication I can see other firms in the business pulling out and setting up in Aberdeen.'

Other oil companies blamed the local authorities. John Moorhouse, director of communications for Shell UK in the 1980s and 1990s, acknowledged that when they were preparing to hook-up their Fulmar field 190 miles to the east, the company could have diverted to Dundee. 'But Dundee were so disorganised they would never have been able to cope. That's why we didn't go although it was the more logical place. We didn't really know at that time we were going to get the stuff in the far north.'

Roger Ramshaw, who worked in Dundee as a petroleum engineer with Conoco and ended as president of the merged Conoco Phillips UK, took a similar position. 'The irony was that Dundee was a better port than Aberdeen from the pure supply standpoint. But then there was the labour situation and the attitude of the Dundee council. Basically it was: should we stay, or go to Aberdeen. We decided on Aberdeen and never looked back. Dundee were not welcoming.' Over at Queen Elizabeth Wharf, Howard Price saw it differently. 'We tried to enhance the image of BP in Dundee and I think the council appreciated how important we were to the city. We brought a lot of money in and it had a multiplier effect. We were held in very high regard.' That kind of diplomacy earned Howard the job of British Consul in Turin. Like Jack Livingstone, he is now retired to Broughty Ferry. One of his successors, John Titterington, agreed that they had got on very well with the authority, especially first of all with Dundee Port Authority. 'We were always made very welcome by the various lord provosts and got their full support.' John Aitken refuses to accept any suggestions of lack of effort from the chamber. 'We felt we were the front runners.' But, he said, 'Personally I really got frustrated with some attitudes that we couldn't go after it. It was like being at Hampden on Cup Final day. You were in front of the goal in the six-yard box, the ball at your feet, the goalie on his back – and your laces were tied together.'

Peter Cockhead, then depute director of planning at Grampian Region, summed up the crucial differences that gave Aberdeen the final edge in a 1983 paper, 'In the early 1970s Aberdeen was ideally located to the oil exploration areas of the middle North Sea, it being the largest community in the north providing major harbour, airport, rail container terminal and research facilities, and unlike Dundee, the local authorities were willing to actively support the oil presence.' The reason lies in all of these points, but the most important aspect to remember is that the industry has a powerful herd instinct. It likes to be with its own kind. So it simply made up its own mind about where it would put down permanent roots. And the deciding factor would have been the bottom-line costs of those six hours' extra steaming down to Dundee.

Today Dundee has done a remarkable job of reinventing itself as the City of Discovery – outwith the oil industry – incorporating modern developments including biotechnology, digital media, biomedicine; it also has one of the world's foremost medical institutes, specialising in cancer research. The city's postwar saviour NCR remains – but with a reduced staff of 1,500. Only journalism survives from the legendary triumvirate that brought the city fame and fortune – jam and jute are long gone.

[6] Blitzkrieg

With the huge flurry of new discoveries and the opening of the production taps in an increasing number of fields through the 1970s and early 1980s, a veritable avalanche of new people, new companies, new demands and new challenges threatened to overwhelm the small local authorities of Aberdeen and the North-East of Scotland. Yet key officials on the front line of the battle to absorb the aggressive new industry remember with affection those frenetic years that so transformed a stagnant community.

Trevor Sprott, planning director for Aberdeenshire (later Grampian Region) said, 'There is no doubt we were faced with an enormous task, but they were exhilarating times.' Bert Sturgeon, estates officer and Aberdeen city assessor, found it all tremendously exciting: 'The best thing to hit not only Aberdeen, but Scotland, since the Industrial Revolution.' John Hutton of the North-East Scotland Development Authority (NESDA) recalled the atmosphere as 'lively, invigorating and stimulating'. But there were critics who claimed these officials were ill-prepared. Architect David Taylor certainly thought so in 1975 in his contribution to the *Red Paper on Scotland* (Edinburgh, 1975), a savage polemic edited by the future chancellor of the exchequer, Gordon Brown. 'The small local authority . . . remote from the context of national priorities is ill-equipped to deal with the massive changes thrust upon it.' Lord Kirkhill, the former lord provost, was adamant the city did very well: 'I think Aberdeen coped. It didn't all happen at once, it took a while.' Another civic leader, James Lamond, was more defensive. 'You mustn't forget that in the middle of all this, Aberdeen was really just a small town with a small town council. For me the thing came like a bolt from the blue.'

The fact that it was also initially cloaked in secrecy by the oil companies hampered the councils' ability to react. Maitland Mackie, as convener of Aberdeenshire County Council, decided to find out what the oilmen really wanted. So he called a meeting in a local hotel in 1971. 'I asked them to tell us how many people, how many houses – just what they were looking for.

The meeting was a damned flop. Nobody would speak. They didn't want their competitors to know their business – separate companies, y'see, and separate individuals. I told John Russell [Mackie's county clerk] to call a halt. So we adjourned to the bar for drinks, then on a one-to-one basis, you got the stories.'

A previously unpublished document for 1971, from the closed files of the Scottish Office (now the Scottish Executive), held in the National Archives for Scotland, gives another account of the same meeting, the first held publicly to discuss the oil situation. It reveals graphically the total lack of knowledge by the community about the new industry, and the initial lack of understanding between the authorities and the oilmen. All the principal oil contractors and service companies, representatives of financial services, local business and the local authorities attended. A civil servant reported that Mackie said the local authorities were anxious to help and would welcome guidance from the oilmen about the future scale of activities. Oil-company representatives stressed the uncertain nature of exploration; they 'didn't know for certain if oil was here in quantity'. A Conoco executive was more forthcoming. From the interest shown in the next round of licenses 'it was obvious there would be a lot of activity in the waters off North-East Scotland'. He added, however, that 'the extent to which companies were attracted to the area was up to the public authority'. Diving consultant Keith Johnson was at the same meeting. His version was rather more blunt. 'One of the oil companies said to the harbour board, "If you don't get your shit together we're just going to cruise up and down the east coast until we stop."'

Such meetings became a regular feature as councillors strove to understand these polite, but tough, corporate newcomers. Lord Kirkhill recalls that BP's Alastair MacLeod Matthews – 'an English gentleman' – set the tone. 'He didn't suddenly send every councillor five gallons of whisky. No, he approached it the right way – a reception for the planning committee, drinks, smoked salmon and a film show to make his point. Or, if he needed real information, it was an informal dinner for a few. The first Yanks would have gone the five gallon route, but they quickly spotted it didn't work.'

As the pressure mounted at the start of the 1970s, the authorities had little time to learn. As Trevor Sprott, Aberdeenshire Planning Director, conceded, the county, which became Grampian Region, was not prepared. 'We were making it up as we went along.' Regional development officer Alan Campbell said it had to be realised that the authorities had neither the planning machinery nor the manpower then. 'As you would expect from a rural council with just some market towns to administer, there simply weren't the staff.' Sprott recalls the staff only grew from thirty-six to forty. 'I remember making a bid for sixty and I was laughed out of court. We had to cut our cloth accordingly.' Sprott's boss, Aberdeenshire's chief executive, John Russell, said in 1973, 'My authority are handling about 4,000 applications per annum. Before oil it was about 2,000.'

A regional council report in 1981 put it concisely: 'The arrival and very sudden expansion of the oil industry brought unprecedented problems for local authorities previously more preoccupied with the problems of declining population rather than dynamic industrial and commercial activity.' And it was not only the small local councils who were caught napping. The chief economic adviser to the Scottish Economic Planning Department, Gavin McCrone, claimed, in a paper presented at Aviemore in 1974, 'Both in magnitude and speed, the pace of development associated with North Sea oil far exceeds the growth of any other industry in Scotland during the last half century. From a position in which the UK had not proven oil reserves, in little more than two years a major oil province has been discovered. It is not surprising that such a major change should impose some strain on existing structuring and systems.'

The councils may have been ill-equipped, as David Taylor maintained, but it would be unfair to fault the abilities of the officials. Political leaders of the time insisted they were of the necessary quality. Lord Kirkhill said the city had formidably capable officers in Tony Colclough, the planning director, the town clerk, JC Rennie, and his depute, JFV Hunter. 'We were well served by these men. Tony was more than a match for the oil people. They were surprised to find somebody like him in a place like Aberdeen – English public schoolboy, Cambridge – no bloody oilman flummoxed him. Rennie was brilliant but detached and Hunter, now there weren't many cleverer than him. He wanted to be part of the action and the passion of the times.' Sir Maitland Mackie had the same kind of faith in John Russell, who became chief executive of Grampian. 'Russell was fit for them.' Shell's director of public affairs in Aberdeen, John Moorehouse, was highly impressed by Sprott and his department: 'Their reports on figures and projections were absolutely brilliant. They were so damn professional. The information was useful for our planning purposes as well.'

Both councils were to need all the local government skills they could muster. The extant planning structure had not been devised to regulate developments that grew so rapidly and on such a scale. The demand in the 1970s by some Labour politicians and industry analysts for a slowdown – like the depletion policy Norway was to introduce – was ignored, although Lord Kirkhill remembers saying no to quite a number of fairly desirable developments. Under the relevant statute, the Planning Act (Scotland), 1947, amended in 1969 and 1972, every planning authority had to prepare a five-year development plan. The plan had to measure the local authority's ability to cope; to guide developers, who 'would not simply be choosing their own areas'; to show expenditure priorities; and – what was described as its 'main virtue' – assure citizens control was being exercised.

Under the Local Government (Scotland) Act, 1973, which brought in new regional and district authorities, strategic planning fell to the regions, which ultimately led to friction between Aberdeen City District and Grampian Region. But the change was fortuitous and timely, giving inquirers one door to open and the region overall control. But officials were worried about the robustness of the system in the new circumstances. A senior Scottish Office planning official told the Scottish Economic Planning Council's newly formed oil taskforce in 1973, 'I am beginning to wonder whether it is reasonable to deal with major industrial development proposals by the same planning procedures used for minor matters like the location of a single house.' The taskforce decided later there was no scope for strengthening the current statutory powers, but remained determined to maintain control.

By 1975, against a barrage of demands for housing, industrial sites, new-build offices and office space, new roads, schools, and the vastly increased burden on water supplies, sewerage and the utility services, the local structure plans had to be revised. At one point in the oil areas, sixty-four plans, impact analyses and research reports were under preparation, and, during a development peak in 1974, there were twenty-seven applications for platform construction yards in one month.

Lord Kirkhill had gone on one of the early local authority trips to Houston to see how the first international oil capital had managed to cope. 'What a mess. Development gone mad – a 36-mile-long main street and absolutely no control over it. There was no way we were going to let that happen to Aberdeen.' Bert Sturgeon, Aberdeen City Assessor and Estates Officer, was of similar mind after visiting Yarmouth in Norfolk. 'To be quite honest, it was awful. Piecemeal, higgledy-piggledy – it made me all the more determined to keep control in the face of sometimes overwhelming demand.' However, not everyone thought like Lord Kirkhill. Malcolm Ford, of Shell Expro, positively recommended Houston's 'aggressive' tactics if Aberdeen wanted to continue to grow. 'They dangled the right carrots: low-cost land, a sympathetic political and economic environment which allowed fast development, and the right tax advantage. Houston was prepared to speculate to accumulate . . . Some [of you] may say, we have had enough disturbance to our traditions and our old way of life. In which case, put up the shutters and politely ask the oil business to go elsewhere, because clearly North Sea oil is going to grow.' Planner Peter Cockhead was invited to Nova Scotia in the 1980s to advise the Canadians on how Aberdeen had integrated the new developments. 'The authorities in St Johns [Aberdeen's Canadian equivalent] were prepared to rip out the city centre to make way for oil. Aberdonians would never have agreed to that.'

Because the development structure was hopelessly inadequate, new mechanisms had to be manufactured. Aberdeen, where land was in short supply, drew up a new town map, Moray and Nairn produced a new strategic framework, while the other authorities used existing statutory planning reports. As Trevor Sprott explained, 'We were struggling at the time and thinking to ourselves: "My God, what are we going to do here?" Finally we worked out an environmental impact statement and we were able to keep the Government and the council on side with us.' Under new local government legislation, the region produced a system of structure and local plans plus an overarching strategy which covered the main areas under pressure in Aberdeen and 20 miles around up to 1986. In addition, Sprott's environmental scheme identified fourteen significant areas to be safeguarded. 'We told the companies they would have to show us what was to happen on a site. There was a great deal of fuss, but there was too much at stake. We had to know. Eventually they worked with us and we kept control. We also had the Gaskin Report, which despite missing oil, had done the planning groundwork.' Former NESDA official Malcolm Bruce believed that Gaskin's prophecy of 'doom and gloom' had encouraged a fortunate attitude. 'The councils had already marked land for industrial development – Tullos and Altens in the city and Dyce and the Bridge of Don in the county.'

In 1974, the North-East Scotland Joint Planning Advisory Committee (NESJPAC), an ad hoc body established after Gaskin to influence planning strategy, set out a 'holding' development policy to prevent the proliferation of new small communities, avoid major strains on resources, provide infra-structure, and relieve the pressures on the construction industry. There was still public scepticism about the staying power of the new industry. In 1975 another report urged local authorities to adopt this containment policy warning it would be 'disastrous if oil development lasted only ten years and indigenous industries, with better long-term prospects, were irretrievably damaged'. It also suggested 'giving indigenous industries preference over incoming oil firms'. Fortunately the planners ignored this advice. Oil has outlived indigenous industries that either failed to grow or have disappeared entirely. The general fear was that if the NESJPAC advice went unheeded there would be 'uncon-trolled development'. This is arguably true in the explosion of dormitory housing satellites such as the Bridge of Don, but it is certainly not the case with the controlled placement of industrial estates in and around Aberdeen and the discreet location of large individual industrial concerns such as pipe farms.

Sprott maintained that his regional council, controlled by Conservatives for fourteen of the sixteen years he worked there, was fortunate in having continuity of political rule. He said it made for quicker decisions to meet the speed of developments. He was less positive about the Labour-controlled town council's relations with his council. 'That was very bad for a time. I suppose it stemmed from local government reorganisation. They didn't like the city being downgraded and the region having all the powers over matters such as planning.' Shell's John Moorehouse was aware of the difficulties. 'Hats off to the local authorities – particularly the regional council who were absolutely great. We had very few dealings with Aberdeen City Council – they were seen as an irritant rather than being particularly impressive. Nothing to do with politics but everything to do with the decisions they were able to make compared to the region.' Reorganisation brought party politics into the rural areas where councillors were largely independent. Maitland Mackie lost his seat and therefore the Aberdeenshire convenership. Grampian Region's first convener, the Conservative Sandy Mutch, said his party's majority of thirty over his term in office, 'made things easier when we wanted to push something through'.

The greatest single pressure that the new government infrastructure faced was the clamour for thousands of new homes. According to Trevor Sprott, 'The real dilemma was trying to estimate the number needed. A report I produced in 1974 said it would be 16,500 and that shocked everybody – but that was a vast underestimate. We needed more houses than the services could supply. At that time we were trying to rationalise about sixty-eight different water schemes under one authority and we were miles behind.' The strategy Sprott ultimately devised was to spread phased housing developments around the area. But other significant problems surfaced as the building rate increased. Gaskin, in 1975, highlighted the severe shortage of building labour caused by the desertion of skilled staff – initially a circular problem. A local businessman, Stanley Low, pointed out in 1973. 'The key to the labour problem is housing, and we don't have the labour to build the houses. So we will have to bring it in to build houses for the workers who are coming in to staff the oil industry.' A prime example is that of the owner of a small joinery business in Maud who closed his company in 1975 and moved into Aberdeen to set up a totally new business after twelve of his eighteen staff defected to a builder paying higher rates to match oil-industry wages. The enterprising joiner, Bryan Keith, ultimately built his Bon Accord Glass company into a multimillion-pound concern. Another element was that the construction companies, under heavy pressure, opted to take the more lucrative oil work rather than housing. Eventually the construction industry expanded its workforce by more than 5,000.

For the city there was also the vexed question of a dearth of land for any development, complicating relationships between local authorities, where the demands on one had to be met by another. The new districts, Gordon and Kincardine and Deeside, were more than happy to supply land for housing outside Aberdeen, creating a net loss of population to the city. By contrast, by 1985 the population of Gordon had increased by 23,000, and Kincardine and Deeside, by 12,000.

By 1975, an annual average of 4,000 new houses was being completed, 55 per cent public rented accomodation with priority to new key workers. In the following three years house construction averaged 5,500 a year. The record, 6,300, was in 1976 – a rate of seventeen new homes daily and the majority public. From 1976 to 1981, 41 per cent of all new building was by local authorities and the Government's Scottish Special Housing Association (SSHA), which invested £55 million in 4,600 houses in the oil areas from 1972 to 1976. The prime reason was to house local residents under pressure from rising house prices and rent levels caused by the sudden housing demands by immigrants. To alleviate the situation, from 1971 to 1981 the SSHA built 1,750 new units for oil-related key workers. These were the homes provided for the families of Pauline Baxter from Dorset and John Brodie from Dundee. Ted Roberts of BP said they were worried they were jumping the queue and offending a lot of Aberdeen people who couldn't get a house. 'The council said they would just build more. Then we wanted short-term housing, which we got for two years. But we still felt guilty.'

By 1982, the balance between private and public sector housing had shifted completely, with council property representing only 23 per cent. The building rate had also reduced dramatically, largely because of Government financial restrictions. By then private developers, thwarted in the 1960s by a political squeeze on urban space, had joined the building boom, producing 2,000 new homes a year. By 1994, the total housing stock in Grampian had increased by 40 per cent to 65,000 new houses spread, as Sprott had planned, to every available gap site in and around the city. The area's Structure Plan Forecast for 1999 noted, 'House building has continued at a rate of approximately 9,000 to 11,000 homes a year up to 1999 and still more are planned. Aberdeen and Aberdeenshire councils [restored to full autonomy in the 1996 merry-go-round of local government reforms] have since estimated that a further 25,000 homes will need to be built over the next eighteen years.'

But for all these remarkable and commendable efforts the planning

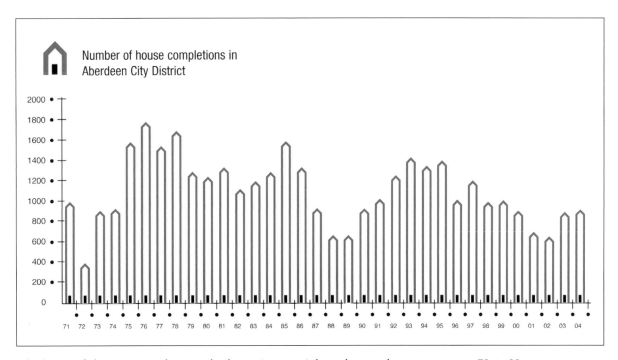

Number of house completions in Aberdeen City District

Blitzkrieg of the 1970s and 1980s had a serious social weakness: the concentration was on buildings and not communities, the priority, bricks and mortar. Within the expanded city boundaries, the farmlands of Old Machar/Bridge of Don had become the biggest and fastest-growing suburb, a virtual town, with sprawling estates of mixed private and public sector properties with a population of 30,000, almost twice as large as Peterhead. But the area was developed at such a speed – and it is still growing – the concomitant services required to bind together a social community lagged behind and are still lacking. Shopping centres on a scale to befit the population are of very recent origin. Until the 1990s there were no adequate medical facilities and similarly churches were slow to establish. Only the provision of schools in the Bridge of Don matched the growth of population: two academies, eight primaries – five with nurseries attached – and a feeder primary at Balmedie. The area's biggest school, Oldmachar Academy, was originally built to take 1,000 pupils; the current roll in the now over-crowded buildings, is now more than that. That the area is very much an oil workers' settlement was demonstrated during the 1986 oil-price collapse, when it had the highest rate of unemployment in the region.

The only other area to match it is the market village of Ellon further up the Don, which doubled in size in less than ten years. Because of a shortage of land, Gordon District, which took approximately 20 per cent of the new housing, ultimately called a temporary halt in the 1980s, as did its companion district in the new commuter belt, Kincardine and Deeside. An other

Plate 33.

(*Boxtree Creative*)

significant oil-related expansion was at Westhill, 5 miles west of the city centre, where there was a dramatic change, mainly in new private sector housing and a growing industrial estate. The settlement now has a population of nearly 9,000. Growing even more swiftly, nearer Aberdeen, is the former hamlet of Kingswells, also a significant oil-industry dormitory. Since 1991, when there were 1,100 people in new private housing, the number of new homes has trebled in 2000, to 3,270. Old coastal hamlets such as Portlethen and Findon were also reinvigorated, as was Balmedie northwards up the coast. Each experienced a 200 per cent increase in housing. Further afield in Banff and Buchan a growth of 20 per cent reflected the wide sphere of the oil industry's influence.

In his survey Gaskin drew attention to the reluctance of the rurally based North-Eastern worker to commute any distance to find work. Any movement had been migratory and permanent. From the 1970s onwards, that reluctance vanished. Some 70,000 daily car journeys were made in and out of Aberdeen in 1999 and the numbers are still rising, creating the modern phenomenon of urban gridlock. Peter Cockhead, who joined the regional planning department in 1975, and succeeded Trevor Sprott as director, thinks the early development plans were not the cleverest way to do it, citing the Bridge of Don estates as an example. 'Some of the traffic problems now and the effects of the settlement growth can be traced back to the strategies of twenty-five to thirty years ago, although they enabled the area to cope at the time in a relatively cost-efficient way.' Cockhead, who later became the council's director of planning and strategic development, said, 'The consequences are also seen in excessive speculative building not always in the appropriate location and [in] currently vacant office blocks.'

The influx of new families greatly increased demand for school places. Over the thirty years the regional and county councils built a total of fifty-two schools, far surpassing the school-building record of any other area in Scotland, or in the UK for that matter. Former convener Sandy Mutch was as proud of that record as of any other. 'That was really something – fifty-two schools at a cost of £81 million. How about that for forward thinking, eh? God knows what they would have cost today.'

The house-building boom created a new and lasting dimension to the North-East's domestic property market. The initial consequence was the abnormally high cost of land, but there was also a phenomenal rise in house prices (see Chapter 4). It was described by Tony Mackay and Anne Moir in *North Sea Oil and the Aberdeen Economy* (Aberdeen 1980), as 'demon-strating the worst effects of the advent of the oil industry'. In the 1970s, the balance of rental and home-ownership in the city was weighted in favour of the public sector rental, 47 per cent of households, with 20 per cent renting from the private sector and 33 per cent owning their own homes. By the 1990s, two of three houses in the area were privately owned while private rented stock in both city and region dropped sharply by almost a third.

Aberdeen soared nearly to the top of the national house-price table. The foundations were laid when prices rose by five and a half times, over the early 1970s, 40 per cent above the British average. Eventually the cost of a home moved from 20 per cent below the UK average to 10 per cent above, making the city's housing prices 'generally higher than for any other UK region except London and the South-East of England' according to local property surveys. Fortunately, average earnings in the area rose by a similar rate. In hard figures, in 1971 an average home sold for £4,100; by 1983, the price was between £35,000 and £39,000. By 1994 – the peak era – the price was in the region of £70,000 and it has continued to rise. Oil made property a remarkable investment. Beyond the city, prices have always been lower. Up the coast new homes cost 20 per cent less, while the opposite has occurred in Deeside, especially in the desirable suburbs of Cults, Bieldside and Milltimber, where prices have remained exorbitantly high.

The related cost of land to buy and to lease for business underwent a similar rapid escalation. Up to 1973, 30 acres a year were set aside by the planning authorities; during the following five years, that more than doubled to 75 acres. Because of the planning regulations, however, development was not so simple. Aberdeen Town Council fought a bruising five-year battle to re-zone 'green belt' farmland at Altens on the southern outskirts. Lord Kirkhill

Plate 34.

(Boxtree Creative)

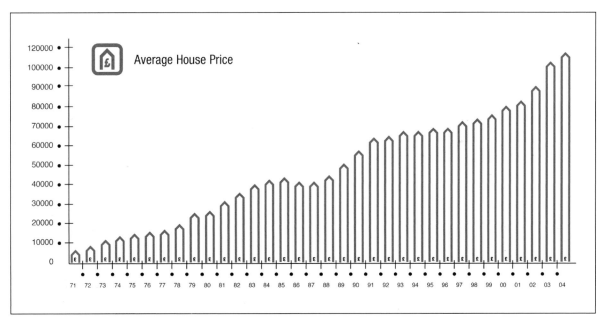

remembers people 'sniffing around the boundaries of the city, looking for parcels of land to buy in the hope they would be needed for development. I've no doubt some of these people made a killing.' It wasn't only the incomers who struck lucky. Sydney Reid, the farmer who sold the first slab of land (60 acres) to make way for the new housing development that was to become Kingswells, was delighted with the sale and 'wished he could have done it more than once'. He added, 'I am sorry I only got one crop out of them.'

Just how much of a 'killing' was made has been illustrated by several surveys. Researchers Pamela and Malcolm Baldwin found in their 1975 book, *Onshore Planning for Offshore Oil: Lessons from Scotland* (Washington) that when Michelin bought land for its tyre factory in 1969 the company paid just under £1,239 per acre; in 1974, an industrial site opposite went for £41,322 an acre. Other comparisons, by A McGregor Hutcheson and Alexander Hogg in *Scotland and Oil* (Edinburgh, 1975), show that a regular lease of 1 acre at £200 in the early 1960s had increased tenfold in the 1970s. The French oil company Total Marine had to pay £3,500 per acre for a 15-acre site at Altens. Later that year, the last remaining site at the adjacent West Tullos estate was leased at more than £5,800 per acre. A yet more startling example of the escalation of prices was a tract of land that went in 1970 for £2,500 per acre, while in 1980 similar land was leased for £5,500, implying a selling price of £50,000 to £60,000.

From a few sparse plots and scattered advance factories the councils had been pushed to fill and largely occupied by relocated local firms, a total of eleven industrial estates – seventeen in Aberdeenshire – developed organically as new companies rushed in to provide the oil support sector. The take-up of land reached unprecedented levels: from 1960 the 148 acres of East Tullos estate took 20 years to develop; from 1974 the 300 acres of Altens were filled in just 12 years. Lord Kirkhill recalls during 1972, Aberdeen had '200 firm inquiries and approximately 30 casual inquiries' for land. 'At that point the

Plate 35.

Ultra-modern facades of some of the many hundred oil company offices in Aberdeen's industrial estates.

(*Allan Montgomery*)

council were only able to accommodate a few. The majority were left to the private market.' NESDA was facing a similar barrage: 236 enquiries in the region; 121 were from established companies wanting to expand or relocate, while several were from key oil-company staff wishing to set up on their own. In many cases the former lord provost admits the council were forced to resort to compulsory purchase orders. Between 1981 and 1985, the councils were back in control of the market – some 70 per cent of new industrial and commercial development occupied local authority industrial estates. There were also purpose-built factories at Peterhead, Inverurie, Ellon and Forres. In all, more than a thousand acres of land were developed in that period.

Another problem was the availability of office space. From the start, demand for offices increased every year and the availability of floor space went from 46,500 square metres to 200,000 in ten years. Nearly half the offices were developed by speculators, a fifth purpose-built, giving Aberdeen more office floorspace per head of population than Glasgow and Dundee. The city also boasted higher rent levels – on a par with London and the South-East of England. Curiously, the initial demand came from the public sector, because of a nationwide rise in civil service employment, and in response to local government reorganisation. By the mid-1970s the oil industry began to catch up, with oil-related companies set up in revamped buildings and in a series of modern office blocks, altering the cityscape with imaginative designs and use of contemporary materials. At the end of 1974, only 4,300 square metres of new office accommodation were occupied by oil firms, but in seven years they had taken over 115,000 square metres – one third of the total office space. At the end of 1985 the figure was 270,000 square metres.

As the dynamic new industry underwent almost perpetual change with new companies, new acquisitions and mergers, so did the development of their premises. The upward movement of Shell Expro (who occupied the largest amount of office space among the oil majors) is the quintessential example of

Plate 36.

The foundations of the first phase of the complex that became Shell's UK Exploration headquarters at Altens industrial estate, Aberdeen. (*Shell UK*)

an onshore base growing in tandem with exploitation offshore. It developed from an increasingly scattered number of premises in the city, to the exponential development of a prominent site on Nigg Brae overlooking Torry and the harbour. Shell Expro, who first used Aberdeen Harbour as early as 1962, began with only a few dozen people in Union Street, and in a warehouse in a former tramcar depot in Market Street. The extended granite building is still home to oil firms. As more staff arrived, stacked portacabins were added to the warehouse. Another office was established while a site was leased in Tullos in 1966. By 1972, following the finding of the massive Brent Field, drilling and production were transported to Aberdeen where the roll had grown to 228. The company enlarged its Tullos site and set in motion plans for a two-storey building. The first phase opened in 1973, the next in 1974 and, a year later, the building housed 433 people, almost equalling the complement at Shell Centre in London. The next stages followed in 1974 and 1977 and the total building was finally completed in 1984.

At its peak there were more than 5,000 people working in and out of Aberdeen (there are currently 1,200 at Altens). The scale of building was for a long time behind the development needs, which was, according to Peter Cockhead, 'A classic demonstration that not even a major oil company such as Shell had any knowledge of their future needs. If the likes of Shell and BP

Plate 37.
The Shell buildings today.
(*Allan Montgomery*)

didn't know, how much more difficult was it for the local authority to try to respond?' Shell's great rival, BP, has undergone similar massive expansion in the city. Its North Sea headquarters occupied a virtual industrial estate on its own with a multi-storey car park. The company have now set in motion ambitious plans for an innovatively designed new exploration and production complex adjacent to their existing offices. The company says the development is a symbol of their long-term commitment to the North Sea.

Both authorities, city and region, endeavoured to control and direct the new developments. Many companies reached out to the West End, utilising the large granite houses for prestigious offices. Far from being overwhelmed, the local authorities regarded it as an unexpected bonus for improvement and development in the city. To service the influx of new business the region had also to build hundreds of miles of feeder roads for the greatly increased traffic and install new water and sewage pipelines to cope with the greater pressures. The demand for new offices dried up following the big oil slump in 1986 and never again touched the same heights. The industry's onshore support sector was firmly embedded, however, in the commercial fabric of the city and out into the satellite settlements within a 16-mile radius.

So, from the 1980s onwards the city was established as the administrative hub of the North Sea oil and gas industry. In retrospect the local polity may

Plate 38.
BP's North Sea headquarters begin to rise at Dyce, Aberdeen.
(*Aberdeen Journals Ltd*)

Plate 39.
The old and the new – Aberdeen's famous granite quarry, long deserted and full of water, overlooked by the Hill of Rubislaw – home to several major oil companies.
(*Allan Montgomery*)

have been slow to react at the beginning of the North Sea adventure, but it is also true they were forced to improvise quickly on a totally unsuitable planning regime designed for less expansive industrial and commercial development. But the overall pressures were enormous and whether or not they were helped sufficiently by successive governments, either financially or practically, is a contentious question about a politically volatile era. For if the councils were slow to respond, the governments appeared to be equally so.

Oil and Politics – A Potent Brew

7]

The vainglorious prediction about the potential of North Sea oil was not grounded in known facts outside the industry. 'Scotland could become the Texas of Europe,' proclaimed Gordon Campbell, the Conservative Secretary of State for Scotland, in speeches and newspaper articles in 1972, and it was a comparison his advisers wished he would stop making. Professor Gavin McCrone, a former Government economic adviser, admitted, 'We didn't really know enough about it to make statements like that. No one really knew at that time. There had only been a few discoveries since Forties.' Campbell himself told the Scottish Grand Committee at Westminster in 1972, 'Two and a half thousand jobs have been created directly so far, and this figure is likely to rise to about 8,000 in the next two years.' Hardly Texas, hardly Houston, which even now are on a scale neither Scotland nor Aberdeen can ever attain.

Like the councillors from small towns, no national politician appeared to possess the nous to tackle the powerful forces crowding in on them. Lessons should have been derived from the new gas industry in the southern sector of the North Sea. For the accommodation of an even larger development further north there now appears to have been little or no preparation. Opposition Labour MP Bruce Millan told the Scottish Grand Committee, 'There is a lack of a coherent policy and a lack of expertise in the Government. That applies to the Scottish Office and to the Department of Trade and Industry [DTI] in dealing with North Sea oil.' His Government was hardly blameless either. In fact, neither of the two parties who swapped office in the 1970s should be credited with any great awareness. The journalist who broke the news of the first find, Ted Strachan, wrote in the *Press and Journal* in 1972, 'Government response to the onshore situation created in the past year by the discovery of oil . . . underlined how little thought had been given in previous years to any such situation arising – or at least to positive consequences to Scotland. This is, of course, not a criticism of the present Government only but of their predecessors also.' But Strachan did concede, 'In the circumstances the

How would you like your children to stay in Scotland?

With £825 million every year from Scotland's oil they could afford to stay

It's Scotland's Oil ✕

Plate 40.

The clever nationalist battle cry of the 1970s – 'It's Scotland's Oil', one of a million leaflets that flooded the country during the 'devolution wars'. (*Gordon Wright*)

Government have improvised quite manfully.'

The Scottish National Party did more than just improvise. In September 1972, they unleashed their most famous slogan, 'It's Scotland's Oil', followed a year later by the equally potent, 'Rich Scots or Poor Britons'. As Andrew Marr says in *The Battle for Scotland* (London, 1992), 'Oil had blown away the central anti-nationalist argument made by Labour . . . that Scotland was simply too poor to go it alone.' The most successful campaign in the SNP's history was the brainchild of a Glasgow lawyer and leading party official, Gordon Wilson. He had recognised the potential of oil in 1970 but found there was little information at the time. He had just finished a term as national secretary and was taking a sabbatical. 'I could see the propaganda aspects if oil were properly projected. That was the genesis of the campaign. I persuaded the executive to spend an awful lot of money the party didn't have.' Gordon said the credit for the research should go to Donald Bain, an economist, who built the case that there was a lot more oil than people were giving out and conjured up a budget surplus. 'The other parties were not dumb – but they started from a London-centric approach and what they saw was more money for Britain.' From the SNP campaign group came the famous slogan. 'The title was masterly because we meant it to belong to the land and to the country – not to the ethnic group. And that was what began chiming with people.' The first leaflet, 'To London with Love – Scotland's Oil', ending, 'but only with self-government', sold something like a million copies in a country of five million, producing a very large response. 'We

Plate 41.

Leading SNP politician Gordon Wilson, on the stump in Dundee as he fights for a parliamentary seat. (*Gordon Wright*)

developed the theme of what we would do with the money in press conferences. Nobody wanted to offer Scotland anything.'

For a time, the SNP had both Downing Street and St Andrews House on high alert. In February 1972, in a letter stored in the National Archives, Conservative Prime Minister Edward Heath asked the DTI to prepare a case against the argument that the benefits flowing from North Sea oil production 'should accrue to the Scottish economy'. This was 'hypothecation': targeting revenue to related projects. In other archive documents the DTI raised the difficulties of cross-border taxation, but the main thrust of the proposed Government attack was that the 'closely integrated nature of the UK economy makes it impossible to split revenues into national and regional compart-ments', and 'oil revenues fell short of the differential element Scotland enjoyed from Central Government funds'. The Whitehall officials warned finally that radical changes in the present financial relationship would 'resurrect difficult and controversial issues now dormant'. The warning came too late. The 'difficult and controversial issues', which were Home Rule and independence, had already been 'resurrected' and oil played its part.

The two 1974 elections, which brought Labour back to power, were fought by the SNP on the 'It's Scotland's Oil' campaign, and Gordon Wilson won in Dundee East. Labour managed to stabilise their position politically by offering devolution – a decision that split the party in Scotland – and by basing the British National Oil Corporation headquarters in Scotland. The impact of the SNP campaign showed in the ballot box. They won first seven

Plate 42.

A victory for 'It's Scotland's Oil' – the Scottish National Party's new MPs, who won an extraordinary eleven seats in the Westminster Parliament in 1974. (*Gordon Wright*)

and then eleven seats in Parliament and a record 30 per cent of the vote. Alarmed, Labour pushed through legislation on devolution, but failed to win a majority in a referendum. Hitherto secret 1974 Cabinet papers, released recently, explain their reasons for concern. A memorandum produced by Sir Kenneth Berrill, head of the Central Policy Review Staff in Whitehall, entitled 'The End of the Rainbow: Offshore Oil and British Foreign Policy', speculated that Scotland 'on fairly reasonable assumptions about the profits made from North Sea oil could go it alone quite comfortably'. He called for a concerted policy drive to convince the Scottish electorate that despite this their best interest lay in remining part of the UK. This was followed by a survey by Scottish Office economic adviser Gavin McCrone, recently unearthed by the SNP, which forecast that the offshore industry could generate about £3,000 million. 'Properly managed, an independent Scotland could enjoy massive surpluses from North Sea oil for a long time.' He claimed this created for the first time a credible economic argument for Scotland breaking away from the UK. This highly controversial prediction – far more that the £100 million which the Government forecast – was never made public. By the 1979 election, when the Tories returned under Margaret Thatcher, the SNP lost all but two of their Westminister seats, and the oil campaign withered and died as a political issue. In the judgement of political analysts Prof. Bill Miller, J Brand and M Morgan in *Oil and the Scottish Voter, 1974–79* (London, 1980), 'The SNP oil campaign succeeded more in establishing the economic possibility than the political desirability of independence.'

During the devolution wars, the SNP's concept of an oil fund, fed from a share of UK oil revenues, also subscribed to by the Liberals and Labour, and, despite the Tory Government having earlier dismissed the possibility, their energy spokesman, Patrick Jenkin, demanded such money should be used to alleviate 'the additional heavy burden of ratepayers in the North-East'. Based on a Norwegian scheme, the idea was rehabilitated in the 1990s as 'The Scottish Fund for Future Generations'. The argument over whether or not Scotland could survive fiscal autonomy based on North Sea oil revenues is back on the political agenda. In an interview with the author, SNP leader Alex Salmond said the Norwegians had only begun their oil fund in 1996. 'Now it stands at £85 billion pounds and the revenue this year is higher than their oil revenue. That fund will last forever.' He added, 'Right, these are the years of plenty, let's start an oil fund now – and of course it will grow like Topsy.' The party have rekindled the 'Scotland's Oil' initiative with a new campaign.

It is clear from the official files that if the Government in London and the Scottish Office had any single overriding oil policy in 1972, it was simply to ensure that the fossil fuels – and the revenues – were extracted from the seabed as swiftly as possible. How they and the local authorities were to deal with developments onshore was to be very much 'improvised', as the deputy secretary for the Energy Department, JG Liverman, told a meeting in London in 1975. 'The Government's energy policy is the sum total of all the decisions on specific projects and plans taken from time to time in the light of prevailing circumstances.' In Alex Salmond's view, Whitehall had pursued economic policies as if oil production were a short-term phenomenon which would peak in 1990. 'It was just so absurd and bore absolutely no relation to any reasonable projection. This policy still maintains. These people have been so wrong so many times they merely extend their wrong arguments to the next generation.'

A Scottish Development Department (SDD) official formalised a hastily improvised onshore policy in 1973 at a meeting with Shetland Island authorities, who were concerned about being swamped by developers. That policy comprised: rapid exploration and extraction of oil within control of the planning system; striking a balance between the conflicting concerns of conservationists and developers; and using development plans for forward thinking and planning before the applications arose. From the North-East experience the development plans were never designed to cope with the unique circumstances of North Sea oil.

For the Government, rapid exploration was certainly the key. The under-secretary of state at the Scottish Office, George Younger, told representatives of the major oil companies and the Scottish industrial, political, financial and commercial establishment at a meeting in Edinburgh, 'The Government is anxious on the one hand not to interfere with the legitimate commercial operation of the oil companies in whose judgement must lie the decisions and anxious on the other hand to see no unnecessary difficulties or delays impede progress.' A twice-yearly standing conference was established to monitor onshore developments in the first few years. What was really behind the meeting was explained in a briefing note: 'The reason is to demonstrate the Secretary of State's concern and interest, so as to disarm any criticism [which had begun to be heard, particularly in the North-East] that the Scottish Office is not giving the lead it should in a situation which has such a great potential for the Scottish economy.' In an unprecedented expedition of procedures, between 1970 and 1979 some seventy applications were processed; of these, five were major oil-gas terminals, all the service bases, four land pipelines, fifteen platform yards and fifty other projects were approved.

From an analysis of the Scottish Industry Department (SID) files for the early 1970s, it would appear that the Scottish Office was trying to give as much of a lead as it was being allowed by Whitehall. The department was responsible for onshore support, but Prime Minister Heath had allocated overall stewardship for oil partly to the DTI but mostly to the Department of Energy (DoE). A delegation from Scotland warned Heath they were afraid oil development would overwhelm local authority resources. They wanted direct Government intervention in the North-East, even to the extent of buying land to shut out 'cowboy' speculators. Heath expressed his confidence that with the creation of two super ministries there would be no problem in controlling the new industry. But there was certainly little genuine guidance about onshore development on offer from London. Professor McCrone remembers the cross-border dealings: 'There was a certain amount of tension between the DoE and St Andrews House and something of a personality clash. But by the time I became chief economic adviser I had no real problems.'

The conflict of opinion was explained by a SID official to the chairman of the Scottish Economic Planning Council. 'I am not at all sure the Government generally has awakened to the full significance of the development, or of the fact that there might be areas of activity which were not best left to the ordinary commercial forces. This might be thought to be particularly true at No. 10.' When Gavin McCrone joined the Scottish Office in the 1970s he was fully aware that the development potential of oil was becoming an important factor in the Scottish economy. 'But I don't think Whitehall ever really grasped what was going on at that time. When they eventually did, they just wanted to get the oil out. As a result, I think they threw away a tremendous opportunity by being so lenient with the oil companies during the first licensing rounds. They could have made more money than they did at first.'

Scots political journalist Dan McGeachie was hired by the American oil company Conoco (now Conoco Phillips) in 1976 to establish working relationships with UK politicians and civil servants. They wanted Dan, with his broad experience, to advise on prevailing political thought. 'Some of the Whitehall officials tended to be a little suspicious to begin with, but after a very short time we got on extremely well, developing a close bond and a good relationship. A lot of the politicians and civil servants really liked the Americans, who realised they could have more influence on the political side here than in their own country.'

Dan, who was appointed to the company board, considers the Scottish Office were more supportive and less political about oil. 'They wanted the jobs and they wanted the oil and they had the Nationalists operating in the background – but that was a side issue that didn't concern us. We were involved, of course, in Shetland.' The islands council were won a lucrative share of the revenues from the Sullom Voe oil terminal (see Chapter 12). 'To reach that settlement and then not to do something similar for the rest of the country – that cost a bit of pain and money for an awful lot of people, including the tax payers and the oil industry.'

When Dan came on the scene the industry had a very odd relationship with Labour: 'The energy minister, Tony Benn was very distant and not at all friendly, while his number two, the Scot, Dr J Dickson Mabon, was being very friendly.' When the Tories came to power in 1979 many of Dan's colleagues thought life would become a lot easier. 'There was really no difference,' Dan laughed. 'In fact most of the nasty things that happened occurred under a Tory Government. The oil price started going up, the oil was flowing and it was time to start turning the screws.'

The president of the Scottish Trades Union Congress, Raymond Macdonald, saw it differently. He told an industrial conference in Scotland in 1973, 'The [Conservative] Government appears to have been paralysed by the enormous potential of the oil discoveries. When it wakened from its petrified state, it gallumphed around frantically setting up committees and councils without any definite pattern of control or planning emerging. The North Sea remains firmly in the clutches of the oil companies. Little of the possible profit from oil will return to Scotland, or Britain.' At the same conference, held by

Plate 43.

The author (left) interviews the energy secretary, Tony Benn, for a documentary on North Sea gas in the 1970s. The minister had the disconcerting practice of personally taping the recording for future reference.

the Scottish Council (Development) and Industry at Aviemore, David Knapp, vice president of Chevron asked, 'I wonder if Scotland really appreciates the monumental impact of North Sea oil? Without a plan for growth and the financing and management of the infrastructure, there would be a possibility the benefit would by-pass Scotland and go elsewhere.'

After the first proven discoveries a plethora of Government bodies sprang up, thirteen all told. Ray Macdonald was on the Scottish Oil Development Council, chaired by Lord Polwarth, minister with special responsibility for oil. The peer achieved immortality as 'Lord of the Oil' in John McGrath's biting political satire *The Cheviot, the Stag and the Black, Black Oil* (1977). His character proclaimed, 'I am Lord Polwarth and I have a plan . . . I am not a supremo. In this way the people of Scotland – or at least the Bank of Scotland – will benefit from the destruction of their country.'

There were periodic calls from Opposition politicians for the establishment of an over-arching Scottish Oil Development Authority, but a Scottish Planning Department told the Treasury in a letter in 1973, 'This we have fended off by saying the ordinary planning machine – although creaking a bit – has so far been able to cope; and we are most anxious to maintain this line.' The nearest the Government came to an executive body was the Scottish Development Agency. Christopher Harvie claimed, however, in his 1994 book, *Fool's Gold*, that it was 'specifically barred from oil-related activity'. Guy Arnold, an economic journalist, suggested in *Britain's Oil* (London 1978), 'In time to come the Aberdeen story might be seen as a classic example of how the interests of central government have overridden – again and again – the interests of a particular region.'

From the Scottish Office files at the beginning of the 1970s, however, it is apparent that the relevant officials were as ignorant as anyone else – outside the oil industry itself – about the scale of future demands onshore. This now seems extraordinary for a government organisation. But oilmen were not surprised. Dan McGeachie was told by his boss, Jack Reynolds, 'I have just met a bunch of important and highly intelligent people who thought oil was contained in a big undersea lake. Maybe if they knew more, they would be more sympathetic to the amount of cost, effort and risk we are taking.' From this conversation emerged Conoco's influential Gleneagles Seminar, an annual two-day 'teach-in' at the famous Perthshire hotel, which over nearly twenty years was attended by most of the leading politicians, including Cabinet members. The seminars ended when Conservative MPs claimed Prime Minister Tony Blair and his deputy, John Prescott, had been at Gleneagles with their families and had not declared it. The company, instead, funds an international environmental prize, administered by St Andrews University.

The inexplicable lack of political awareness back in the 1970s came as no surprise to Aberdeenshire planning officer, Peter Cockhead. 'There was a genuine wish to be of assistance, but much of their policy advice was inclined to come after the event.' The Scottish Office were initially obsessed with particular aspects of onshore development that were to prove impractical – and costly – such as concrete platform yards (see Chapter 10). Most of the attention was heavily focused on the need to spread the benefits of oil and gas to the larger centres of population. An official told the Treasury in 1973, 'In the long run, the areas will become little more than transit areas through which the vast wealth of oil and gas will pass on the way to refineries situated according to market requirements [only one in Scotland] or to mass consumption centres like the central belt of Scotland.' He added, 'Certainly no large-scale industrial spin-offs will be created in the transit areas.'

Their ambiguous attitude, on the other hand, to those 'transit areas' of Aberdeen and the North-East had a well-established historical provenance. Over the years politicians of all complexions have castigated the Scottish Office (and now the Scottish Executive) for ignoring the region's structural and financial problems. In December 2000, the announcement by the Scottish Executive of a new three-year budget system, which gives the region a sizeable increase in money and a measure of financial stability, was greeted with a little more gratitude by the councils. Planner Trevor Sprott insisted they were always clear they would get no financial help. 'The Scottish Office always had the same policy: they gave money to those people they thought needed it.

They never gave any money to those who were on the up. Today you have the horrible example of how they have stuck to that policy, in the state of the road system we still have in the North-East.' He was speaking in 1992. A survey in *The Economist* in 1973 described the country as 'a divided land', with oil in the East and in the West 'still doubt and even depression'. Industrial editor, Ted Strachan, believed these competing divisions were encouraged by the attitude of the Government. 'So the new situation of Scotland on the doorstep of the world's third biggest offshore oil province is met by a dusting off of old plans, acceleration of piecemeal road programmes which were overdue anyway and a resolve to avoid the financial embarrassment of actually having to provide more houses, schools and roads in Aberdeen and the North of Scotland by diverting as much of the incoming industry as possible to Central Scotland.'

Political myopia about life beyond the Central Belt is totally inevitable and understandable. Since the last war, the most heavily populated region and former wealth-generating heart of Scotland has suffered a greater accumulation of economic and social problems than any other region. In contrast, the North-East economy has been, by common perception, at worst static and at best comfortable, with low unemployment. The reality is that the northern region has been beset by problems that are different from the Central Belt but, in their own way, just as needful of a solution. So the irony of onshore oil development, according to Gavin McCrone, has been that, 'Much of the impact was in areas where unemployment was already low . . . while the main industrial areas of Scotland still see no early prospect of their problems being resolved.' Lord Kirkhill, a former Scottish Office minister, maintains oil was discovered in entirely the wrong place. 'If it had been found off either of the firths of Clyde or Forth, the economic benefits and the industrial opportunities would have gone a considerable way to alleviating some of these problems, producing maximum benefits to Scotland.' It is also highly probable that it might have generated more participatory interest from Scottish industry than ultimately has been the case. In the opinion of Sir Ian Wood, foremost Scots oil industrialist, 'Glasgow and Edinburgh missed the boat terribly when oil came. If it had gone to the Clyde, there would have been a huge spread right across the whole of Central Scotland and they would have been in it in a big way.' Only a few Central Belt companies responded, although some in the financial sector did become involved. For example, the Clydesdale Bank funded all of Scotland's platform construction yards originally. Early on, a number of exploration companies were set up: Pict Petroleum, Caledonian Offshore, Viking Oil and Caber Oil, plus a number of leading trusts who invested in exploration syndicates. North Sea Assets was later established to finance exploitation and production. Other Edinburgh-based oil companies included Thompson and Cairn Energy. Only Cairn now remains, still investing heavily on the Indian subcontinent with a great deal of success.

So the Government did endeavour valiantly to control and direct the oil companies and developers to sites in the West and Central Scotland. In 1974 the SDD issued a coastal strategy to guide developers to 'preferred development zones'. Priority was given to the Forth, Clyde and Tay Estuaries rather than the Highlands and North-East. Bruce Millan, Minister of State for Scotland in the Labour Government of 1975, told an investment conference, 'The government is not prepared simply to concentrate its attentions on supporting the development of regions most affected by oil development, but would give equal and urgent priority to the older industrial areas, especially in West Central Scotland.' McCrone warned at the time, however, that although it was essential oil should help to resolve Scotland's traditional problems 'many of the oil-related activities are quite specific in their locational require-ments. There is less scope for steering them to areas of unemployment than exists for most other industries'.

There were many tussles between the Government and the Grampian authorities over the placing of important agencies in what was the UK's putative oil capital. Peter Cockhead wrote in 1982, 'While central government may wish to see onshore development more evenly spread, the only tangible evidence has been the government influence on the decisions of the British National Oil Corporation [BNOC] and the Offshore Supplies Office [OSO] to locate head offices in Glasgow rather than in Aberdeen.' Oil companies gradually moving their UK headquarters into Aberdeen were puzzled by the gerrymandering attempts by successive governments. John Moorehouse of Shell said, 'The BNOC and OSO decisions showed how completely out of touch the politicians were with the reality of running a business. There was absolutely no logic to it. They would have been as well having them in London as in Glasgow.' What in fact became obvious was that, as Gavin McCrone had realised, the industry generally chose its own locations based on purely economic judgements, with the main base centred on Aberdeen, which ultimately gained the oil and gas division of the DoE and the National Energy Institute.

Certainly the St Andrews House documents show that the civil servants were only expected to advise and guide. George Younger told a meeting of the various oil interest groups on the eve of the 1972 licensing round, 'I am most anxious that the Scottish Office should not be thought to be trying to interfere with the normal operations of the local planning authorities. The Scottish Office, who can see the total picture, can help in the consideration of applications for planning permission by ensuring that all the right questions are asked, and asked at the right time.' Such a passive stance was regarded by contemporary commentators and opposition politicians as entirely inappropriate. They were disturbed at the lack of a cohesive national oil development plan or of a policy of re-investing revenue in the regions which had borne the brunt of exploitation.

Eventually the Scottish Office did provide tangible financial aid and, by 1974, allocated £400 million to onshore public expenditure. Gavin McCrone, who provided that estimate, said at an Institute of Petroleum seminar, 'Sometimes one gets the impression that public opinion sees the development of North Sea oil almost exclusively in terms of energy policy and licensing, perhaps it is time that the significance and cost of the support activities by the public sector were more widely realised.' He described the scale of the onshore industry as 'more substantial than any new town'.

However, according to Alick Buchanan Smith, the former Tory energy minister, in later years, 'The administrative machine – Central Scotland-based – remained somewhat surprised by what was happening to the North. The Government should be prepared to take more positive action than hitherto to encourage such developments.' An OSO official, concerned at the effects of a shortage of labour, told the oil taskforce in 1975, 'This was due to a general unwillingness within government to believe that the opportunities offered by oil-related developments were other than short-term ones.'

Buchanan Smith qualified his view by pointing out that successive governments eventually stepped up the provision and investment of resources. He was talking in 1989 about the designation of an extra oil-related component of the rate support grant paid to local authorities in affected areas, the largest proportion of which fell to Aberdeen and the Grampian region. It had taken some time, however, before the oil money arrived because the Treasury in Whitehall were still refusing to recognise the special needs of oil areas. The resistance was based on a total lack of understanding, illustrated in an exchange of missives with the Scottish Office during 1972 and 1973. The Edinburgh officials had begun to realise the local authorities would need financial help and they were generally sympathetic. So they suggested to the Treasury the affected areas should get 75 per cent to meet the added expense. The Treasury, very emphatically, did not agree. They didn't see why costs could not be met through the normal rates and rate support grant. Their reasoning was extraordinary. 'The problems they have to deal with are essentially local ones and not necessarily national because they result from the oil industry. The proposition for a direct grant raises very difficult issues because of the precedent it would create.'

The inevitable compromise was that the Scottish Development Department agreed to contribute towards new structure plans and planning studies with financial input from the local authorities. The Treasury were worried the relatively small sums in prospect could be used as a precedent for much larger additions to infrastructure services such as schools. Which was, of course, precisely what eventually did happen. The oil-related element to the rate support grant was brought in two years later by a Labour Scottish Secretary, in the Local Government (Scotland) Act, as part of the reorganisation of local government in 1975. But the terms of the grant were strictly limited, work connected with downstream activities was not included, nor was compensation for the higher costs of land or staff pay. By the time the oil 'bonus' arrived, Grampian had already been forced to bear the burden of financing the infrastructure for thousands of new homes, new schools, industrial sites, roads, water and sewage systems.

The initial sum set aside in 1975/76 for helping areas affected by oil was £2.25 million out of a total budget of £664 million. Iain Sproat, the Conservative MP for Aberdeen South, described it in the House of Commons as an insult. 'The money is a totally inadequate response to the oil programme in Scotland.' Minister of State Bruce Millan told him, 'We must maintain a balance of fairness with other local authorities which have special burdens placed upon them.' Grampian's share began at £745,000; by 1978/9 it was £3 million; in 1979/80 it rose to £4.5 million. By the following April, the region had itself expended £38 million. The highest oil grant came in 1983/4 when the council received £8 million, but the North-East had already paid out £50 million. Peter Cockhead does not believe it was enough. 'The reluctance of Central Government to reflect the rate of population growth in its resource allocations seriously delayed essential road improvements and resulted in inadequate capital investments in several areas of public sector service provision.'

Over the onshore expansion period from the 1970s to the mid-1990s, the bill met by the ratepayers of Grampian for oil-related infrastructure was £100 million. In return, the industry contributed millions to the economy in wages and increased expenditure on goods and services. The council's reward came in the rates paid by the hundreds of newcomers. Unfortunately the increased rateable value to the area had been virtually cancelled out by a corresponding reduction in the Government's equalising aid to local authorities, which was intended to place all Scottish councils on the same financial level.

Those were the times when Grampian was given the distinct impression that they were being penalised for success. In 1972, in an attempt to attract new industry, the whole of Scotland was turned into a development area, except for Aberdeen, which was classed as intermediate. Thus, even though they came of their own volition, oil companies such as the American-owned Highland Fabricators, qualified for extremely generous grants. From 1976 to 1979, more than half the £12.5 million paid out in regional aid grants went to incoming oil-related firms; indigenous industry did not qualify. As Guy Arnold interpreted it in *Britain's Oil* (London, 1978) 'as soon as it was clear Aberdeen had become the oil capital with the advantages that therefore accrued to it, a parsimonious government downgraded the city'. The area lost this lucrative status as a medium-grade development area at a crucial time in the summer of 1980, with calamitous effects on the struggling indigenous industries. There was a feeling of bewilderment. A submission from the North-East authorities to Edinburgh pointed out, 'By creating a prosperous image for Grampian in Whitehall, the bulk of the region lost access not only to United Kingdom Government funds for regional grants but also to regional financial assistance.' By 1982 the North-East had also lost discretionary assistance under the Industry Act, removing their entitlement to most of the European grants and tourist-related and employment grants. The litany of setbacks continued: in 1977/8 Labour Scottish Secretary Bruce Millan reduced the rate support grant by 4 per cent. Sandy Mutch former Grampian convener described it as a 'terrific blow' to the council. 'That 4 per cent represented a tremendous amount of money to us at a crucial time when we were trying to put in all the necessary services for the oil industry. But there was nothing we could do. We just had to accept it.' The former chairman of the Conservative and Unionist Party in Scotland also had to fight the region's corner against his own party in Government under Margaret Thatcher. 'I had to plead on bended knee to George Younger [the then Scottish Secretary] to get more money. As far as I was concerned, politics didn't come into it. I was hard as I could be. Perhaps I wasn't all that popular with my own party. But that didn't bother me one whit.'

Despite everything, it is to the abiding credit of the 'rural council with some market towns to administer' and the 'small town with a small town council' and the councils that followed them, that they were able – over a relatively short and unprecedented time scale – to absorb and integrate such a gigantic industrial invasion and to service it successfully by providing new houses, offices, industrial estates, schools and many miles of roads and pipelines for sewage and drainage. Grampian's retired director of planning, Trevor Sprott, was extremely philosophical when he talked in 1993 about the enforced learning curve of the oil years and about the role of the Scottish Office and Westminster: 'We were pretty much on our own in the early days – we just had to get on with it.'

Other than imposing legal and fiscal restraints on the industry, no Government has as yet pursued a coherent onshore oil or energy policy. It is perhaps a measure of the politicians' corrosive lack of belief in the lifespan of the North Sea oil and gas industry that the industry now has to deal with the seventh energy minister in eight years.

[8] Fish Versus Oil – Geese Versus Gas

The twin ports

The windswept wetlands lie just off the shoulder of Scotland, a grey loch guarded from the North Sea by a narrow bulwark of beach and marram grass; a small flotilla of wintering geese bob contentedly at the water's edge; the peace of the cold late afternoon is disturbed frequently by the harsh appeals of seabirds, outriders to the hosts of migrants to one of the country's most important nature reserves.

Yet the tranquility of the Loch of Strathbeg, halfway between Fraserburgh and Peterhead, belies its once turbulent history: popular legend has it that more than thirty years ago a flock of pink-footed geese forced the mighty hydrocarbon industry to think again. Or at least that is how conservationists of the day liked to tell it.

Half a dozen miles up the coast, at about the same time, under the grim

Plate 44.

A heron fishes the Tower Pool in the unique Loch of Strathbeg on the Buchan coast – migratory staging post for the pink-footed goose and first choice for the siting of a gas terminal that was eventually built at St Fergus.

(*Allan Montgomery*)

ramparts of Peterhead Prison, a relay of alien vessels – massive barges, tugs,
survey ships and supply boats – had begun seeking shelter in the spacious Bay
of Refuge, alongside the long protective granite arm built by convenient
convict labour. For this fertile neuk of farmers and fishermen a new and very
different epoch had begun. In the late 1960s the Buchan corner, where
Peterhead and Fraserburgh are the principal centres of population, was
becalmed in the same doldrums, identified by Maxwell Gaskin, as Aberdeen
and the rest of the North-East: growth had stalled, there was no realistic hope
of new industry, but, more significantly, the traditional migration of the
young, skilled and ambitious was sucking the life out of the area and
obscuring the true rate of unemployment. In the dozens of farms in the fertile
hinterland agriculture was still holding its own, despite the strictures of the
European Economic Community, but the staple industry for the ports at both
Peterhead and Fraserburgh was fishing and its ancillary services and trades,
including a busy shipbuilding yard. After the loss of the herring fisheries, the
skilled Buchan and Moray catchers were gradually building up the white
fishing industry, but the two ports had contrasting fortunes at the end of the
1960s. At one stage Peterhead's fishing authorities were barely able to cover
their employees' wages, while the rival harbour was enjoying a run of success.
Up to 1972 Fraserburgh had the edge and was the first to top the £1 million-
mark in white fish landings. Local lawyer George Macrae has performed a
number of pivotal roles in the North-East's fishing industry for many years.
He became clerk and legal adviser to Fraserburgh Harbour Commissioners in
1969 and is currently secretary of the Scottish White Fish Producers'
Association and of the North-East Fishermens' Trading Association. Macrae
recalls, 'Peterhead had hardly two brass farthings to rub together with no
fishing boats using the place at all, whereas Fraserburgh had a significant
white fish fleet. It was also the principal pelagic port in Britain and still houses
more than 50 per cent of the UK fleet.'

Both towns were also unique in the North-East in profiting from postwar
investment by American companies. Cleveland Twist Drill were in Peterhead,
along with Euclid (Great Britain Ltd), who made gear boxes, and the
automotive engineering firm General Motors. Consolidated Pneumatic Tools
(CPT) from Chicago had set up in Fraserburgh. Peterhead had two other
major economic contributors: the prison and RAF Buchan, the NATO base at
Boddam. Despite the two burghs' key roles, Maxwell Gaskin's survey had
bypassed them in favour of Elgin. The omission incensed Buchan politicians
and the business community. Then suddenly all planning strategies were
blown apart. The North Sea oil and gas industry and Scotland's white fish
fleet had better ideas, and the earliest beneficiary was Peterhead.

Blue Toon – boom town

First on the scene was the assorted armada of oil-related vessels that had begun to use the old jetties in Peterhead's Bay of Refuge to rest and reload at a port on the direct line to and from the central North Sea. Then the pace of exploration quickened offshore with the first half-dozen discoveries, while the pipeline system was well underway. Marine traffic became heavy. Local woman Isla Armour, who has worked for the Peterhead Bay Authority for more than thirty years, was fascinated. 'The oil came as quite a surprise. There had been a few boats, but in the summer of 1974 everything arrived and people embraced the business because there were a lot of good jobs to be had. I don't think they encountered hostility, except that the fishing harbour was reluctant to get involved.'

The colloquially named Blue Toon had known boom times before while Britain's biggest whaling fleet in the 1800s and then during the extraordinary years when herring was king. But, while the harbour was recovering through white fish landings, the bay had been underused. Isla Armour remembers, 'There was just the one harbour for fishing and nothing else. At the Harbour of Refuge there were only rocks and sand. Then Peterhead became THE place

Plate 45.

Before the onslaught of oil – Peterhead Bay harbour and fishing harbour. (*Peterhead Harbour Authority*)

for oil servicing. Congestion had begun to build up in Aberdeen, where the port was closed if there was a storm. We had problems with weather but the boats could always get out.'

This strategic importance of the town had also attracted perceptive developers and land speculators. A flurry of early deals and proposals sent land prices soaring. Eventually the North-East Scotland Development Authority (NESDA), who had also identified this 'second oil front', began to press the Scottish Office to act. In 1972, in an unprecedented measure, the Scottish Secretary, Gordon Campbell, concerned lest additional activity and employment would be lost to Scotland, assumed powers through the Harbour Development (Scotland) Act to improve the Harbour of Refuge. Through the Admiralty they already had regulatory powers. A new quay and berthage was built on the south side to house an oil service base costing £2.5 million. The Bill was hastened through Parliament in four months and the Bay Authority was formed under Government administration. It was to be the only onshore venture where the Scottish Office took a hand. Oil industrialist Sir Ian Wood's company, in conjunction with food and shipping company Christian Salvesen, was invited to tender for the contract to run the base, but it was won by Jimmy Simpson's pioneering Aberdeen Service Company (North Sea) Limited

Plate 46.

Peterhead Bay now, with the fishing harbours (top) fronted by ASCO's north base. The original south base is in the foreground. (*Peterhead Harbour Authority*)

Plate 47.

Peterhead's Greenhill fish market – after the seine net fleet had decamped north from Aberdeen.

Plate 48.

Captain Alex Auld, former master of Peterhead's fishing harbours.

(now ASCO). But a company called Arunta had been first in leasing land on the north side from the Harbour Trustees for a service base.

Then came the second invasion, which was to turn the old port into one of the busiest in the country. The UK's premier white fish market was at Aberdeen, along with the Scottish inshore fleet. For some time, however, the fishermen had been unhappy with conditions and costs at the shabby, run-down market. Their main quarrels were with the restrictive and costly dock labour scheme and the fact that Aberdeen-registered boats owned by the big trawl companies were always given priority. So during 1972, virtually en masse, the 400 boats in the fleet sailed the short sea miles to Peterhead and a warm welcome from the fishing harbour trustees. By then, anyway, in Aberdeen, oil had been gradually usurping fish.

Captain Alex Auld, later master at the fishing harbour, described the effect as 'a flood of fish with an almost instant twenty-fold increase in landings – up from hundreds of boxes to twelve to fourteen thousand'. So after a period of relative inactivity Peterhead had to deal with two invasion fleets competing for access. Throughout the mid-1970s there was another explosive clash of interests as the Bay of Refuge and the fishing harbour vied for overall control until St Andrews House announced there would be no single port authority. They had already appointed an overall unitary controller, Captain Oliver Signorini, an Aberdeen man who had been serving in tankers. He was master for the Bay Authority, a quango dealing with the oil traffic, and the captain pilot for the fishing harbour. A civil servant was the first chief executive of the Bay Authority, which eventually became a Trust empowered to reinvest its own funds.

Captain Signorini explained why the fishermen picked Peterhead and not its arch-rival Fraserburgh. 'Quite simply, the Bay of Refuge. If you have a south-easterly gale you have to be well moored and the Bay was where vessels could make a run into.' Alex Auld, Signorini's deputy with responsibility for the fish harbour, said the market at that time couldn't cope. They had to land on the open pier. The Board then decided to build a covered market and, as the landings increased, the first of the new fish markets was built on the other side. Peterhead, said the voluble Signorini, had gone mad but there was space for both.

Those growing demands on Peterhead are difficult to visualise: vessels from both industries turning up any time, day or night. Yet despite the national importance of oil, it was never in doubt who had prior access. Peterhead was in the first instance – and still is – a fishing port; at its peak it was the biggest white fish market in the United Kingdom. Alex Auld said, 'A fishing boat has priority over everything.' Oliver Signorini had that enshrined in a byelaw: 'The fishermen had to get in by seven in the morning, if they didn't, they missed the sales.' Twelve berthing masters handled some four hundred boats. Alex said, 'The merchants came up from Aberdeen every morning, 10,000 boxes and sometimes second sales.'

Said Oliver, 'Meantime you might have a drilling rig coming – that took two or three hours. Then a flotilla of pipeline barges wanting out. The fishermen were having to slow down.' So he came up with another byelaw, which restricted the movement of oil traffic for an hour before the sales to make sure the fishermen got in. 'But oil was big and the companies said, "Are you going to stop the oil traffic for a couple of hours to let these bloody fishing boats in?" Well, I got my way. When the market was fully modernised they were landing 40,000 boxes a week. For the oil industry, you had 30 or 40 supply boats and pipelaying vessels a day.' There were more skirmishes ahead. 'During a maintenance engineering period there was big heat from the companies and the Bay harbour to bring in rigs. I said no. "I know the weather and I won't allow these big heavy drilling rigs in after September or before April." I got hell over that but I got my way. Any weakness and you would have been destroyed by either.'

An equally fiercely contested battle to develop oil- and gas-related plants was also continuing. There were two main proposals: one from Scanitro, a Scandinavian consortium, for an ammonia plant; the other from Shell/Esso for a £93 million natural gas liquids (NGL) plant. The NGL was to be piped from

Plate 49.

Captain Oliver Signorini, first overall master of Peterhead bay and fishing harbours.

the gas terminal and processing plant rising at the village of St Fergus, 5 miles up the coast road, and then tankered out of Peterhead. Oliver Signorini remembers, 'The town was about exploding – the fishing was going crazy – the oil industry was going crazy. But these schemes were over the top. The locals knew the limitations of the bay harbour and were worried about safety.' Despite objections by Banff and Buchan District Council, the Scanitro application was approved by the Scottish Secretary. The plant, however, was never built. Shell/Esso had already aborted their plans in the midst of a public inquiry and set their sights on Mossmorran on the Fife coast (see Chapter 12). The companies had discovered the breakwater would have to be rebuilt at great expense and it would have been too costly to operate the size of vessels they planned to use. Oliver Signorini claimed, 'Essentially the inquiry chairman said they couldn't continue as there hadn't been enough research into how well these vessels could perform in south-east gales.' Maitland Mackie, chairman of NESDA, was also chairman of the Harbour Trustees. 'The Shell situation was the only time I was blamed for any of my actions. But they had always had a contingency plan for Mossmorran. The downtime for the tankers – and the size of them – was the whole secret.' Since then, tankers almost twice as large, and huge drilling rigs, have anchored in the Bay.

The failure of these additional projects was perhaps fortuitous as Peterhead was already under enormous pressures, particularly for labour. Work had begun in 1973 on a giant £230 million power station employing 160 people at Boddam. A tanker jetty was being built and the two oil service bases were under construction. A further £2 million was spent by ASCO and the seven-berth logistics and service base opened in 1974. On the north side, Arunta had developed on an island at Keith Inch with a jetty running out into the bay on stilts. There were four berths for supply boats and a huge warehouse. Arunta sold out to their partners, the British Oxygen Company (BOC), in 1974. They operated the second base until it was taken over by ASCO.

Like Aberdeen, Peterhead experienced the shockwaves that inevitably follow the impact of such a powerful industry. The indigenous industries suffered a loss of staff for a time, but once the flurry of construction ended the labour shortage became less acute. There was also a housing crisis for local families, according to a local minister, the Rev. Ian MacKenzie. 'Every week, I meet couples who have nowhere to live once they are married. I don't think the housing plans are adequate.' New housing was later built in the town.

During one spell in the 1980s, there were sixty to a hundred shipping movements in the bay alone and every one needed a pilot. 'We were employed nearly full time,' said Alex Auld. 'During the day I worked at the harbour and

Tuesday, 15th August, 1972.   THE BUCHAN OBSERVER AND EAST ABERDEENSHIRE ADVERTIS

THE RAPE OF PETERHEAD
"Gullibility is not Faith" - says Rev. Iain

All else is Speculation!

THE North of Scotland Hydro-Electric Board have decided to proceed with an oil-fired station at Boddam, near Peterhead.

The announcement made by the Government on Tuesday, about the arrangements for the nuclear industry, makes it clear that within the time scale available, it is not possible to meet the anticipated load growth in the North of Scotland with a nuclear station at Stake Ness, Banffshire.

The station at Peterhead will be commissioned in 1978. It will have an output capacity of 1,320 MW. and will be designed to burn gas as well as oil. There is now the possibility of substantial quantities of associated gas being available from the North Sea oil finds.

The total cost of the station at Peterhead, where the Board own a suitable site, will be about £100 million and during its construction the labour force employed on site will be about 1,200 men. The operation of the station after completion will give regular employment to about 300 staff.

The Secretary of State for Scotland is being asked to consider the Board's application for consent to this station as a matter of urgency and an early announcement will be made about invitations to tender for the construction of the station.

The Stake Ness site, which is particularly suitable for a nuclear station, will be retained for a later development.

EVERYTHING has its appointed hour — read the Rev. Iain Mackenzie from the pulpit of the Muckle Kirk on Sunday — a time for gathering stones and a time for throwing them, a time to think and a time not to think.

But, he added, there comes a time when a body can't think, when events engulf them — such as is happening in Peterhead right now under the shadow of mystery developments in the South Bay, at Sandford, and if the leak-source is right, at Longside drome.

An acquaintance had challenged the Reverend Iain as to his Faith in line with the projected developments around Peterhead at this time. "Where is your Faith?" he was asked The reverend reply — " Gullibility is not Faith."

There is one hell of gullibility floating around this part of the North East just now, and has been for some time — aided and abetted by public figures, government, local and national.

So much so that many people of Peterhead are utterly confused in their minds, quite bewildered as to the future of their community, and fearful at heart as to the role the native is to be

South Bay site — only the plans for a site, below H.M. Prison, thereby putting the Prison, worth probably a thousand pounds a week to Peterhead, at risk.

Would the Government take that risk? We do not know Influence "can do a lot, and apparently "influence" cannot be ruled out in the projected developments conjured up for Peterhead.

There is another plan in existence: it projects Sandford oil-fired station. We have not had access to it, but long before the New Year we recorded that the proposals included the erection of some 14 oil storage tanks, to be topped up with residue oil from Grangemouth and Rotterdam.

When the news broke on Wednesday that the decision to site the oil-fired station at Sandford had been taken, this by special announcement in Parliament and from Edinburgh HQ of the Hydro-Board, we contacted the latter with the request that an artist's impression of the project would be of great interest to our readers, together with relevant detail as to what it was going to mean in all its spects.

Courteously but firmly, the spokesman for the Board told us that no other information was available other than what had already been given out and which we had to hand. We did

Bishop Easson to retire
to Edinburgh end of Church Year

The Right Reverend Edward Frederick Easson D.D., Bishop of Aberdeen and Orkney in the Scottish Episcopal Church will be resigning from his diocese on 6th November next. The forty congregations throughout the diocese will have heard this news in Church on Sunday, 13th August.

and devoted pastor. He has travelled frequently to the United States where the Protestant Episcopal Church has close links with the Episcopal Church of Scotland. This connection was first formed when Samuel Seabury, the first Bishop in America was consecrated in Aberdeen in 1784, when the Bishops of the Church of England for

Plate 50.
As the development frenzy mounts in Peterhead, a local newspaper, the *Buchan Observer*, mirrors the fears of the townsfolk – that the town was going to suffer from the oil boom.

at night I worked as a pilot – just two of us – fifteen or sixteen pilot jobs a night. One time I wasn't home for two days, we were so busy.' It was a seven-days-a-week operation. 'Supply boats couldn't wait – it had to be now. All the Forties pipe was loaded from Peterhead.' Oliver said, 'The quays were so busy at ASCO they had to anchor in the Bay, bow to stern maybe four or five altogether.' Captain Auld recalls one risky episode. 'Oliver was taking a rig in to the south side and I was guiding a massive 30,000-ton ship in at the same time. I had four tugs and then the towlines on the forward tugs parted. She kept coming ahead and I just managed to stick her alongside the breakwater. The tide kept her there until Captain Signorini got the rig in – but that was hairy.' However, the incident Peterhead people most remember was the beaching of the oil rig Ali Baba, in the winter after Signorini left to return to the oil industry. 'It was moored at the tanker jetty and a south-east snorter drove it right on to the rocks. Eventually they managed to get her out and towed her to Rotterdam. The repairs cost millions.' The already congested Bay harbours also had to contend with another armada of incomers, the seasonal arrival of the Eastern bloc Klondyke fleet of fourteen factory ships. 'They took 75 per cent of the fish landed then,' said Alex Auld. 'They had maybe 150 to 200 men on board and they all came ashore. It was amazing.'

The Boddam campsite had accommodation for 600 single men and 160 families and there were other camps and caravan sites set up for workers at the

Plate 51.

Storm clouds over Peterhead's Bay of Refuge in the 1970s – the entrance shared among oil traffic, fishing vessels and the giant Soviet factory ships, the Klondykers.

village of Crimond. At night they were joined in the town by oilmen and seamen of all nationalities – all looking for amusement. 'The town was buzzing and the pubs were mobbed,' said Oliver, 'It was very exciting times. They tried to control the guys building the power station with the camp, which had its own catering, pub and a club with entertainment. Arunta recognised they could make money by ferrying people in and out from the Bay. Safe enough but it wouldn't be allowed now.' The town fathers feared for a time all this unaccustomed revelry would put a usually douce community's social and moral welfare under severe strain. For a time intense national and international media attention was focused on the uproarious lifestyle of the incomers and their attendant camp followers. Captain Auld said it was common knowledge prostitutes were coming up from England. 'They plied their trade, made a fortune and went back again. That was when the Italians were here. I also think that was the first sign of drugs in Peterhead.' The Italian divers and crews on the pipe barges were a magnet for the local girls. Brian Porter spent a year as a BP inspector on the barges laying pipe to Forties. 'The divers were wild when you got onshore. Peterhead was a cowboy town then. One time we had a good few drinks and went to this dance hall. As you went in there were women waiting, wanting money to go round the back. But it was the Italians they were after. They would buy them whisky, which the women wouldn't touch. Then the boyfriends would arrive and they drank the whisky. The poor Italians fell for it every time.' Isla Armour maintained that despite the flood of foreigners there wasn't a lot of trouble. 'You could still walk down the town streets at night – there would be the odd fight in a pub but it wasn't wild. Not like today. Nowadays I wouldn't go down Queen Street on a Friday or a Saturday night – nothing but drink and drugs.'

For more than twenty years the Buchan port enjoyed a period of unrivalled prosperity from both fish and oil. The three fishing harbours, North, South and Port Henry, were a huge source of revenue, reaching a remarkable peak in 1990 when more than 1.5 million boxes were sold at a value in excess of £81 million. Sadly the markets are now a shadow of those heady days, with a ghost of a white fish fleet devastated by punitive conservation legislation imposed by the European Commission. The fishermens' organisations fight on to secure a more generous regime for the crews who are left. But there are some signs of a revival. 'Pelagic fishing is on the up again,' said Alex Auld. 'Last year there was quite a lot of mackerel and herring landed.' Of the other sizeable economic sources only the prison survives; the RAF base has been sold and the American engineering companies have long gone. Now the two authorities – the bay and the fishing harbours have been merged into one.

The oil industry remains the main employer, although it too has suffered from cycles of recession and change. The ASCO operation has been a remarkable success. The company expanded with a second facility for construction, hook-up, fabrication, craneage, storage and accommodation for semi-submersible rigs. Then, in 1994, there was further extension in the form of a new £4.25 million jetty and breakwater and a £1 million leisure marina. One of the main clients, BP, who had moved their support operations to Peterhead from Lerwick and Dundee, went to Aberdeen. Although ASCO still provide services to BP in the city, a number of jobs had to go in Peterhead. Now centred in Aberdeen, with three other bases at Immingham, Great Yarmouth and Liverpool Bay, the company has grown through acquisitions and was the subject of a management buyout in 1996. It has been described as the leading logistics specialist in the North Sea.

Local MP Alex Salmond forecasts a new era for the port. 'Peterhead is a frontier port. The big companies will always have their base in Aberdeen. But the argument will be: if you are a new player, go to Peterhead.' A cluster of engineering, fabrication and service companies are now based around the Bay, including the impressive engineers Score (Europe) Ltd.

Isla Armour thinks the town has never been the same since oil. 'You knew everybody before – or knew about them – then there were strange faces everywhere. Of course, the town expanded – it had to. That was the most prosperous time in the '70s and '80s and into the early '90s. Lots of the people who came in stayed. But once the pipe-laying barges left, business trickled to a steady stream. Then when BP pulled out, a lot of town people lost their jobs. So oil workers who live here now commute to Aberdeen. Then when the fishing declined, people went to work offshore. There will be a lot of unemployment when the oil goes.' Alex Auld, who took over from Oliver Signorini as joint harbour-master, is now retired. 'It was definitely good for Peterhead. I would like to see it again to tell you the truth. I think it made the town, the shops were all bursting. Now the place is nearly dead.'

The reluctant suitor

'When the oil came Fraserburgh was doing reasonably well fishing-wise. But a mistake was made when the town council said they would prefer Fraserburgh to continue to develop its fishing interests. They argued that fishing would always be here and oil not necessarily. I don't think that was a right decision but they made it and I have to say it was supported by the harbour board.' These words from one of one of the leaders of the Scottish fishing industry were unexpected, but Fraserburgh lawyer George Macrae is also a businessman with the future well-being of the Buchan port in his mind. 'I am no visionary, but I could see a mile away there was potential. You don't get companies investing millions unless there are significant returns. It is wrong to have all your eggs in one basket. They should have diversified but they didn't.'

George knows well the nature of the folk he has served in a number of key public offices over many years. 'You have got to remember, the North-East triangle from Aberdeen to Elgin has been the victim of under-investment for generations. That still prevails and while the people are among the best in the world, they are not the most outward-looking.' He said the belief was that oil and gas exploration was something that happened somewhere else. 'Here, generation after generation had been born into fishing and farming and it is very difficult to change. After all, arguably, fishing is Scotland's oldest industry.'

So, unlike Peterhead, Fraserburgh has had no major oil interests to take up slack in the fishing industry, which had always been at the core of its economy. Before the arrival of the inshore fleet in Peterhead, Fraserburgh just had the edge in attracting fish business and was first to top £1 million in

white fish landings. Three principal employers, MacFisheries, British Fish Canners and Associated Fisheries had a total labour force of 1,500.

In the latter part of the 1970s, two planners from Banff and Buchan District Council set up an enterprise trust called Fraserburgh Ltd. George Macrae, the chairman, said it was business-led but supported by the council. 'Fraserburgh's unemployment had really begun to rise – up to about 17.5 – 18 per cent. Local authorities here move extremely slowly and involve themselves in narrow-minded politics that achieve nothing except to frustrate the business community on which the whole economy should depend. I am afraid that sort of approach was reflected then in the town of Fraserburgh.' But Fraserburgh Ltd contributed to reducing unemployment to about 5 per cent in its seven-year lifespan. 'For every pound we invested we attracted £11 from other sources. So it was one of the top three enterprise trusts in its day.'

The fishing industry had already begun to pick up in the mid-1970s to early 1980s, and there was an explosion of new vessels funded by significant grants from Europe. George Macrae said, 'The years of plenty in the white fish sector began. Prawns weren't on the go then. On the pelagic side, Fraserburgh was cluttered with Russian factory ships. It looked as if the good days would never end. We spent £44 million modernising the harbour for fishing and commercial traffic. That has been a great benefit.' Another bonus has come from the landing of more than half of the North-East's highly lucrative Norway lobster (prawns). The 1998 total of 5,807 tonnes (twice as

Plate 52.

The harbour at Fraserburgh – quiet in contrast to its rival down the coast. (*Fraserburgh Harbour Board*)

many as at Peterhead) worth £10.94 million, compared to 12,872 tons of white fish, valued at £12.09 million. Currently it is the biggest shellfish port in Europe. Six of the fifteen largest firms are in fish processing now, while only one engineering company remains. The town is also home to Banff and Buchan College, a technical education establishment.

One of the previous stars of the Fraserburgh economy was the highly skilled American company Consolidated Pneumatic Tools (CPT), who specialised in compressors and electric tools. In full production, they trained and employed more than 1,500 people. They should have been ideally placed to profit from the St Fergus gas terminal only 5 miles away. That simply did not happen. George Macrae said local firms had never been able to get into the oil industry in any significant way. 'CPT is a major example. Oil service work could and should have been done in this area, not Aberdeen. Industry should have been told a certain percentage had to be located in Buchan. That would have given economic stability, rather than people travelling to Aberdeen.' But it is CPT's failure to seek business at St Fergus that is the real mystery.

Fraserburgh lad John Burns served his apprenticeship there as a mechanical technician. 'They could have involved themselves, but they would have had to diversify which would have been a major change.' John blames the management. 'They didn't have the foresight. We had this industry on our doorstep and we made compressors needed by them.' Instead of pursuing the opportunity, CPT and its sister branch in Aberdeen went into decline and finally closed in 1981 with the loss of hundreds of jobs. A final twist to the story is that CPT compressors continued to be used at St Fergus, while a number of former workers are still at the terminal. But contracts with the plant were not easy to win, as Ian Moir discovered when he moved from NESDA in 1982 to become chief executive at Fraserburgh Ltd. 'One hurdle was organising the complicated pre-qualifications for tenders. The local contractors also had to have money in the bank as a bond and they didn't like that either.' The work had to be done immediately. 'That meant dropping regular customers. Once the contract finished they had gone elsewhere. So there was a great deal of reticence. To be honest they really haven't gone hell for leather to get the work.' Ian said competition for labour in Fraserburgh was bad for a while. 'The engineering industry was the loser. Guys with a relative degree of skill found they could earn an awful lot more going offshore.'

On the social front, like Peterhead, Fraserburgh has had to deal with a number of problems, notably an unwanted reputation for widespread drug abuse among its young people, but the port's concentration on fish rather than oil should indicate the phenomenon cannot realistically be linked in this instance to the influences of the new industry.

George Macrae once produced his own definition of what makes a Fraserburgh person or 'Brocher', although he say it applies equally to Peterhead and the North-East generally: 'A Brocher is someone who wants things done, isn't prepared to do them himself, is quite happy for an outsider to do them. If the outsider does it well he gets no credit. If he does it in a way the Brocher doesn't like, the Brocher will say, "Fit the hell does he ken aboot it? He's nae a Brocher anyway."'

The loon fae the Broch

'I never thought that I would finish up like this – in this position. I can say that hand on heart. A loon fae the Broch – and I am Total's head of operations for the St Fergus gas terminal. There you go.' So said John Burns, an inspiring example of the meritocracy of an industry that has always encouraged local workers with ability and ambition. A trainee from a town notoriously reluctant to become involved in the developments on its doorstep, he now controls Europe's biggest North Sea gas complex. 'I started here in 1976 and we had six months off-the-job training. There was just a field at that time. Phase one construction of the plant was ongoing. It was an industry we weren't used to. It was alien. "Natural gas? Fits 'at?" But it was an opportunity to get into oil in its infancy.'

The succession of gleaming metal spires of St Fergus, with their yellow gas flares, rising from a conglomeration of silvery steel pipelines and low plant buildings are an impressive sight on the flat coastline of Buchan. Despite its massive scale, stretching across 500 acres, the terminal is sufficiently well landscaped to blend relatively unobtrusively into such a peaceful littoral setting. It has become an acceptable neighbour to the community. More than thirty years ago it was a different tale. The dispute that raged around the gas industry's proposals redefined local government planning strategy and subsequently dictated the companies' own approach to environmentally sensitive areas. And at first it appeared that wildlife and not community life had frustrated the industry juggernaut.

The controversy centred on Britain's biggest coastal loch and the hunt for a suitable landfall for the first gas pipeline from the northern North Sea. The Loch of Strathbeg is internationally important: a Grade 1 Site of Special Scientific Interest because of its significance as a staging post for thousands of migratory birds, including the pink-footed goose, and because of the unique

Plate 53.

Total's operations manager at St Fergus, Fraserburgh man, John Burns. (*Total*)

Plate 54.

Once Europe's largest gas terminal, the processing plant at St Fergus, in Aberdeenshire. (*Allan Montgomery*)

ecosystem in its shallow, brackish water. With its unstable sand-dune structure, one of only a few of its kind in Western Europe, it is also a Grade 1 Coastal Site. In 1972 the vicinity was chosen by British Gas for a reception point for a gas pipeline from the Frigg Field, a huge discovery, just declared commercially viable, straddling the border of the UK and Norwegian sectors. The nearby, disused Crimond airfield was to be the site for the terminal.

There was an immediate and angry response from local and national conservation bodies, coordinated by the biology and geographic departments of the University of Aberdeen, who formed an advisory environmental liaison group to Aberdeen County Council. Public meetings also demonstrated the feelings of residents in nearby villages at Crimond and St Fergus. However, there was another strong and probably more influential objector to the scheme: the Ministry of Defence (MOD) already had planning permission for a strategic radio station at Crimond.

The county council (subsequently part of Grampian Region) were anxious to encourage the development of the gas terminal, and they set up a negotiating group. After months of discussion, the convener, Maitland

Mackie, and the executive, John Russell, met the developers on the shore. 'Look, there's miles of beach in either direction – why does your pipeline particularly have to be here?' British Gas had apparently not thought to look for alternatives. They finally conceded it would be better to find a less contentious landfall. That was St Fergus.

One of the environmental leaders, biologist Dr Bill Bourne, was delighted, calling it 'A very excellent settlement which everyone hopes will benefit the developers, the public and everybody. It was a very satisfactory result.' So the decision to move became regarded as a win for the wildlife. 'Geese triumph over gas?' George Macrae dismisses this. He was chairman of the community council at Crimond, where he lived. 'I was heavily involved as I also acted for the owner of the land they wanted to buy. One meeting, which I chaired, was full of environmental interests – not local people. There was a huge debate but it was people with no proprietorial or residential interests, saying what should happen. To me it was obvious the area needed investment and it was good to have diversification. But they were all scuppered when the Ministry of Defence re-acquired the land and erected three major masts to link with the Mormond Hill NATO early warning system. The environmentalists didn't win. The MOD wanted it for national security and that took precedence. People were happy and it gave a kick up the backside to the local authorities.' British Gas used new location and assessment procedures to anticipate similar possible clashes. Now called 'environmental impact analyses' they are incorporated in European planning directives.

The great debate was all over when John Burns arrived in 1976 to begin work with Total Oil Marine, the French company who operated the site for British Gas. 'I had served my apprenticeship at CPT and came out with academic qualifications. But I also had to work part-time to bring in more money. CPT took on twelve apprentices every six months and they were ahead of their time for training. Quite a few early terminal staff were ex-CPT, good-quality guys, and there are others spread throughout the industry. I think that says a lot. But it hurt to discover St Fergus were using compressors made by CPT's major competitor and we were only up the road. But I was twenty-six at the time, a wife and two children and I wanted to get something more secure for them.' He knew very little about oil and gas. 'There was a difference in money, but not considerable at that time because it was an onshore site. You got more going offshore.' While the plant was being built there were two classrooms with groups of twelve.' On the first day there was a surprise for the new recruits. 'This was November and this guy from admin-istration told us, "This is a Christmas present for your kids and an invitation to the company dance." This was totally alien. The kids got £15 each – a helluva lot of money in 1975 – and we weren't even in the door.' Across a career of almost thirty years John still remembers the feeling of excitement as St Fergus grew. 'We were into something completely new to our corner of the North-East. We had an opportunity to be involved and to me that was a challenge. I set out every day to learn something new and that way I was going to progress.'

Not unexpectedly, the impact of the terminal was great – as was the cost to the local authority. Some idea of the financial scale came when British Gas applied to add a second terminal, at a cost of £500 million. Grampian Regional Council were told they would have to find £14 million to cover infrastructure and service costs. The project, based on a massive gas-gathering scheme, was ultimately moved to Teeside.

The disruptive passage of heavy freight to and from St Fergus had one definite effect on the community: it focused public attention on the poor quality of a road system whose improvement should have been an integral element of the onshore development of oil and gas. In the 1970s the network was pounded daily by regular convoys of huge, slow-moving transporters going to and from Peterhead as well as St Fergus laden with massive pipes and machinery. Grampian's director of roads, William Turner, said: 'The route south has perhaps one of the highest percentage of heavy goods vehicles in Britain – between 20 and 25 per cent of the vehicles travelling on the A92 and the A94 are heavy goods vehicles.' At one point, a railway bridge had to be raised 6 feet to allow a 135-foot long, 205-ton pressure vessel to pass under. The vessel, shipped to Fraserburgh from Dunkirk, was moved the 6 miles to St Fergus by two special transporters from England. The twisting Buchan route was already being tested by the sudden influx of fishing industry transport after the inshore fleet moved. Today, other than the painfully slow dualling of the A90 to Peterhead, which took thirty years to complete, limited changes to the A9 and some trunk road alterations, the North-East routes remain severely overloaded.

Back at the terminal, John Burns and his fellow trainees were allocated shifts after six months, ending with a one-week trip offshore to the MCP 01, a manifold compressor plant, located halfway between Frigg and St Fergus. Burns remembers, 'The training was fantastic and there was such a variation in staff; one guy had been a lion tamer in a circus, another had been a Royal Navy cook.' When the plant started up there was only one field, Frigg, and one customer, British Gas. After the first gas began to flow in 1977 from Frigg field, which at one time supplied a quarter of the total annual production, the seaside site grew hugely into a £340 million complex of four terminals, handling natural gas liquids and oil. Shell UK has a plant and Transco (British Gas) transmits to the national grid. The overall operator and owner is Total E & P UK.

The heroic endeavour to transport the North Sea gas can be judged by the statistics. On its way south the original St Fergus line crosses 486 rivers and water courses, 576 roads and 23 railways. Grampian is now spanned by five major hydrocarbon pipelines: three are main land routes; the others are oil from Cruden Bay to Grangemouth and natural gas from Crimond to Mossmorran in Fife. The St Fergus plant also supplied gas from Brent to Mossmorran. The NGL pipeline survived a number of objections from authorities concerned. It was the first of its kind in the UK, although they were common in the United States. There were some compensation agreements with local farmers but other land needed compulsory purchase orders. There is no direct planning control over the routing of pipelines and Buchan's local authorities pressed for a national policy.

Great care – at the behest of the council – was taken with the amenities of the St Fergus site: special acoustic techniques were used to minimise an inevitably noisy operation; and a strict safety regime was instituted. Conservation measures were imposed as a condition of planning permission, and the companies commissioned environmentalists to restore and manage the unique dune system. Banff and Buchan District Council were also given a £250,000 guarantee by Shell UK against damage to the landfall section of the company's FLAGS pipeline, the first 'environmental insurance' of its kind. The council's planning director, Peter Suttie, said, 'The issue [of the Loch of Strathbeg] had the effect of wakening planning authorities to the environ-mental impact of many proposed developments and led to much greater requirements being imposed on developers.'

In 1981 John Burns and some of his colleagues transferred offshore to MCP 01, which eventually took tie-ins from Piper Alpha, Tartan, Claymore and Amerada Hess. He was duty supervisor the night Piper Alpha exploded and later gave evidence at the Cullen Inquiry. 'I got the Mayday round about ten. Couldn't believe it. We were in thick fog so we didn't see the explosions although we were only about thirty miles away.' The Total team depressured the Piper line, which had actually ruptured at the final explosion and doubled back on itself. They got rid of the gas by flaring all night. 'We were helpless. We just sat and listened to the radio traffic. We could put faces to the names of those Piper guys. There were some I had been with in the Boys' Brigade.'

The operations boss maintains that Total have always been very safety conscious. 'It's bred into us – No. 1 on the agenda long before safety became flavour of the month. We were ahead of our time with safety committees which are now governed by legislation. You cannot work in this industry and be unsafe. If you are offshore you are sitting on top of it. It is the same here.

These pipelines are full of gas. You treat it with respect. If this was an unsafe plant the guys wouldn't work here. Last year we clocked over a thousand days without an incident.'

When Banff and Buchan MP Alex Salmond was elected in 1987 he was surprised there was no policy to ensure a local labour content: 'Now each new developer has accepted it. It was done for Shell's Goldeneye project. The college also have a skills scheme which is working very well.' Total have a daily staff of 120, who are all local. 'It is a stipulation. We have a new service and maintenance contract with Aker Kvaerner and part of that agreement is that everybody has to be local.' According to John Burns, the company sponsors four or five young apprentices on the Government's Cogent training scheme. They also try to buy locally as much as possible. 'We have quite a good relationship with Dales Engineering in Peterhead and are generally very pro-active in using local firms, otherwise I would be failing as a local myself.' As for other benefits to the community, Burns said Total has never maintained a high profile. 'We tend to do things quietly, sponsorships, funds towards a sheltered housing complex and donations.' However, despite all this good work, one anomaly mystified people from St Fergus and other small villages for a long time: even though they lived next to the biggest gas terminal in Europe, it took fifteen years before they got their own domestic gas supply.

John is now on his third spell at the terminal. Apart from the MCP, he was out on the Alwyn field for five years and also worked in Aberdeen on a project to convert the MCP into the first installation to be controlled remotely from onshore. 'That was interesting, but you were up at seven to avoid the traffic and it would be seven at night before you got home. I didn't enjoy that, it was a nightmare.'

The St Fergus site, which now houses operations run by Shell, Exxon Mobil, BP, ConocoPhillips, Gassled (a Norwegian consortium) and Transco, currently produces in excess of 20 per cent of the total national gas network. We are currently producing 65 million cubic feet a day from the Norwegian sector, plus about 26,000 barrels of natural gas liquid. That gives us another twenty to twenty-five years, plant life.' They are currently looking for any other gas supplies. There is spare capacity, but the bottleneck is in building more pipelines. John believes there is a good future for his side of the industry: 'The UK is very much dependent on gas for power. We have to continue to be pro-active, it is still out there. As technology advances we will reach areas maybe unworkable before. With the high price of oil, future development will go ahead.' He concluded, 'By then it will be time to hang up my hard hat and let the youngsters come through. From what I have seen here, we have a lot of kids who can do it.' Just like the loon fae the Broch.

He Ain't No Hillbilly

9

And far abin the Angus straths I saw the wild geese flee
A lang, lang skein o' beatin' wings wi' their heids towards the sea

The Wild Geese, *Violet Jacob, 1915*

In the intimidating room in the huge London tower block, the young inexperienced Montrose lawyer looked round the table at the panoply of representatives of the Department of Transport, the British Ports Council and the Scottish Office, all leading civil servants. And he told them, 'If that is your attitude I know I can speak on behalf of my Trust when I say that we won't be doing the development. We would rather keep the facility local.' Thirty-three years on, Sandy Jessop, who is now a Scottish sheriff, relived that moment. 'I walked out. But as I reached the lift they came after me and asked me back again. We started talking again about what we required and they then realised we had a serious facility planned and there was potential.'

The ambitious plan Sandy had put forward in that appeal for Government assistance and support was for a £2 million transformation of part of the Montrose Basin into a North Sea oil and gas service base. The Government officials had told him that as Montrose was just a wee authority any development of this nature would have to be taken over by Dundee. 'But the Harbour Trust were determined to retain control on the basis that the industry might well be only short-term and they didn't want to be left with a derelict eyesore with no value to Montrose. We thought it would be a future asset.' Sandy was later told by Tom Lister, of the Scottish Development Department – who gave him great support – the comment after the meeting was, 'He ain't no hillbilly.' 'That was a wonderful accolade at that time. Quite honestly it was a voyage into the unknown as far as I was concerned. I was only thirty, secretary to a harbour board with a small monthly income.' It wouldn't be the last time he would feel like a wee boy confronting the big battalions.

The sheriff's tale is a remarkable account of how the small Angus port stood firm against big business, and won. The development scheme had begun as the improbable brainchild of the harbour master, former sea captain Gordon Graham, who had become aware of the possibilities of attracting new business from the activities offshore. 'Gordon always had this great belief that the south side of the river at Ferryden could be developed into a magnificent feature. Gordon was a great enthusiast but there was never going to be any money for it – pie in the sky.'

Montrose at that time was the poor relation of the string of east-coast ports, Peterhead, Aberdeen and Dundee, all of which were casting avaricious eyes at an offshore industry in the throes of hunting for suitable landfalls. Sandy, delegated by his law firm in 1967 to act as harbour clerk, said Montrose was an independent port administered by a trust formed by councillors and various other bodies. 'The highlight of the month was the boat coming with wheat for Mackenzie's flour mill. I used to take a great delight in watching it come in.' So Sandy and the trust had to rein in their harbour master's grand plans, although Gordon and the stevedore company manager, Tommy Robertson, another enthusiast, succeeded in bringing in new business.

The port was not governed by the dock labour scheme, but in 1970 it became embroiled in a widespread docks strike. 'We were heavily picketed by dockers from Dundee and Grangemouth and we had a pretty bad couple of days. We weren't a union port and they claimed we were taking business from the other ports.' The strikers were told they could examine the ships' manifests. 'But they didn't want to know. They were quite determined to close us down. We kept them talking until the pubs opened and they got fed up. To their credit, our stevedores worked on and gained a great reputation.'

Sandy said they thought it odd no oil company had made approaches. 'Then I was sent to America on a fact-finding expedition organised by Dundee and Tayside Chamber of Commerce although we had always realised we were at a geographical disadvantage.' Then BP set up in Dundee. 'Maybe there was something for us after all. Gordon produced his plans again but we still felt we couldn't afford them.' Then a company called Site Preparations appeared looking for land. 'They turned out to be – how shall I say – not the greatest of companies. They had very grandiose schemes but we were never quite convinced they were right for us. But undoubtedly they were the catalyst.' Gordon dusted down his plans for a third time and the Trust took the brave policy decision that if they went ahead at all they would keep control of the facility for Montrose. That was when the young lawyer staged his walkout in London. A tremendous bluff that came off.

Plate 55.

Montrose Harbour

in the 1960s.

(*Van Werninck Studio*)

'At that meeting I was told we wouldn't be able to do anything without a proper feasibility study and that we had better appoint consultant engineers. But that would cost money.' The harbour decided to go ahead, and appointed Baptie Shaw and Morton. 'They investigated the river to see if it could be dredged and piled and then gave us a cost. That was really the start.' The dredged sand and gravel was to be used to fill in the south side of Rossie Island creating new land for the base directly in front of the old fishing village of Ferryden. The projected costs were £75,000 for dredging and about £1 million to construct the jetties. 'We were talking about £2 million for a harbour with a monthly income of £2,000. I remember saying, "How many more noughts are to come, because I have never seen anything like this in my life."' Tom Lister told the young clerk, 'You can go ahead provided you have a customer. You make sure of the income and we will help you get a loan from the DTI [Department of Trade and Industry] – so don't worry about that.'

Site Preparations brought in a number of prospective companies, among them Salvesens and P&O. 'But there was nothing concrete and it went very quiet. Site Preparations kept pressing for sole rights but we were equally determined not to give in. We thought it was all going flat.' Then Sandy was told to make a direct approach to P&O. 'Suddenly we got a response but they

Plate 56.

The oil service base
(bottom of the picture)
at Ferryden, Montrose.
(*Van Werninck Studio*)

weren't keen to do business with Site Preparations – only with ourselves. They didn't see the geographical distance as an obstacle, they looked at the feasibility study and thought everything was OK.' They also tried for sole rights. 'But we said no. If anything went wrong we would still have the facility to use for the benefit of the local community.'

The operating company, Sea Oil Services (SOS), was formed by P&O, and Dundee-born Dougal Beedie believes he was the first employee. He came as the accountant, but he also had an unusual background of nautical experience. After a course at Gordonstoun he had gone to sea with the Blue Funnel line. Then, still in his twenties, he trained in accountancy and joined P&O in London. 'Setting up a base in the North was a natural follow-up from Great Yarmouth. The choice was between Montrose and Peterhead. The latter had a bad reputation for weather and it could be a difficult place to sail in and out of, and remember we had to have twenty-four hour access.' P&O didn't want to go to Dundee because it was known there were labour problems. 'So the choice was Montrose, based on the attitude of the locals, the favourable political scene and the climate.' Dougal arrived as construction began in 1973, operated with colleagues from a small office in the High Street.

Plate 57.
Conservative Party Leader, Margaret Thatcher, at the opening of the Montrose Oil Service Base. The clerk to the Harbour Trust, Sandy Jessop, is on her right with his wife. The MP for North Angus and Mearns, Alick Buchanan Smith, later to be Energy Minister, is on the left.
(*Van Werninck Studio*)

There was a tremendous buzz in the town but Sandy Jessop could reveal nothing. Once again he found himself confronting first-division opponents as the negotiations began. The dignified man who now sits on the Sheriff Court bench with all the solemn majesty of the law behind him has a twinkle in his eye when he recalls those tough meetings. 'I was the wee boy again – the country hillbilly – up against the big organisations with all their different accountants.' This time he had support from Gordon Graham with his maritime knowledge and the local *Montrose Review* editor, Councillor Jack Smith, who chaired the harbour trust. 'Jack was great. He would chat up the P&O people, taking the pressure off me when I was negotiating. But it was a long period of hard bargaining and travelling which I must admit took a lot out of me – and I was still doing my other job as a lawyer. It was a tremendous learning curve and I often had doubts about my own ability, but the board never flinched in their faith in me.' They eventually brokered a good deal: P&O would erect their own warehouses and engineering workshops and, in turn, secured a fifteen-year lease at a rent sufficient to cover the loan from the DTI. The harbour board formed their own development committee, chaired by Jack Smith. 'Right from the start Jack told me, "We are not going

Plate 58.

The Insch Burn at Ferryden as work begins to fill in the area for the new base.

to query your expenses. We are not going to have them paid by any proposed developer who wants to control us." That committee never once had a divided vote.' The service company signed and the Trust received the money from the DTI.

Sandy laughs at his own naïveté over the tendering process. 'The tenders were due to be in by twelve noon and Ken Sturrock, one of the engineers came to my office about eleven. I said, "Ken, we are in terrible trouble. Nobody wants this job. We haven't got any tenders in." Well, he laughed. "You won't get them until two minutes to twelve and you will be asked to time-stamp them." I said, "Why is that?" "Because they will all be suspicious that if they put their tenders in too early you will tell somebody else what they are bidding." And right enough the big company representatives had come up overnight and they were sitting having coffee, tenders in their hands. Then there was a queue just before noon to deliver their bids.'

The task of convincing the general public about the need for the development had already begun with public meetings. 'In Montrose terms, it was a huge job with a major impact because there had never been any development on that side before. There was definite loss of amenity.' The Montrose Basin had two arms, one of which was the Insch Burn, nearest Ferryden. 'With that blocked up, Rossie was no longer an island. There was quite a bit of opposition and you could understand what they were worried about.' Montrose man Bill White, a former salmon fisherman who eventually worked at the base as operations manager, explained, 'When the water was in the burn, it was a bonny place – where they laid up the herring boats in the old days. Unfortunately when the mud and sand came down the river, it turned black and it wasn't very pleasant. But a lot of people liked it the way it was and there are some nice houses. I used to live at the east end and we had a beautiful view of the bridges and the basin at sunset. That disappeared. But being sea people, a lot of them enjoyed watching the boats coming in and out. There were quite a few meetings, but eventually it went ahead anyway.'

Sandy said, 'The engineers explained everything and we were quite lucky in Alex Nicol, a county councillor and harbour board member. He was a Ferrydenner and very much for the development. He did a lot to answer the villagers' misgivings.' Another local man, Mike Murray, who worked at the base's machine shop, said the protests petered out after a while. 'There were more people wanting business and jobs. It was amazing when the base opened how many Ferryden people went to get work there. Some people made a tidy wee fortune out of it.' Dougal Beedie felt P&O got off lightly in the protests. 'It was not surprising they were unhappy, but the local political people were very supportive. The key figure was Jack Smith. He saw the potential for the town – not just for oil and the marine side, but for Montrose as a whole.'

Other local industries were concerned about the dredging. There were two

Plate 59.

View from seaward back towards the basin in 1972, the old Ferryden fishing village (left), the entrance to Montrose Harbour (right). (*June Hay*)

Plate 60.

Dredging the channel towards the sea at Montrose.

(*Van Werninck Studio*)

vessels involved: one drew up the sand and gravel to deepen the seaward channel, the other piped the dredged material back to build up the site. Bill White worked on the dredgers. 'The Esk is a very volatile river and the sand is very fine. The tide brings it in and it silts up and has to be dredged again every year. That cost a lot of money.' The annual dredging bill was written into the lease agreement with Sea Oil. The giant chemical manufacturer Glaxo, who had an important factory on the north bank, were worried. Their executives asked the engineer what would happen if it all went wrong. 'Don't worry,' he said. 'It won't. If it does it will just suck it in one end and spit it out the other!' The site was landscaped with a screen of trees camouflaging the buildings. It was a bold move by the trust, heralding twenty-five years of prosperity for the port and for the town.

SOS took over the base in 1975. Total construction costs were £5 million. About a hundred staff were recruited, some skilled engineers who worked in the machine shop. The 30 or 40 casually employed stevedores went full time. During the busiest period the total workforce among the companies on the base numbered between 700 and 800. With an income rising to about £1 million a year from landing fees and increased pilotage, the harbour no longer needed the support of the local rates. The trustees paid off their loan and acquired more buildings to improve the site. Even more importantly,

Plate 61.

The oil base quayside at Montrose at the height of the North Sea oil business. (*Montrose Harbour Board*)

Montrose appeared on the map as a prime location for oil development.

But its geographical position was, in fact, a problem from the beginning. 'By the time the base was completed,' explained Dougal Beedie, who had become marketing manager, 'the major oil finds had moved north and that had a huge impact. There was also the Arab–Israeli war in 1973 and fuel prices went through the roof. Suddenly, we had to convince people that servicing rigs drilling further north out of Montrose was as economic as Peterhead. By that time ASCO had set up in Peterhead so we had to change from the purely platform side to general oil field equipment and we started manufacturing under licence and selling things in the machine shop.'

Marketing the base fell to Dougal and Alex Barnard, who later became Managing Director of SOS. 'Our first target was Canada, where the early contracts came from. The two main players were Home Oil and Bow Valley.' Other companies later joined SOS on the new base, including Otis, a subsidiary of Halliburton; Varco; Vetco Gray; Salvesens; Drexell and a variety of ancillary oil-related industries. Sandy Jessop said, 'The base was never an end in itself. I always saw it as a magnet for other companies ' For the twenty-five years of its existence, Montrose was a busy, vibrant outpost of the oil and gas industry.

Captain Niall McNab recalls, 'They were just completing construction when I arrived at the end of 1974.' Niall had been Master of Shipping at P&O Aberdeen and took a similar role at Montrose. 'Companies wanted accommodation, so there were portacabin villages all over the place.' Space actually ran out. 'It was very busy – the boats coming and going. Parking cars suddenly became a problem – now you have no trouble finding a place.' As well as Home Oil, an oil company called Pan Ocean were also initial clients, according to Niall. 'They [Pan Ocean] had Oslo Drilling who were totally owned by Fred Olsen. There was also a German company, Demenex, and a number of other drilling operators.

'At the end of 1975 we won a contract to ship out subsea transportation pipes for Total, who were building a concrete platform halfway along their pipeline. Brown and Root did that hook-up from Montrose – it took about three years. The pipe was coated at MK Shand at Invergordon and shipped down, continuous flow joints, 80 foot long – normal joints were 40 foot. But we had plenty space and laid down roads to suit. We got Harry Lawson of Dundee, the transportation company, to join two 40-foot trailers into one 80-foot trailer. We handled a pipe every three minutes – great stuff, all go night and day.'

The base began with two supply boats a day but the eventual upward curve is astonishing. In January 1977 there were 47 oil-related ships using the port; by the end of the year the total rose to 591. The figures dip and soar in tempo with the boom and bust nature of the industry. The peak years were between 1981 and 1985, when the highest volume was 653 oil-related vessels in a year. From 1977 to 2002 the port handled 37,700 million gross tonnage in oil-based shipping. Companies came and went: Consafe, Hydrotech, Aker and Shell. Niall said Farquhars of Huntly, who began by building garden sheds, fabricated accommodation modules on the SOS quay.

Niall said, 'We loaded them out, modules up to 1,000 tonnes. We had Shell's hook-up for Brent Charlie. That contract lasted four years, followed by their Fulmar platform. There was Brown and Root Wimpey on the construction side. So we would have 300–400-foot barges laying alongside as well as tugs.' SOS also hired mobile cranes that could handle 1,000 tonnes. 'They could go through an 8 foot gap – the size of a normal lorry.' But everything came in by the roads which were often blocked by the volume of convoys. 'The counterweights themselves occupied twenty or thirty lorry loads. We also had large A-frame cranes and crane barges – quite spectacular stuff. We did it ourselves first of all and then contracted it out to the specialists.'

Bill White said when they brought in barges for other people like Shell he was the only person with the experience and knowledge to handle them. 'I managed to teach other guys about dealing with barges and huge heavy weights. You can't just bring a weight like that to a standstill. The big thick nylon ropes came off so fast from those barges. That's how some guys got their legs broken.'

The Montrose crews had an excellent reputation for getting things done and done well. Niall McNab talked about the major dock strike in Aberdeen docks. 'We did reasonably well out of that. Our men didn't strike, although they were unionised. Most of the stevedores couldn't care less as long as they got the work. We paid good money and they earned a lot in overtime.' Bill White was not a supporter of the unions. 'We had our troubles here. I was never a union member. One time the nurses were striking and the stevedores went out in support – nothing to do with them at all. Here we were working hard to bring business in and things like that were happening. But generally it was a bonanza time. Once I worked for thirty-six hours straight – the lads didn't do that. We made a lot of money.'

'It was really a great job, different all the time. The big projects were the most satisfying – the modules or the heli-decks. On one Shell job we worked all with a big module and crane – those cranes cost £10,000 and then maybe £500 an hour working. At midnight a wind got up just as the big lift was beginning. I said, "Stop. We are not going to go with it." The jib was swinging so far it would have pulled the lot over. Remember, this is at £500 an hour, "We will come back in the morning." But I thought, "How am I going to explain to the client on a fine calm day, what had happened at twelve o'clock at night." But I got the men back working and told the client it had been too dangerous. He looked at me and said, "Worry no more. I will sign it off." They trusted me because I got the job done. An American once said to me, "The good jobs are written in sand – the bad jobs are carved in rock – there forever."'

SOS had a second operation at the base, Sea Oil Subsea, which built remote submarines. An occasional visitor was Sea Oil Mobile Lab, which carried out tests at construction yards and was based at Ardersier. In the machine shop highly skilled engineers dealt with drill bits, drill collars and other downhole equipment. Mike Murray had heard about the prospects at the base. He called up the manager machine shop, Bert Low. 'I had been his apprentice and he asked me to work for him. People kept saying I was stupid. But I said, "I will get ten years out of it." That's what they were saying in those days. "Ten years it will dry up and what are you going to do." I ended up working there until 1980.

'We were just a jobbing shop but very very busy. Worked for a number of companies, including McAvoy Hughes, which is now absorbed into Vetco.

Vetco eventually came out of the base and started out in what we called the tattie sheds', the area north of Montrose, now a small industrial estate. 'Vetco in Montrose is now one of the most sophisticated machine shops in Britain.'

Probably the most profitable venture for P&O's Sea Oil group was Homeco, which had premises in Aberdeen. Dougal said the company made some tools in the UK but most came from the States. The main money-spinner was from drilling equipment, bought in America, rented out and refurbished in the Montrose machine shop. 'Homeco was a great business – we didn't believe the figures – we thought we had the dot in the wrong place.' Sea Oil Homeco is now Premier Oil Aberdeen. Mike Murray said they also repaired the supply boats out of the machine shop. 'Sea Oil wouldn't let anyone else service them, it was all very lively.' In 1980 he was made redundant. 'They were starting to sell off and a French company, SMF, bought the machine shop. Then the local council offered grants to attract business to Arbroath which had severe unemployment problems. So SMF went there. Some of the other companies followed.' Dougal Beedie said that was one of those decisions that didn't make sense. 'They got so much per person per job created in a development area. That caused ill-feeling among their competitors in Montrose.'

Niall said the base was one of the biggest employers in the Angus area. 'Brown and Root employed a lot of local people – welders and fabricators. There never seemed to be a shortage of skilled men. Our best people were ex-farm lads – fork-lift truck drivers. As for safety, we worked well within the existing rules. There was no merit in not doing that. You lost too much if people got injured and were off work.' There were incidents over the years. 'One truck driver drove over the side. We picked him up by crane, hosed him down and that was it. Then there was a German tug ended up on the rocks one night. The biggest incident was the *Seaforth Highlander* going aground on the bank – we got her off eventually. No loss of life.'

There was constant movement from the base, Niall said. 'Marathon bought out Pan Ocean and decided to go to Peterhead. Otis went as well. Then Sea Oil Subsea closed in 1979.' Dougal said, 'It just folded. They were into manned submersibles which weren't very popular. One got something stuck round the propellor – that got a lot of bad publicity. The group had a cruise business and that was not really what they wanted.'

The closure created what could be termed a spin-off company, Merpro, located on the appropriately named Brent Avenue close to Vetco Gray. When Mike Murray was made redundant he contacted an engineer called Bert Smith, who had set up on his own after being paid off by Subsea. Mike was asked to set up a machine shop, which became Merpro, with Bert Smith as managing director and another former Subsea man, John Adams, as chairman. 'Twenty-six years I have been with them, along with other guys who were paid off.' The highly successful company provides a range of products and technologies for the oil and gas industry 'We are really busy – absolute crazy – purely oil work, nothing developed here, simply customer requirements.' In the slump year, 1986, Mike had to pay thirteen workers off. 'But like the base we work twenty-four hours a day, two twelve-hour shifts. Nowadays the wages are so good people won't work the same overtime.'

Another oil-related newcomer to the town was the Petroleum Industries Training School. Ensuring the establishment of the school in 1975 was one of Sandy Jessop's last responsibilities before he joined the fiscal service. 'That's been a tremendous boon to Montrose, because they have brought in all these people staying in local hotels, going out for meals, using taxis.' The school is now RGIT Montrose, part of the training and safety division of Petrofac. It originally merged with the world-famous Offshore Survival Centre at Robert Gordon's Institute of Technology, now the Robert Gordon University. Following a management buy-out, the organisation was taken over by the oil services company.

After the oil price dropped in 1986, Sea Oil finally left Montrose. 'We could see no future here at all,' claimed Niall. 'With the prices oil companies were charging there was a great tightening of belts. There were also the local rates and the lease was about to expire. But mainly we were slightly on the periphery – too far south steaming time. P&O could see no great future, so they sold the base to the Harbour Board.

'At the end of the day they got their location wrong. I think we should have gone to Peterhead. The distance from the oil field is crucial and costs became vital when ships of 10,000 horsepower came in – massive engines requiring massive amounts of fuel. It all worked to our detriment. Mind you P&O did well. It was a sound investment for them. I don't think they regretted it one bit.' Neither did Montrose.

Between working for Glaxo and Sea Oil, Mike Murray had a spell as a policeman. 'The base brought a lot of work – for the pubs as well from the men off the supply boats, especially the Esk Hotel in Ferryden, which used to be called Diamond Lil's after the landlady.' But he saw a change in the town. 'There wasn't a great deal of trouble. But there was a lot of drunkenness – a lot more people with money to spend.' He said the money was fantastic. 'I was paying more in tax than I was getting paid in the police.' Bill White's family did well out of oil. 'I worked for Sea Oil, my wife for Panocean, my daughter was with a number of companies on the base and my son-in-law is a master on supply ships.' Bill was made redundant when Sea Oil moved out.

Sandy Jessop said when the oil base began Montrose still had the jam-makers Chivers Hartley. 'With Glaxo and the harbour they were the major employers. Now like the jute mills they are closed. The peak period for the Ferryden base lasted twenty years. Those were great days, exciting, more good than bad.' The chemical company, now GlaxoSmithKline, recently won a temporary reprieve against closure.

The Port Authority opened up the 40-acre base for general commercial cargo, but there is still an involvement with the oil industry. Some of the originals remain there, including Schlumberger. There is still occasional fabrication, oil equipment shipped in and still a lot of pipe refurbished. But the base is now cast in a support role rather than day-to-day supply. Retired businessman John Aitken, who moved to Montrose from Perth to work for an oil-related company, Ultraglide, said the greatest benefit to the town was the spending power that the employment created. 'In a way it was a counter balance to Glaxo, the main employer up to that time. It produced an awful lot of opportunities and encouraged more house building. It was definitely a good thing. I think we could well be doing with another one.'

On a sunny autumn afternoon, almost on cue, a ragged skein of the poet's Norlan geese flew southwards like an arrow across Montrose's peaceful wide saltwater basin 'their heids towards the sea'. It was quiet on the reclaimed land of the base except for a jet-ski pilot preparing to launch from the estuary bank where nets once hung drying below the line of fishermens' cottages. What is essential to the Angus port now is that the base is wholly owned by the harbour authorities – just as the determined young lawyer, the journalist, the harbour master and the trustees planned back in the 1970s.

The Colossus of Kishorn

10

We're the Kishorn Commandos way up in Wester Ross
We've never had a gaffer, we've never had a boss
But we'll build the biggest oil-rig you've ever come across
Remember we're the Kishorn Commandos
        The Kishorn Commandos, *Gordon Menzies, Gaberlunzie, 1976*

The land rush

Scarcely had the first traces of hydrocarbons in the sand and rock core samples from the first oil and gas wells in the North Sea been recognised at the opening of the 1970s as indications of huge commercial potential than the first platform construction companies launched an urgent race for land. American and European firms with proven track records, hastily cobbled together consortiums and rank newcomers all competed, and the bewildered northern councils were swamped with applications for planning approval for a variety of sites as the builders chased the lucrative contracts to fabricate the dozens of offshore production structures the oil companies urgently required. A whole new industry was being born and Scotland, with its proximity to the oil and gas fields, had to be in pole position against international competition.

By the end of 1973 paperwork for seventeen ambitious schemes lay on the council desks, with one further project waiting in the wings. From the islands of Orkney to Argyll in the South-West; from Caithness on the northern tip of mainland Scotland to the island of Lewis; from the Cromarty Firth on the east coast to Fife in the south, there was a clamour for permission to develop an array of remote locations round the ragged coastline of Scotland. Most were in sparsely populated areas of great natural beauty and were vulnerable to the certain depredations of a heavy industry and a mass invasion of workers of the sort not witnessed in the Highlands since the building of the hydro-electric dams.

By the end of the 1990s only six yards were fully operational and fighting

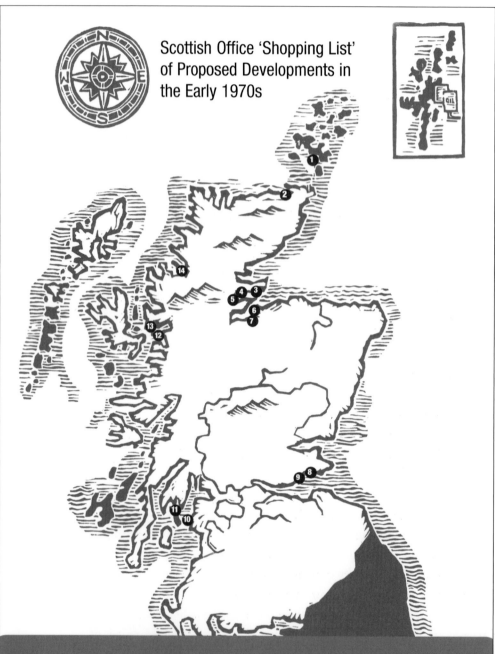

Scottish Office 'Shopping List' of Proposed Developments in the Early 1970s

1   Christiani and Nielson – Houton Bay Orkney
2   Chicago Brge – Dunnet Bay
3   Highland Fabricators (Brown & Root Wimpey) – Nigg Bay, Easter Ross
4   Mid-Continent Supply – Alness
    Taylor Woodrow – Alness
    Costain – Alness
5   Brital Marine – Evanton E. Ross
6   Costain – Fort George
7   Oceanic Contractors (J Ray McDermott) – Ardersier
8   Redpath Dorman Long – Methil, Fife
9   Angle Dutch Offshore – Burntisland, Fife
10 Costain – Hunterston
11 Sir Robert McAlpine – Ardyne Point, Argyll
    Peter Lind – Toward Quay, Argyll
12 Taylor Woodrow – Drumbuie, Wester Ross
    John Mowlem – Drumbuie
13 Howard Doris – Loch Kishorn, Wester Ross
14 John Mowlem – Ullapool

for continuity in orders. Three of them were struggling. The Scottish Office 'folly' – the most expensive hole in the world created for a fabrication yard at Portavadie in Argyll and paid for by the taxpayer – remained just that, an unused gaping chasm. At the turn of the century the orders for structures in the UK dried up, and thirty years on from the initial surge the industry is non-existent in Scotland save only for one viable fabricator at Burntisland/Methil. Their most recent order, appropriately enough, was for the biggest new field discovered since the 1970s, the 550-million-barrel Buzzard field. The last two big contracts, for Shell's Goldeneye and BP's long-awaited Clair field, went abroad, signalling the end for the yards at Nigg and Ardersier. The concepts of North Sea oil and gas production technology had radically altered; the days of the offshore giants were over and the economic strategies of Big Oil, in other words the industry majors, had gone global.

Yet in the beginning the short-term future had seemed so bright: the dawn of a major new manufacturing enterprise onshore to complement the developments offshore. The Government body set up to generate industry business for UK companies, the Offshore Supplies Office (OSO), estimated fifty-three major platforms could be required by the end of 1980. Beyond that there was a great degree of uncertainty. Ominously, only half the number of initial orders eventually went to British yards. The prevailing fashion appeared to be for concrete structures. The Norwegians had successfully built and installed their Condeep design in their sector and potential developers in Scotland sought to emulate them; of the eighteen applications for yards, twelve were for concrete.

Realising the enormous and welcome fillip the new industry could give to the Scottish economy, and the prospective bounty for onshore employment, the Scottish Office sought, through a special oil taskforce, to streamline the planning system; they favoured the massive concrete platforms too, but they were also determined to steer the companies to the West of Scotland where unemployment was heavy and manufacturing in decline. This, too, was the preference of the all-powerful unions who ruled British shipbuilding, the industry most akin to platform fabrication and which they were now also seeking to control. Jimmy Gray, a former Amalgamated Engineering Union (AEU) convener of shop stewards at both Ardersier in Moray and Nigg in Easter Ross, attended national union meetings where sixteen fabrication yards in the UK were represented. 'There was always tension with the boilermakers, which you could understand. Their traditional areas were the shipyards and construction, so their skilled membership had a vested interest. They were opposed to the yards coming up to the Highlands. They wanted them for Teeside and Tyneside, the Clyde and at Dundee and Leith.'

Plate 62.

(*Boxtree Creative*)

The oil operators and the fabricators – not people who took kindly to being directed – thought differently. Ultimately three yards were set up in the Highlands, one on the island of Lewis, two short-lived ventures in Argyll and Ayrshire and two at sites in Fife.

The world's biggest floating structure

On the face of it, in the 1970s the Highland authorities and the Highlands and Islands Development Board (HIDB) were seeking new industry and new employment for a vast and remote region in permanent decline. The environmental lobbies didn't wield the same influence then, but there was widespread public concern about the effect of these large industrial enterprises on the social fabric of the Highland communities. The test case was the pivotal Drumbuie Inquiry, at the time the longest-running public examination of a new industrial development. The six-month inquiry heard evidence on planning applications by Mowlem and Taylor Woodrow, to build concrete Condeep platforms on two areas held by the National Trust at Port Cam, Drumbuie, and at the mouth of Loch Carron. There were objections from 300 individuals and 17 organisations, mainly on the basis of social and environmental disruption and the anticipated burden on the local authorities. Despite a plea that Port Cam was the only site for such platforms, which were needed 'in the national interest', the Scottish Secretary rejected the applications.

While attention focused on Drumbuie, across the loch a shrewd UK builder was quietly negotiating with one of Britain's richest industrial families, the Wills tobacco dynasty, who owned the Applecross peninsula, for a lease on a similar location at the mouth of Loch Kishorn. Sir John Howard had formed a consortium with the French company CG Doris; he had experience of major civil engineering, while Doris had just built a concrete oil-storage tank for the Norwegian Ekofisk field. Former Ross and Cromarty councillor and local farmer John Macdonald, who was on the planning committee, was involved in the negotiations. 'Sir John was friendly with the Wills family and they had assured him he would get in if he got planning consent.' John added, 'About 80 per cent of the people in the area were in favour. But people are astonishing. The day after I told Sir John his planning application had been approved, the first person I met coming out of office was the managing director of a construction company. He had been negotiating to build the road into the site. He was also chairman of a local anti-oil yard campaign.'

The local council were generally in favour of the development but, in fact, drove a hard bargain to safeguard the community's interests. Kishorn and

Plate 63.

(*Boxtree Creative*)

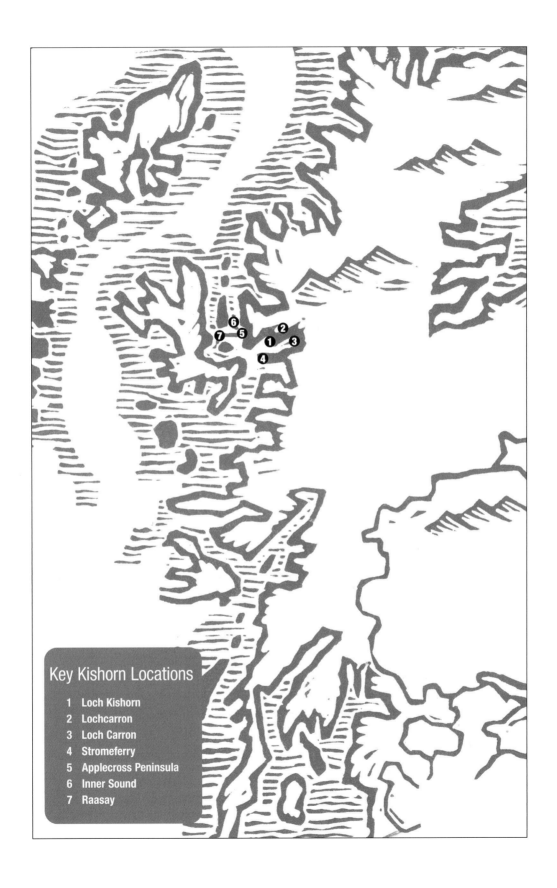

Key Kishorn Locations

1 Loch Kishorn
2 Lochcarron
3 Loch Carron
4 Stromeferry
5 Applecross Peninsula
6 Inner Sound
7 Raasay

Plate 64.

A muddy swamp on a Highland hillside destined to become the birthplace of a monster oil production platform.

Lochcarron were tiny scatters of houses clinging to lochsides on the fringes of Wester Ross, supported economically by forestry, farming and some fishing. The landscape was wild and unspoiled. But the development was approved on the concept of a self-contained 'island' site: heavy material would be transported by sea, avoiding the area's single-track road system. The 'island' was a planning chimera, the location was land-based, but the promise was enough to ensure planning approval in 1974 from the Scottish Secretary, Willie Ross. He also recognised the 'very real economic losses suffered by this country' if the yard didn't go ahead.

There was another powerful local interest to be placated – the fundamentalist Free Presbyterian Church. The council inserted a clause in the planning conditions: 'There will be no work on the construction or operation of the site on any Sunday except that which is necessary for treatment and repair and for continuous concrete slip-forming process.' They also set a limit of 400 for the

Plate 65.
Peaceful now, the cottages of Lochcarron, strung along the the shore of the Wester Ross loch.
(*Allan Montgomery*)

Plate 66.
All that is left from the days of the giant, a flooded chasm in the hillside above Loch Kishorn.
(*Allan Montgomery*)

total labour force, but that was to be far exceeded.

Major John Wills later gave his reasons for leasing the land in the first edition of the company's *Kishorn News*. 'People would return to the depopulated Highlands and young men would not go away while money would be put back into the peninsula in different ways.' No one, however, quite anticipated the impact the yard and its workforce would have on the community. Sir John had already won a £60 million order from Scotland's largest company, Burmah Oil, for a concrete platform to form the hub of their Ninian field. During construction, Ninian was bought by the American company Chevron.

Historically the placid sea loch had a tradition of marine construction: Norsemen had built their galleys there. But the great longships would have been hugely dwarfed by the astonishing Colossus of Kishorn. The completed carcass of this modern behemoth weighed nearly 0.5 million tonnes; it

contained 150,000 cubic metres of concrete with a base 140 metres in diameter, the highest wall some 550 feet. It was, at the time, the biggest man-made floating structure in the world. For its dry dock 1.5 million tonnes of rock had to be carved out of the hillside, a pit 30 feet deep, with a diameter twice that of Murrayfield rugby stadium. There was also a taskforce of 12,000 tonnes of shipping: seven supply ships, two ocean-going ships and two smaller tugs, five coasters, five personnel ferries, and a crane ship capable of lifting 800 tonnes. The cement was churned out from one of the world's largest floating plants at 100 cubic metres an hour. Compared to the ten years needed to construct a power station, this miracle of civil engineering had to be completed in two years before being towed to the Sound of Raasay for the installation of the deck sections and modules. There were great battalions of men and ranks of machinery; for the bemused inhabitants of the tiny hamlets this was an invasion beyond anyone's experience. But it seemed to be generally welcomed. One correspondent wrote in the company magazine, 'It is a beautiful sight across the loch this long and stormy winter. We have saved a fortune in batteries. The piling hammer at 7.30 a.m. is the best alarm clock ever!'

In the peak construction years Sir John's workforce estimate had to be doubled again and again. At one time 3,000–4,000 were engaged at Kishorn, including the camp's service staff; there were also 34 different contractors on the site. The wage bill began at £60,000 a week and reached £108,000 during the busiest period. As the site developed, a £1.25 million workers' village was constructed for 480 people, with restaurant, bar, cinema, gym, shops, launderette, barber, post office, bank, bowling green, sports field and a caravan site for married employees. Two former cruise ships, the *Rangitira* and the *Odysseus* sat at the jetty and accommodated another 300–400 hundred men. The management team, half a dozen of them French, were housed in a small estate in the village.

In the beginning the company's employment agent was virtually overwhelmed by applicants, 4,000 eventually whittled down to 800. Among them were many local people: three villages, for example, Loch Torridon, Shieldaig and Lochcarron, supplied 60 who commuted daily, while 150 regularly used a new sea link between Kyleakin on Skye and Loch Carron. The main employment agent was a legendary Irishman, Charlie Fergus. 'You would go to a club with him,' John Macdonald said, 'and he literally couldn't get peace to drink. Hundreds of men would come up. "Any chance of a start, Charlie? Anything going?" They were desperate to get up here.' He recalled a crisis when the platform was out in the loch. 'When the wind rose the cranes couldn't work and all the steel had to be manhandled up great heights. More men were needed. Charlie would fly planeloads from Ireland into Inverness –

Plate 67.
Opposite. Ninian Central. The preparatory work begins.

Plates 68 a–d (overleaf).
a. the gigantic carcase fills the dock;
b. the Kishorn Commandos at work;
c. Ninian Central ready to move;
d. flanked by tanks, the platform heads for Raasay Sound.

b.

c.

load after load.' The general workforce, immortalised in song as the 'Kishorn Commandos', also called the Bears, flooded in from all over Britain.

Local boy Ruaridh Baird-Ferguson had just left school. 'There wasn't much in employment, but the yard was quite an exciting thing so a lot of people went that way.' He began as a chain boy helping surveyors and engineers who were constructing the dock and laying out slabs for the platform's steel skirting. 'Looking back, the amazing thing was the number of people involved – it was just like a small town.' Six months on he became one of the yard's first apprentices, serving his time in maintenance and mechanics. 'Nigg was far more organised. We had a school for welders but there were very few apprentices. Certainly we were put to Inverness College. You had to put in the hours but I just liked the work. I got £35 per week which was good for an apprentice at that time.'

Another local, Jocky Brown, worked as a subcontractor at the yard, steel erecting and rigging. 'They were a good enough company. I know one man who saved enough to build his house. He worked every shift for five months – £4,000 – enough for a three- or four-bedroom bungalow.' John Macdonald believed the yard wages caused problems for local companies. 'I had run a seaweed-buying agency where we paid £9 a week; it was £7 at the local authority and the forestry. We were inundated, £2 a week was a big difference

Plate 69.

Emergency accommodation for the overflow of the workforce at Kishorn, one of the former cruise ships moored at the jetty.

Ruaridh's big day

Medallion for the Prince

During his visit to Loch Kishorn Prince Charles was presented with a silver gilt commemorative medallion by 17-year-old Ruaridh Baird-Ferguson, an apprentice fitter, whose home is at nearby Lochcarron.

Ruaridh is the longest serving apprentice at the Howard Doris platform yard. He was educated at Plockton Secondary School, joined Howard Doris as a chain boy in July 1975 and was transferred to the mechanical repair workshop last year.

The medallion (pictured left) has the head of the Prince of Wales on the face and an illustration of the Ninian Central Platform on the reverse.

A limited number of these medallions were struck in bronze and the die has been destroyed so that no further coins can be made.

Plate 70.

A proud moment for the yard's first apprentice, Ruaridh Baird-Ferguson receiving a commemorative medal from the young Prince Charles – captured in the special souvenir brochure marking the launch of Ninian Central.

in your take-home pay. So locals didn't want anyone else disturbing the balance. The difference at the yard was enormous, because there were no restrictions and twelve-hour days were very common. The rates were better too.' Marion Mackenzie, whose car mechanic husband was busy with yard contracts, worked in the camp canteen. 'Sixteen-year-olds leaving school came home with £300 a week clear on twelve-hour shifts. A lot of money in the 1970s – they got about £18 in Lochcarron.'

Life in the canteen was unforgettable. 'When you opened up at eight o'clock at night, if you didn't get out of the way quick enough you could get trampled on by the Bears – about 3,000 squeezing in for meals. There were two bars – including the famous Wellie bar. They came every Wednesday night – pay night.' She laughed, 'Just like Wacky Races – they would be jumping over the tables trying to get to the bank first. All to get their money out before their wives could get their hands on it.'

Jocky lived on the *Rangitira*: 'I was on the bottom deck – Room 34, great. A good bunch of lads . . . Couldn't understand a word you were saying [Jocky has a pronounced Wester Ross accent]. Crazy bunch, they used to go to the nightclub in Inverness, nine or ten in a car. I stayed in the camp as well. You never had to leave – everything was there and the bars were good. We had the "shithouse choir". After the bar closed, we went into the toilets for a sing-song.'

Medic Steve Russell Price, from Trinidad, also remembered life at Kishorn. 'It was like the Wild West. I was there a couple of times on three-year spells – the last for the Maureen contract in 1980–83. It was rough. We had portacabins but some just slept in their cars. They crawled through the wire to have a shower, came to the bars at night and then crawled back out again.

There just wasn't enough accommodation. We had two bars, the Pigs' Bar – which speaks for itself – and one for staff like myself. It wasn't as rough. We worked twelve-hour shifts for three or four weeks at a time. But I lived in Inverness and came home for two weeks. It was a ridiculous shift, but the money was very, very good. I wasn't complaining.'

Steve said he met some characters at Kishorn. 'People nicked an awful lot to offset their salaries. There was the famous "Skye boy, fly boy". He used to strap equipment like chainsaws to scaffolding boards, throw the boards into the water and the tide took them over to Skye, where his mates picked them up and sold them. Then there were the guys who disappeared after they came on shift. You didn't see them again until three minutes before the end of shift or at mealtimes. Ninian Central was so big they could go down into the column and vanish.'

As Steve indicated, the camp had its own medical facilities, with medics, nurses and an attending doctor. Helen Murchison, who came from Kishorn, trained in the South as a nurse. She returned in the 1960s, married with two children, with very little prospect of work – until Howard Doris started. 'I just leaped at the chance to go back to my old profession. Grand Metropolitan, who ran the medical side, were surprised there was someone so well-qualified in the community.' Most of her patients suffered sparks in their eyes from the welding. 'In the early days blasting at the site was a regular event.' She was absorbed one day in removing an object from a worker's eye when the siren sounded. 'I just carried on. Then the doors burst open and both of us were gathered up in brawny arms and rushed along the corridor. That was too close for comfort.' Helen remembered very few serious injuries on the site. 'There were two fatalities and inevitably a large number of minor accidents.'

When the yard started there was no fence and anybody could get in. 'Quite often people were living there who weren't employed at all,' said Helen. 'I was called out in the middle of the night. The clinic was a shambles. Three men who looked as if they had been in a road accident, broken ribs but nothing life-threatening. In the ward, a man with his face slit, another chap's hands were slashed. On a trolley was a fellow we called the Old Man. He wasn't old at all – he had just led an adventurous life. You couldn't see him under all the mud. But we cleaned him up and he had pretty serious injuries, the worst to his head. The doctor, a locum, was stamping about shouting, "Animals, just animals!" Anyway it turned out the Old Man wasn't even employed there, he was just dossing, on the run from the police. I think it was for murder. Once he recovered he was jailed for six months. When he came out he was transported back to wherever he had come from. But he wasn't the only one. They hid in the shower blocks in a space between the showers and

Plate 71.

The former senior nurse at the yard's medical centre, Mrs Helen Murchison, outside her home at the lochside. (*Allan Montgomery*)

the ceiling – slept there every night until the company cottoned on.'

Inevitably this flood of strangers made its presence felt in the surrounding villages, but there was a convenient forum for mutual contact in a joint local liaison committee. John Macdonald eventually became chairman. He described its makeup: 'Representatives from the camp, landowners, the inevitable ministers and church people, even men from the Admiralty in Kyle. We had no difficulty with the yard because the control mechanisms worked perfectly.' What most people seem to remember is the onrush of cars and buses twice daily through Lochcarron and Kishorn. Said Helen, 'There was a single track and hundreds of men with no experience of these roads, but they would drive to the pub and back. The number that crashed was absolutely phenomenal. It was amazing there was only one fatality.' Steve had similar memories of wintertime. 'Over at Achnasheen there were about six or seven miles of black ice, so the cars spun off the road. But they had so much money they just used to leave them, take the radios out and jump into a mate's car.' Inevitably top of the liaison committee's agenda were regular complaints about cars littering the lochside. Eventually Howard Doris agreed to tow the vehicles away if the community agreed to pay for them to be dumped.

The locals claimed there wasn't a great deal of trouble from the yard workforce. Jocky did tell, however, of one big fight in the Welly Bar. 'The place was full of Irish. Somebody asked for the water and instead of passing it, the guy threw it. There were about six policemen in the camp. Everybody involved was down the road immediately – no messing. If you got into any trouble anywhere within a 65-mile radius, including Inverness, and the boss got to hear, you were sacked.' John said, 'They were out of here on the train on Monday, whatever their seniority.' Helen maintained that was Sir John Howard's promise: troublemakers went out the door. According to John the local hoteliers enjoyed a massive increase in business. 'They went from £5 or £10 turnover in a night to £1,000 – and that was not unusual for both pubs in Lochcarron.' John Cowell, a genial Englishman, owned the village store during two busy years. 'One of the first crimes in living memory happened at that time. The oil was nicked from a petrol station – £4 4s.-worth – that created a great stir in the 1970s. Folk said this was what the site had brought – crime and so on. There was also the case of a man who broke down in the Glens on the way to work. When he walked back to get his car, it had been stripped of anything that could be taken away. Nowadays you don't bother locking doors – but at that time, folks were wary for a while.'

One contentious matter raised with the committee came from one of the churchmen, said John Macdonald. 'He said how sad it was to see mothers with little children in church on Sunday when their fathers had to work. So we demanded the names in confidence and checked them out. The men were on site right enough, but they were in the bars. The ministers had to back down.' The catering staff girls lived in separate accommodation in the village. 'That was like a convent,' said Helen. 'One house was opposite a prominent minister's home and he used to watch them with an eagle eye. He would phone the camp and tell them he had seen a man going into the house. But, of course, by the time the security boys got over, the man had disappeared out the back window.'

In the early days there were a few clashes with the influential Kirk ministers until their power began to wane. 'That was one of the biggest changes. The Church's grip weakening. In spite of the rule about Sunday working, the company continued to press for it. They held a secret ballot in the village and the vote was tight – 87 in favour and 81 against. But the restriction continued and John Cowell's progressive marketing ideas brought him into conflict with the Kirk. 'I had noticed Sunday was a day when people were out and about or were working and they wanted things. So I opened the shop, but there were quite a few churchgoers who were quite upset. They said they weren't going to shop with me anymore. That lasted about four months – until they found it very inconvenient. I also got a licence to sell wine, and the guys were paying fifty quid a case. The passing trade was enormous. The guys would buy not one can of beer but twenty-four and it was all gone by Inverness.' But he was threatened by the Kirk. 'They said the wrath of the Lord would descend upon me. But I am still here.' He is one of the majority of villagers who thoroughly welcomed the incomers. His turnover went up three-fold in twelve months and he bought his cottage with the profits. 'When I did the post office on a Thursday night I could tell where they came from by their registered letters, in which they sent money home. Whatever was left after they paid their camp bill went into those envelopes. Queues of them, and I was just banging away with the stamp like a good 'un.'

For the community another important council condition was the Sir John Howard Trust Fund, into which the company paid £25,000 per year for the benefit of the local inhabitants. 'That money was invested,' said John Macdonald, the former liaison chairman and a fund director. 'The 1970s were very good years for investments. That largely built the Howard Doris Centre in Lochcarron, which provides residential care for the elderly.' Helen added, 'It also gives employment to twenty-five local women in their home village.' Another attribute of the fund was that it helped local youngsters with their education. 'We have disbursed all the monies now. We gave the final few thousand pounds to the secondary schools at Plockton and Gareloch.'

By the end of the 1970s the yard had to change to meet new concepts in platform requirements. Ninian Central was the last big concrete platform built in the UK. Then Howard Doris won a new contract in 1979: an 18,000-ton integrated deck for Phillips' Maureen field, the first steel structure built at Kishorn. The company invested £1.2 million redesigning the yard and the facilities. Managing Director Albert Granville said the yard had to be as flexible as possible, capable of producing concrete and steel gravity platforms, steel jackets and hybrids in both materials in order to ride the boom-and-bust nature of the business. The Maureen contract was finished on time.

The company had always felt restricted by the 'island concept', although they had continued to transport some of the material by road. So in 1978 they applied for the clause to be removed in order to speed up the supply process and allow them to compete more favourably for orders. They faced a barrage of criticism, including a petition from fifteen local residents who wrote, 'It would aggravate an already dangerous situation caused by the volume of heavy traffic on the roads. If all this exists when it is an "island site", the results of the abolition of this status are too horrifying to contemplate.' Helen Murchison believed the council had made a major mistake accepting the island site idea originally: 'The traffic was ten times what they had anticipated. You had to time your journey to keep off the roads when they were busy.' A major railhead had been created at Strome and all the materials were barged to the site and the lorry traffic diminished greatly. John Macdonald claimed, 'The council did what they could. They remodelled the road to Stromeferry and improved bridges to give major access. But they didn't have the financial resources to go further.'

Ross and Cromarty planning committee, supported by the liaison committee, recommended altering the original planning permission. The Scottish Secretary turned down the application. He aggravated the situation further by pronouncing that onshore developments did not qualify for capital expenditure, such as roads, unlike offshore exploration and extraction. The logic was that if the material was shipped in under the island concept – there was no need for improved roads. After months of arguments the council decided to treat the Scottish Secretary's decision as only advisory. They lifted the restriction.

Later in 1979, Mr Granville claimed the yard was in Kishorn to stay. 'I can assure you that we have not invested £30 million for one operation. I see no reason why Howard Doris should not remain in Wester Ross for another fifteen years.' Fateful words. Despite valiant efforts, the yard only lasted another six fragmented years as they endured the cyclical ups and downs of the industry. They secured two sizeable contracts in the 1980s for structures for the Morecambe Bay gas fields. Then they secured an interest in the Clyde shipbuilders Scott Lithgow. The idea was to combine the shipbuilder's ability to construct pontoons for semi-submersible rigs with Kishorn's capacity to build complicated integrated topsides. The collaboration never succeeded. In 1984, the yard did conversion and maintenance work on BP's Buchan Alpha

Plate 72.

Ruaridh Baird-Ferguson outside the marine engineering repair and maintenance base built on the former helipad at the yard. (*Allan Montgomery*)

platform, and in 1985 it built two gas compressors and treatment modules for Total's Alwyn North field. This was the final major contract. In September 1988 national newspapers were carrying advertisements offering the yard's facilities for sale. The incredible adventure that created the floating island was over. John Macdonald said the community had been under no illusions that it was going to last. 'The dry dock is still there. It will be of use some day.'

Since the closure the lochs have been used for fish farming, while a local haulier transports material from the jetty on to small coasters. There have been attempts to revive the yard: in 1999 Highland Council gave planning permission to convert it to an oil supply and rig decommissioning centre. But basically the village simply slipped back into the peaceful rhythms of a remote Highland community although with a population of 100, as opposed to 60 before the yard, and with more new life, 36 children compared to only 2 in the 1960s. If proposals for a large quarry at the site are approved that tranquillity may be disturbed, and residents fear the effects on aquaculture and tourism. No such concerns trouble the yard's first apprentice, Ruaridh Baird-Ferguson. He and four or five others, including Nigg apprentice Ewan Gillies, run a marine engineering shop built over the yard's helipad. All self-employed and flexible, they find other jobs when necessary. 'That is the Highland way. Some people are against the quarry but I would take any work.'

Jobs for your sons and your sons' sons

The men from the island of Lewis in exile at the Methil fabrication yard in Fife looked on in dismay when they heard yet another foreign company was bidding to take over the redundant oil construction site in their home town of Stornoway. 'We had Norwegians,' said Norman MacAskill, a foreman engineer from the site at Arnish, 'we had Dutch and it looked as if we were going to have French. We thought, "Why the devil don't we do something?" So we did.' The buy-out by the four former employees in 1989 was to be the third occupation of the site at Arnish over an eventful thirty-year period. It was also to be the last oil-related venture.

Former provost of Stornoway, Sandy Matheson, later convener of Western Isles Council, described the steady parade of 'entrepreneurs, conmen and speculators', who arrived on the island seeking land for development; the town council had already repelled one London company in 1972. So the council armed themselves with a development fund and an industry committee to deal with any prospective enterprises. 'We were well-positioned to capture a slice of the oil action.'

Plate 73.

Provost of Stornoway, Sandy Matheson (right), with DM Smith, Crown Estates factor, who played an important role in the island's negotiations with Fred Olsen.

The main target of interest was Arnish, a tenanted coastal farm with access to deep water at Glumaig Harbour. The land, donated by the soap magnate Lord Leverhulme, was owned by the Stornoway Trust, landlord for a large part of the island, including the town. Although the site didn't figure in the 1973 Scottish Office list of prospective yards, negotiations with the Norwegian company Fred Olsen (UK) Ltd were already well underway.

Sandy, ex-officio chairman of the trust, said they resolutely opposed an outright sale. 'But the Trust was very short of liquid capital and the prospect of a good, paying and secure tenant seemed too good to miss, especially as the Lewis economy, which was never strong, was going through one of its cyclical downturns.' Another historical problem was the continuing migration of people from the island. Roger Howarth was planning officer at Ross and Cromarty County Council, which, before reorganisation in 1975, was the planning authority for the Western Isles. He handled the Olsen application. 'There were no great issues about using the site. It didn't go to a public inquiry, which shows there wasn't a great deal of opposition.' Sandy said the Trust was in a powerful bargaining position. 'We were able to set standards and enforce lease conditions on the primacy of local employment, skill training and, to a certain extent, the use of local suppliers.'

When the proposed £8 million development eventually became public, however, in the autumn of 1973, many townspeople were surprised; they had expected a supply base. Instead they were to get a fabrication yard with the eventual promise of 1,000 jobs. Doubts were expressed about the long-term nature of the industry, but Roger Howarth recalls the company representative promising, 'There will be jobs here for you, your sons and your sons' sons.'

Olsen took a 60-year lease on 93.2 acres of land at an annual rent of £32,620.

A number of issues emerged; one was the inevitable spectre of Sunday working on an island ruled by the strict Free Kirk. Olsen's managing director, Michael Thompson, warned he couldn't give a blanket assurance it would never happen. If it was to be a condition, it would 'colour' their decision to move in or not. In reality, the Trust was later assured by the company that because of the 'strong feelings', apart from essential maintenance, 'no construction or commercial work would be carried out on the Sabbath'. Another problem was the expected return of Lewismen to take up jobs. It didn't happen to any great extent but there was a flurry of house-building in the 1970s. The local workforce was, however, outnumbered by travelling men who possessed the necessary skills lacking on the island; 500 were ultimately accommodated in a cruise liner. Local businessmen – in particular the traditional Harris tweed manufacturers who were suffering a downturn – also complained about unfair wage competition and the possible loss of skilled workers. Olsen paid for utility services and access to the site, which could only be reached by boat or a single-track road. The yard, operated by Aker Offshore Services, a division of Olsen, and named Lewis Offshore, finally opened for business in 1975.

Young Murdo MacIver had just left school when he applied for a job at the yard. 'Anything engineering-related had always been my interest and I would have had to leave the island to get it. I can't remember any negative reaction to the yard. Everyone saw the opportunity to work at home, and the promise of jobs.' Sponsored by Olsen, he went straight to Lewes College to train as a plater for two years, including on-the-job training at the yard. He was just finishing when Arnish won what was to be their biggest oil contract: converting BP's drilling rig Drill Master to a production structure for the Buchan field. 'Before that they were primarily involved in structures related to the industry, barges and floating structures – or components for them.'

At that time Norman MacAskill was working as a welding foreman in Glasgow. With very few opportunities for engineering or maritime cadets, young men from the Western Isles always had to train on the mainland. 'Quite a lot never came back – and still haven't. I heard about the yard by word of mouth. Something like that was big, big news.' He eventually came back to Stornoway in 1978. By then the yard had built a couple of barges, two small roll-on-roll-off ferries and a couple of landing craft. The Drill Master was on the stocks. Murdo reckoned 1,500–2,000 people, including contractors, were working on the site. 'At the peak maybe 500 were local – the rest were travelling people.' The yard had its own training school. It dealt with 'A dozen

Plate 74.

Murdo MacIver, who served his apprenticeship at Arnish and is now a director of the successful service company SBS in Aberdeen.

Plate 75.

Structures take shape in the giant shed at Arnish Point.

(*Aberdeen Journals Ltd*)

pipe fitters, twenty platers at a time,' said Norman. 'There was a huge influx of unskilled people. Today you will find joiners in their late forties and fifties who actually have two trades.' Norman was an instructor for a spell. 'The training was intense but I hated it. My trade was pipe-fitting and welding – I was good at it. Then they made me a foreman.'

The Drill Master period meant good times for Stornoway. 'Every hotel, every guest house in the town or on Lewis was filled,' according to Murdo. Norman said people hoped it would be continuous because of the work and the amount of money injected into the community. 'Forget the travelling men who spent money, you have to look at what the local people earned and then spent on the local economy. People were building houses and that created its own knock-on effect – the place was absolutely booming.'

But there was also a downside. 'You used to go into the yard on a Thursday night,' said Murdo, 'and you never knew if you were going to start work or not. There were a lot of industrial issues primarily raised by incoming labour. It was a closed shop then, the main union was the Amalgamated Engineering Union (AEU). Strike after strike – probably my main memory of that time – and a lot weren't justified. For a three-month period over the

whole contract, it was chaos – and the union supported them.' The first strike was six months after the yard started. 'An apprentice accidentally or otherwise knocked a foreman's hat off and got suspended. So the men went on strike for three weeks. The apprentice was on full pay. So while he was sitting quite happily at home and getting paid for it the rest of us lost three weeks' money.' The sporadic industrial unrest continued until Aker brought in new senior management and stabilised the situation, just before they sold the yard.

After Buchan Alpha sailed off in 1980 most of the travelling men went too, but there was still enough work; fabrication for the Maureen platform being built at Kishorn, and modules for Marathon. Then, in 1982, Arnish closed down and most of the remaining 300-strong workforce was paid off. For a time local politicians and union officials campaigned nationally to bring more work but they were unsuccessful. Murdo, who had moved into the planning office as a planning engineer, and was later to become a production control engineer, was among those released. It was the second time he had been paid off. Norman MacAskill, who found employment at Inverurie in Aberdeenshire, thought the reason for closure was not just a lack of orders. 'I would never decry what Olsens did for Stornoway, but they also owned

Plate 76.

The BP rig Drillmaster lies off Arnish Point in Broad Bay in the process of conversion to a production structure for the BP Buchan Alpha field. An accommodation vessel is moored near the yard. (*Aker/Angus Smith*)

Timex in Dundee, which went bust. They needed cash, so what they did was to shut down Arnish to save themselves a fortune.'

Next in was the Dutch company Hereema, which began by completing a barge Olsen had set aside. Murdo found they had a different plan for the yard. 'Their vision was to build semi-submersible platforms to sell all over the world. But there was always a problem with location when you were building structures primarily for the North Sea. That caused difficulties in terms of transportation.' Norman, who had studied for a quality manager's ticket, went back in 1982, first as a fabrication inspector on a few projects and then as quality manager. 'In 1985 we were building small gas field jackets for Amoco and BP – plenty of work for the 200–300 people.' The yard continued to be busy, with only one slack period, until 1988, when it was closed down again. Murdo's view is that a downturn in the industry was the main reason. There was also the transportation problem. 'It had become a handicap, something you always had to fight against. As an estimating manager, I became involved with pricing projects. First you had to overcome the cost of bringing barges round. We largely ended up including these in the price. But Hereema had other yards at Hartlepool and Holland with easier access from either side of the North Sea.'

At that time the Dutch company had joined forces with McDermotts at Ardersier (see Chapter 11) and Norman believed one of the conditions of the merger was that Arnish had to go. 'We were a lot more competitive and taking a lot of work from Ardersier.' That was when the former general manager, the late Colin MacIver; another Arnish man, Peter Webster; and Norman decided to join forces to buy out the company. They were working at Methil for Bluewater Engineering. Murdo, who had followed a contract from Germany to Brazil, was invited to join them. Norman said the money came from their own pockets. 'Half a million of it, some risk – but we decided it was worth taking, because we knew there was a lot of work in the offing.' Murdo had moved in to the yard to set up. 'We all had a belief in it – maybe a little bit too much, but we knew the capability of the place. We had a lot of contacts and the industry looked to be picking up.' The first contract was for a barites (mud) tank for McDermotts at Ardersier. 'That was about £130,000, very small,' said Norman, 'What it did though was re-open the doors and we employed about seventy-five guys.' Then they bid for three medium-sized projects for Shell, BP and Amoco worth about £1 million to £2 million each. Murdo said, 'We thought we might get one but we got all three. We had looked for steady growth but the curve just kept going up and from a dozen people we took on about 150–180.' One of the difficulties was attracting skilled Lewismen back. 'We had to convince people who had been paid off twice or three times for long periods that there was a future. Once we got them back it became established again.'

They kept the yard running for ten years. 'One of the biggest jobs was the Elgin Franklyn project – two jackets – when we employed 250 to 400 people. Looking at the yard's whole cycle in terms of sustainability and jobs – that was its most successful period – other than converting Drillmaster.' To keep men employed they hired-out labour to other oil yards and to the Harland and Wolf shipyard in Belfast. As a Lewisman, Murdo believed what they were doing had a lot of meaning. 'It is hard to describe. It was a community thing as much as anything – bringing jobs and success to the community. And it took teamwork from everybody throughout the whole yard. We had good people.'

It all went wrong when they were completing a contract for the Dutch company Bluewater Engineering: a turret for the Jotun project being built in Finland. Severe contractual disagreements arose and Murdo and two of his colleagues spent nearly a year in Holland trying to negotiate a financial settlement. Bluewater wouldn't budge and the receivers were called in. 'Those were hard times – the hole in our finances was just too big.' The administrator called it a day and the yard's assets were sold off. That was the end of Arnish as an oil fabrication facility.

Norman said, 'It was a shame really. We were still training people and we had nearly thirty apprentices attending Inverness College.' Murdo still felt bitter about the closure. 'There was a lot of emotion. We felt very much for the men. I had taken a lot of pride in going out and winning work. We saw ourselves filling the gap left by Ardersier and Nigg. There were only Burntisland and ourselves left. Given a little bit more support we could have got through. In comparison with what has been invested in the yard today, a very small fraction would have kept us going as a success.' Ironically they had started to explore the field of renewable energy technology as a means of diversifying, precisely the kind of work now secured by the new owners of the yard, still called Lewis Offshore.

Murdo is now based in Aberdeen as a director of SBS Logistics, which originally began operations in Shetland in 1973. Despite his disappointment on Lewis, he joined three colleagues in a management buy-out of the firm in 2003. They have since bought over one of the original service companies, Seaforth Maritime, increasing their turnover from £7 million to £75 million; included among their customers are several new North Sea entrants as well as Shell, Texaco and Conoco Phillips. 'It is probably all down to my experiences at Arnish. I wouldn't be where I am today without it.'

Norman, who runs two companies in Stornoway, believed in its heyday the yard was of great benefit to the island. 'It brought a significant amount of work opportunities for people in different skills and it certainly opened people's eyes to the possibilities that existed.' Murdo estimates that in wages alone the yard must have pumped between £2- and £5 million annually into the economy. Other sources of revenue were the annual rent to the Stornoway Trust of £60,000, and a yearly rates bill of £250,000.

Former provost, Sandy Matheson, who had a distinguished career in local politics over the lifespan of the yard, said, 'There was a substantial creation of wealth right across the economic spectrum. Islanders suddenly found they could borrow for mortgages.' He also believed there was a more subtle effect. 'It was to do with the community psyche, self-confidence and the outside world. Suddenly the place was buzzing with expatriates and newcomers. We had taken control of our own destiny and we were seen to be capable of holding our own with big business and with Central Government, who for a century had viewed the "querulous crofters and the dependence society" with deep suspicion and distrust.'

The world's most expensive hole in the ground

In the platform yard planning frenzy of the 1970s, three other West-coast sites ventured boldly into business; but none lasted long and only two actually produced structures for the North Sea. The yards were all granted planning permission in 1974: one at Ardyne Point, Argyll, in the Firth of Clyde, operated by McAlpine Sea Tank; the second at Hunterston on the Ayrshire coast, run by Costain's Ayrshire Marine Constructors; and the third, operated by Subtank Constructors UK, a Government-financed Anglo-Dutch consortium, at Portavadie on lower Loch Fyne. A number of other applications had been refused: a second at Hunterston from Bredero/Costain/Babcock and Wilcox; and in Argyll, yards at Toward, Ardentinny, Chiskan. Macringan's Point and a refinery at Peninver. None made it off the drawing board.

Ardyne, which closed its doors four years later, built two concrete structures for Shell, designed for the Brent and South Cormorant fields. They also had an order for an Elf platform, but it missed the appointed launch window – reportedly because of labour difficulties – and was completed in Loch Fyne. Hunterston survived a little longer. It produced a unique construction for Phillips Petroleum's Maureen field in the northern North Sea – a large tripod steel gravity flotation, ballasting and oil storage platform. The base, with its distinctive cylindrical tanks, was towed to Loch Kishorn, where Howard Doris added the deck section. The yard closed after the installation of the platform in 1983.

Plate 77.

The unique construction built at Hunterston for Phillips Petroleum's Maureen field – a large tripod platform. The deck was added at Kishorn. (*Phillips Petroleum*)

The Portavadie venture appeared to be full of exciting economic promise when it was announced in 1974 by the consortium of Marples Ridgeway Ltd/ Cementation Construction Ltd/ Royal Netherlands Harbour Works Co. The yard, said to be tendering for four orders for concrete platforms, was predicted to inject £2 million annually into the local economy and provide 500 much-needed jobs. The Scottish Office, anxious to establish Scotland as the concrete platform fabrication centre of the North Sea, not only gave the consortium their blessing, they also loaned them £12 million. They had been told by the Offshore Supplies Office (OSO) that oil companies were 'still for the moment' convinced of the merits of Condeep concrete platforms, 'even a Clyde Condeep'. By 1975, however, it was decided not to use public money to finance any more sites.

After planning assent, the remote, scenic bay at Portavadie immediately became a major construction site; 60,000 tons of soil and rocks were gouged out of the earth by the contractor, Sea Platforms Constructors (Scotland) Ltd, creating a massive hole. A complete £3.3 million village was also set up to house the workers. Once the oil rush ended, according to the *Oban Times*, it was to be converted to a holiday and leisure centre.

Nothing was ever built in the yard. The closest it came to the oil industry was when the gas rig Annie, fabricated for Elf at Ardyne, was completed in Loch Fyne. The giant hole in the ground, ultimately believed to have cost £45 million, remained just that. It was an embarrassing and expensive

Plate 78.

Once the UK's most expensive hole in the ground – the abortive site of a proposed oil construction yard at Portavadie on the Argyll coast. (*Ian Y MacIntyre*)

Plate 79.

The gas rig Annie – the closest Portavadie came to the oil industry when the deck section was completed in Loch Fyne, opposite the excavated dry dock. The structure had been built at Ardyne Point. (*Ian Y MacIntyre*)

speculative foray by the Scottish Office into a complex and precarious market. After six years the derelict site was sold for £7,500. And there never was a holiday village.

Looking back in 1989, Alick Buchanan-Smith, a former Tory energy minister, claimed, 'Having burned its fingers with the over-provision of fabrication yards, the Government thereafter tended to react to, rather than lead, events.'

Neighbours Across the Firths

11

Long before the first oil was found, an official from the Scottish Council Development and Industry (SCDI) reconnoitred the length of the east coast of Scotland, hunting for likely locations to accommodate the onshore invasion he firmly believed was coming. Like a modern-day John the Baptist – his own description – Bill Adams also preached tirelessly to whoever would listen. He was one of the few people in Scotland at the end of the 1960s to understand the portents about the valuable energy source hidden beneath the seabed. His exhortations to the engineering and manufacturing companies of the Central Belt were largely disregarded.

But more knowledgeable people were already on the move. Bill, the North-East's representative on the SCDI, was called to London in 1970 to meet engineers from a company called Brown and Root of Houston. 'They wanted to build a dock somewhere on the coast of Scotland and they showed me a drawing of an oil platform used in the Persian Gulf. This was what they

Plate 80.

Sir Phillip Southwell, chairman of Brown and Root UK, accompanies the Queen on a visit to the company's fabrication yard at Nigg Bay in Easter Ross.

Plate 81.

What McDermott's American engineers saw on their aerial survey of the east coast of Scotland – the perfect site for what was to be the oil fabrication yard at Ardersier.

(*Handford Photography*)

were planning to construct for the North Sea. The criteria were: no shipping channels, no bridges nearby.' But, Bill said, there was also one very specific instruction: 'The cruncher was they didn't want to go anywhere with a tradition of shipbuilding, or marine engineering. In other words they wanted a site where there were no unions.'

The company had already discarded existing European shipyards and the UK chairman, Sir Philip Southwell, was keen to build in Britain. Bill said one of the co-founders of the firm, George Brown, walked into the meeting. 'He simply said, "Which way is the industry going to go – south or north?" I said I thought north. "Well," he said, "you pick the site nearest the action", and walked out.' Bill knew another American company, McDermott's, had already settled on likely land at Ardersier on the Moray Firth. So the only other appropriate site was on a neighbouring firth. A Brown and Root engineer described in the official company history, *Offshore Pioneers* (Houston 1997), how he flew over Scotland and saw excellent sites on the west side. 'But it was not the side the damned oil was on. We flew over this area and there it was. It opened right up into the North Sea. You could tell it was deep because of its colour. And of course that was Cromarty Firth.'

So the two firths, one in Easter Ross and the other in Moray, were chosen to house what were to be the most exciting industrial and economic developments in the history of the Highlands: the highly successful platform fabrication yards that created the first mammoth structures to straddle the oil fields of the North Sea. It was an industry no one thought would last but which survived more than twenty years, bringing prosperity and employment to the northern region; and it arrived unexpectedly and unsought.

The bold enterprise was sorely needed in an area where the greatest problem was depopulation. The Highlands and Islands Development Board (HIDB) had been formed in 1956 under the visionary leadership of Prof. Sir Robert Grieve, to attract Highlanders home. They commissioned a study in 1967 by the architects Jack Holmes Group to plan growth for the greater Moray Firth area stretching from Nairn to Nigg. The study favoured Easter Ross as the key locality, centring on the deepwater wartime naval port of Invergordon. Planning consultant Howard Brindley, who came from London to Ross and Cromarty County Council, recalled, 'There wasn't any other major industry at the time, agriculture and forestry were the largest employers and Easter Ross was suffering quite heavily from unemployment and lack of investment. There wasn't a lot of inward population movement either.'

The Holmes study also identified the area round Dalcross – site of the region's airport – halfway between Nairn and Inverness, as a secondary zone. Around Nairn itself, there were to be no new initiatives. Ross and Cromarty council complied by zoning the Invergordon area for industry. Almost immediately, in 1968, British Alcan applied to build an aluminium smelter at Invergordon, with a workforce of 450, representing 85 per cent of the employment growth in Easter Ross.

Then the American oilmen came calling. By 1974 the significance of the two yards to the greater Moray Firth area economy was startling. In Easter Ross there were 5,300 new jobs in oil, manufacturing and in services; in the Inverness/Nairn area the figure was 3,400. At the peak, while the primary

Plate 82.

The redoubtable Duncan Dick – first local hourly paid worker at Ardersier – talks to his squad as they manoeuvre part of a platform jacket into place.

industries went backwards, some 10,000 people worked onshore in oil-related activities.

Young Ian Bain was back home in Nairn from university for the Easter vacation in 1972. His father, the editor of the *Nairnshire Telegraph*, told him it would be worth going to the town council meeting. 'I think you will hear something of historical moment.' It was the announcement that the McDermott construction yard was going ahead at Carse [Ardersier]. Ian said, 'I suppose it was such a surprise the council believed there was no option but to welcome it. People had been crying out for some kind of industrial employment for a long time. Now they had it in spades. Gallus student that I was, I said this was going to have a visual effect. I was told in no uncertain terms to keep my mouth shut. The visual effect was nothing compared to the economic effect. That was the start of a sea-change in Nairn and the environs.'

The fabrication company, J Ray McDermott, had been among the first to build structures for the new offshore industry in the Gulf of Mexico in the 1940s. By the time they arrived in the Moray Firth they were leading marine service contractors, building installations at Morgan City, in Louisiana. Phil McBride was hired in 1974 as an accountant from British Steel and eventually became financial director. He described the creation of the yard on the 860 acres of land bought from the Cawdor estate: 'It was all mud flats, and the whole site had to be reclaimed and dredged. The soil was used to build the site – a major job; some 400 acres were developed including the harbour and the beach area.'

Construction began in 1972 from a caravan perched on a pile of sand to keep it out of the water. The first local hourly paid worker was the formidable Duncan Dick. He had worked all over the UK in construction projects, including the hydro dams. Men of his generation always had to travel for work. Then he heard Americans in his home area were looking for construction workers. He was hired as a construction supervisor. The builders were Tullochs, who eventually benefited hugely from oil contracts. The job was eight to five at £2,750 a year, £750 more than he had earned previously.

Duncan's early experiences with the American style were a revelation. 'I was met by this American, Chet Hudson, who said, "Why are you here?" "To start work." "Who asked you?" "Mr Peterson." "Peterson no longer works here." "So what happens to me now?" "Better come in and meet the people."' A bunch of Americans were talking about 'a hundred thousand dollars here and a hundred thousand there.' Duncan had never heard anything like it. 'Then they said, "Do you have anything to say, Duncan?" "Well," I said, "could you tell me who is my boss?" "Shit man, we're all your bosses."' Duncan's view was that it would have been better for the yard if the

Americans had stayed. 'British people just didn't have what they had – "shit or get off the pot – don't do as I think, do as I say". I tied in very well because that is my way of thinking.' The man in charge was in fact Ike Foster. 'I was number nine at the yard. The others were setting up. Tullochs had started building the road and for a couple of months I supervised.'

Shortly afterwards, the training school, an innovative feature of the yard, was up and running. McDermott wanted to produce their own welders and fitters and had brought 200 welders from Louisiana to teach the locals. It was a twelve-week course. 'The trainees came from all walks of life,' said Ronnie Sharp, an electrician who had joined McDermott after several years working away from home, 'Butchers, farm workers, road sweepers and they had to be adaptable. If you didn't make it that was you finished. Some of the guys couldn't hack it but the average guys saw it as an opportunity to earn good money. They never left until they retired or were made redundant.' Tom Morrison from Inverness had worked in the shipyards on the Clyde. 'There were no conventional five-year apprenticeships. After twelve weeks they were turned out into the field, working alongside trained tradesmen. That burst the bubble for metal workers forever.'

Eddie Campbell from Culloden had been a self-employed forestry worker. He was not impressed with some of the imported American instructors. ' A lot of them were very nice people but it took me about three to four days to figure out the rigging instructor knew less than I did – which was sweet FA. He had come over with his brother, a rigger who did know his job. But they were full of bullshit and very racist; from Louisiana. Anybody with any tinge to their skins they didn't want to know.' Other former workers were more complimentary. Phil McBride said, 'I couldn't criticise any of them in my time here. The one thing they changed: there was none of this "mister" and "sir" – they didn't operate like that.'

When the yard was operational there was a 3,500 workforce; 2,500 were local. 'Then you were into travelling men,' said Phil McBride. 'Because of the shortage of skilled labour the company shipped in people from Glasgow and Newcastle – traditional shipbuilding areas.' He said, 'There was no resentment as long as everyone was getting their share, but the problems started when only a few locals got overtime. On the Tyne they didn't let anybody from outside work in their area. Yet they were coming up here in their droves.' Eddie Campbell fell into the yard job literally by accident. 'I broke an ankle and couldn't work in the forestry. They were trying to build skids at Ardersier using very dense exotic hardwoods and they wanted somebody to maintain and sharpen chainsaws. Once they were blunt they just threw them away. So I thought, a nice wee skive until my foot's better. That was in 1973. The yard was still being built, the big assembly building was under construction – nothing was under cover, even the pipe rolling mill was exposed.' The 18-year-old had a shock introduction to the unconventional industry. 'One of the first people I met was sitting smoking cannabis, although at the time I didn't know what it was. He was from Glasgow but he didn't last long. He got fired.'

Roddy (Wee Dan) Fraser rolled up one day at the site to deliver a load of piling. 'On the way back out, this guy asked me if I would like a job. So I asked about the money. "About twice what you are getting." So I said, "When can I start?"' Eddie Campbell took another view. 'Working in the forestry, self-employed, it was very hard work but good money. At Ardersier it was very easy work but the money was quite poor for seven twelve-hour shifts. The rate was 65 pence an hour. Locally that was fairly good money but not as good as being self-employed.' Jimmy Gray from Thurso was a fitter welder who had been working at the Foyers Hydro Electric scheme until 1975. He only planned to stay at Ardersier until another contract was ready. He lasted twenty-five years, ending up as convener of shop stewards for both the Ardersier and Nigg yards. 'People used to travel daily to Nigg from Wick. They also came from the other side, Keith and Buckie. Some worked a twelve-hour shift, or sometimes a 'ghoster' – twenty-four hours non-stop. Did that a couple of times but I wasn't keen.' He said the wages were on a par with the hydroelectric scheme. 'My big jump in wages was from £18 in Thurso to £40 or £50 at Foyers. For most of us it was a massive difference.'

As the vast yard took shape, Duncan Dick had a new job. 'I was given some men and told to build the pipe mill in ten weeks. I didn't have a damn clue what was going on. But I got it done in about five and that impressed the company.' The yard ultimately had two mills where plate steel was shaped and bent into pipes, highly skilled work. The scale was colossal; the pipe mill installed in the 1980s could produce 40,000 tons of massive tubular pipes per year. The steel was originally all from British Steel. Ken MacDonald, a Clydeside-trained marine engineer from Daviot, said British Steel didn't have the production capacity to provide the vast quantities of steel required. 'So you were pulling steel from Japan and a lot of it wasn't that good.'

After six months, Duncan's contract was supposed to be renewed. 'After eight months I asked my boss. He told me I had been appointed section manager. "Section manager of what?" He said, "Rigging." I knew nothing about rigging. Rigging is cranes, everything that moved, a lot of rope work, hooking up loads and scaffolding. Eventually I was in charge of all rigging.' That kind of rapid promotion for locals was very common. 'The rate of staff progression was astronomical,' said Ken MacDonald, who eventually moved into management. 'It was basically pick a white hat and see if you can cut it.

Plate 83.

Ardersier in full production.

There was very inexperienced supervision because they were just getting churned out.' Frank Peacock, who eventually worked for both yards, was introduced to the oil world when his company, AI Welders, the premier engineering firm in Inverness, was asked to do some of the steelwork. 'The yards seemed to go in different directions. Brown and Root brought a lot of stuff from the States whereas McDermott bought locally.'

The early orders were mainly for Phillips; six small decks, bridges and a heliport, all floated out in barges. The first major construction was in 1975, a jacket for Occidental, the ill-fated Piper Alpha. Ken MacDonald was fabrication group manager. 'The designers were predominantly London-based and the design had originated in the States. It was ropey, because the criteria were unknown. That first jacket was built all over the place, Japan, France and it was still actually being designed while we were building the structures.' McDermotts also produced the replacement for Alpha, Piper Bravo. Ken said, 'For a time, though, throughout the 1970s, we were up with the best at the frontiers of technology. A lot of criteria were developed in the UK, then the lead in new technology swung back to the States.' Jimmy Gray claimed that the structures were over engineered. 'That is probably why costing eventually became problematical.'

Frank Peacock eventually joined McDermott in 1979. 'It was a good-going concern but I had only been there a year when they lost a big contract for Shell and hit their first down cycle. A number were still kept on and we

Plate 84.

The ill-fated Piper Alpha jacket built at Ardersier.

came through it. I was a production engineer, making braces for the jackets, completely different from what I knew. I had served my time on the Clyde on ships' diesel engines. We were actually constructing these enormous platforms. The whole emphasis was on bringing everything in on schedule, so there was round-the-clock working, and it was exciting. There were pressures, but the industry had this really fresh attitude. The local people responded and got behind it.'

As the structures grew, Ronnie Sharp was staggered by their size. 'To lift those weights and to see the structures guys who had only trained for ten weeks were starting to put together – that was just awesome. Then they brought in bigger and bigger cranes, sixteen or seventeen of them.' Duncan Dick asked the American dredging supervisor, "How big is McDermott?" He said, "Shit, man. For every derrick Brown and Root have, we got five."' Working at such heights did not appeal to Jimmy Gray. 'You seemed very exposed. You went up by crane in a basket and these things would spin and you would get a few frights. The scaffolders shimmied down the poles. None of them was ever hurt. I thought, "You are off your heads." But before there

Plate 85.

A bewildering fretwork of steel pipes and rigging as a platform rises on the McDermott site.

was scaffolding they would walk along the top. I once had to do that but I
didn't like it. These tubulars were about 30 feet in diameter and sometimes
you were hanging onto nothing.' Duncan Dick said initially safety was a bit
rough. 'The first guy to be killed had gone down a manhole where there was a
pocket of argon gas. A diver had to get the body out. Then there were two
boys who fell from the top of the jackets. As time went on we got a safety
officer.' David McGarry began as a pipe fitter. 'People said the yards weren't
dangerous, but where I had come from things were quite tightly controlled. I
was working one time on the sand and suddenly a shadow went over me,
something being lifted. Where I had worked before you would have been
warned. That was never the case at McDermott.' According to Jimmy Gray
there were nine fatalities over the twenty-five years. 'It is difficult to put your
finger on why, because safety was always quite a high priority.'

The work was also high-risk in terms of the consequences of failure. There
is a graphic description in one of the staff publications of Duncan Dick at the
point of no return with a multimillion-pound structure. 'Balanced high above
the Occidental jacket the rigger manager talks to the crane operator 220 feet
below using his radio. As a team they inch a 20-tonne section of pipe into
place – the last member to complete the giant. Any miscalculation could
destroy weeks of work and possibly result in loss of life. But they are masters
of the art and twenty minutes from pick-up the welders are locking the pipe
into place. The jacket is ready to load out.'

Frank Peacock lost track of the number of platforms he worked on. 'You
tended to live your life by them. You remembered the jobs you were doing
when your kids were born.' He worked his way up to project management.
He was told his boss was quite happy with his work but he would be staying
on smaller jobs. 'A month later he told me we had a contract for two
platforms for the Scott Field and wanted me as project manager. That
happened quite a lot. It was the American way, thrown into the deep end.'
Frank left Ardersier to work in Canada in 1999. When he returned he joined
Brown and Root at Nigg.

Because Moray was never heavily industrialised the local workforce was
only nominally unionised. McDermott circumvented any potential
demarcation disputes by recognising one union, the Amalgamated Engineering
Union (AEU). 'That was a brand new concept in the 1970s,' claimed Jimmy
Gray, the union organiser. 'Gavin Laird was the AEU Scottish Secretary at the
time and he signed the single union deal also allowing for adult training. The
Boilermakers Union were very sceptical.' The company provided good
facilities. 'There was a full-time union convener and a lot of training was
given. We did have one or two disputes but over the period there was a very

Plate 86.

At the top of Cormorant Alpha's flare boom at Ardersier, general superintendent, Ken MacDonald (right) with Ken McGregor, IR supervisor, and scaffolding foreman, Wilbur McKay.

stable relationship with the management. They came to respect our culture but they always expected a return.'

Phil McBride said there was only one serious strike just before he joined the company in 1974. 'I think having a single union helped. But there was a bad strike when the Boilermakers Union tried to muscle in, quite nasty for a while. These men had come from the shipyards. But they finally gave up.' Ronnie Sharp believed Jimmy Gray's realistic approach as convener was responsible for the relative industrial peace. 'One time on care and maintenance there were only six or seven of us left. The hourly rate was being reduced. Jimmy said he had never agreed. "But," he told us, "We could either have 1,000 people working at £7.50 or nobody working at £8.50."'

The Piper jacket was followed by what Ken MacDonald said was the yard's biggest single contract, Union Oil's 16,500-ton jacket and topsides for the Heather field. 'I was fabrications manager but then I decided to follow the installation offshore as McDermott's representative and I spent two and a half years away.' An even bigger contract was the 27,590-ton Murchison jacket built in 1979 for Conoco. The company's upstream president, Bill Schmoe, described the launch as one of the worst nights in his life. 'Hereema had built

a huge barge just for this jacket and McDermott had poured a sand pad to ballast the barge so it sat on the bottom. The barge rails were lined up with the rails on the shore, but it turned out the barge was slightly high. McDermott claimed it wasn't built to their specs. Hereema said it was; the sand pad was wrong. Nobody would take responsibility. The insurance people said it would buckle the plates and the bulkheads on the barge. Well, we argued all night long. The lawyers got involved, writing "cover-your-rear" types of statements. Finally I kicked all the lawyers out and said, "Here's what we are going to do: I will take responsibility for the barge being damaged but nothing else. Let's do it." They finally agreed and the jacket bent the barge bulkhead but didn't buckle it. That was a long night.'

Ken Macdonald returned to Scotland to oversee the construction of another Conoco contract, the topside for the innovative tension leg platform (TLP) for the Hutton field. Highland Fabricators at Nigg built the hull. 'This was a world first. To date it is still the biggest topside system built in the UK, 20,000 tons, and the first of the TLPs. We assembled the deck, accommodation and derrick and it gave me great satisfaction to have our bit loaded on the barge, waiting six weeks for the hull.' There was a flood of contracts throughout the 1980s, seven for the Beatrice field, others for Chevron, Mobil, Shell and Amoco. Then in 1986, at the height of the big world oil recession, Ardersier had a major clearout. 'Virtually everybody was made redundant,' said Ronnie Smart. 'Only a few were kept. I think that made a lot of people sit up and think. I was fortunate, I was never paid off in twenty-nine years. But the majority were laid off not once but twice.' Duncan Dick was made

redundant along with nine other group managers. 'I often think they were wrong because they lost a lot of experience.' He was eventually awarded the British Empire Medal.

The yard bounced back with a stream of orders from companies including Total, Marathon and Phillips. Up to 1986 they had fabricated topsides, jackets and pilings totalling 363,158 tonnes. In 1987 the yard underwent a £22 million modernisation and automation programme. A year later there was a tie-up with the Dutch barge and crane company Hereema. Half a dozen vessels were built, but the partnership, Hereemac, was short-lived. Phil McBride said the real decline began in 1993, when the orders started to dry up. Scots politicians campaigned for Government assistance for an industry vital to the Highlands, but there was enormous competition from subsidised yards in other countries. Ardersier was finally mothballed in 1995. But that was not the end of it. Later that year it burst back into life in a merger between the neighbours: McDermott International and Brown and Root Energy pooled their resources and skills creating a joint operating venture christened BARMAC.

Plate 89.

Diggers move in to break the soil at the site which was to become Highland Fabricators.

A yard too far

'It took two days to get up here from Wales, where I had been working on the construction of a dam for Wimpey,' said John Wood. 'This was in 1972 and I knew very little about North Sea oil. They just told me: go to Nigg and build a fabrication yard. "What's a fabrication yard?" "We are still designing it so we are not sure." "And where's Nigg?" "About as far north as you can go."' The young civil engineer drove across the Drumochter Pass on the old A9. 'When I got to Nigg, there was nothing – only sand dunes.'

John was one of the first to arrive on the remote site on the Cromarty Firth peninsula which became the offshore construction yard Highland Fabricators, a joint venture between Brown and Root of Texas and the UK builders George Wimpey. They had bought half the land from the author Eric Linklater for £140,000. The other part, which gave access, was leased because the landowner living in Cromarty refused to sell. Tom Clement was an accountant in Glasgow before joining HiFab (as the yard became known) in

Plate 90.

Highland One – Nigg's first big contract – heads out into the Cromarty Firth for BP's Forties field.

1973. He was the final manager. 'It was a lovely beach and people were still arriving with their caravans, not realising it was being developed. There were some people in croft houses who opted to move out.' Economic consultant Howard Brindley said permission was granted fairly quickly. 'In those days there weren't massive inquiries and although the site was not zoned for development it went through in about three to four months. That wasn't unusual. The Dounreay Atomic plant got permission within four weeks. The environmentalists didn't get involved although the firth had sites of scientific interest.'

Apart from Nigg, in the space of two years the full parade of the international oil industry had descended on Easter Ross brandishing briefcases of proposals: platform construction yards at Evanton and Alness, a heliport and oil service base at Fearn, an oil refinery at Nigg Point, and a pipe-coating plant at Saltburn. The whole battle to develop on the Cromarty Firth is well documented in George Rosie's *Cromarty: The Scramble for Oil* (Edinburgh, 1974). Only the Saltburn project by MK Shand became operational.

The location had been chosen by Brown and Root, a subsidiary of the oil service giant Halliburton, for clear deepwater access to BP's Forties field, where they had contracted to manage the whole project and to build two of the massive jackets, Highland One and Highland Two. So the yard, with half the tonnage capacity of Ardersier, was starting with the most challenging of North Sea structures, both in scale and design. Said John, 'This was completely different from what the Americans had been used to. They had never done anything like a Highland One – a whole new technology.'

He looked out that first day over to where the dock was planned. 'There were just sandbanks and salt marsh, low-lying. At high tide, the water would come right in. A load of equipment had arrived by barge, but they hadn't actually started work. I remember planning the dock. A bit of pacing and a bit of looking and then the foot down. That would be the corner. All the while the guys in London were still designing the yard. "How long has this dock got to be?" "We are not sure yet."' While Ardersier were planning to use a traditional slipway with barges, Nigg plumped for the dock. 'There wasn't a barge big enough to take these huge platforms. So they established this ramp and built the structure on top of it.' As with all North Sea projects there was an element of uncertainty about the life span of the yard. BP thought it might be only ten years. 'So they couldn't make up their minds to build a gate or just a temporary sand bung. They decided on the gate.' John left when that was completed, returning in 1975. The dock was described as a 'crude affair' by Evan Maclean, who came from British Steel in the Central Belt, where he had been a plant engineer, to work as a production engineer. His salary

Plate 91.

The first intake of apprentices at Nigg – it is doubtful if the unfettered long hair of the 1970s would be permissible now for safety reasons.

immediately rose 25 per cent. 'It was just a big hole with a big floating concrete gate and a ramp. There were no significant pumping facilities. Any time you emptied it the walls collapsed and there were landslides.'

The yard was finished in two years, with its three fabrication shops, dock, pipe mill and 200,000 square feet of buildings. All the while, the workforce grew rapidly from the original 200 men who built the yard. Like Ardersier, HiFab knew there was no ready pool of skilled labour. But the smelter, which had attracted experienced men, immediately felt the full force of competition as staff left to work at either MK Shand or HiFab. At a stroke the county's unemployment problem was solved, to the extent that labour had to be shipped in. So, like Ardersier, the yard set up its own training school, operated by American instructors, and recruited local men. That was a council stipulation; 94 per cent had to come from the area. In two years almost 2,000 men were trained in specialist welding, fabricating, rigging and pipe fitting.

One of the apprentices was Ewan Gillies from Muir of Ord. 'I served my time as a fabrication technician at the training school. They took on thirty apprentices every year. The money was good; when I was a fourth-year apprentice I got more than my college lecturers and they resented that; £30 a week – double what my mates were getting as tradesmen. In the yard it was £48. We also got travel money, £18 a week, but coaches picked you up free.' The welders were trained and tested to international Lloyds codes, the highest standards at that time in the UK, and they were retested all the time they were at both Highland yards.

Tom Clement said that the plan had been to fabricate, assemble and

Plate 92.

The *Highland Queen* and
the *Hermes* alongside the
pier – home to hundreds
of the yard's travelling
people.

construct the whole Highland One (Forties Charlie) platform. 'But it became evident they couldn't complete all those elements in time. So they sub-contracted fabrication mostly to Japan bringing in the pieces to assemble.' He outlined three elements that distinguished HiFab: 'There was the civil engineering feat of creating the yard and the biggest graving dock in Europe from literally nothing on 175 acres of mudflats; producing a highly trained workforce where there had been none – some of those youngsters are now senior men in the global oil industry; and finally constructing structures like Forties Charlie – even the Yanks had never done that.' Highland One began to tower above the yard – 31,000 tonnes and one and a half times bigger than the Statue of Liberty. After eighteen months of delays, watched by thousands of people, the jacket headed out past the Soutars headland, to its home for the next thirty years. A second massive platform followed a year later.

The workforce had grown exponentially with the platforms from 1,500 on some jobs, reaching a peak of 5,500 for the Hutton TLP. Frank Peacock said, 'What was very important was this was a very young workforce – under thirty or forty, even the senior management.' He first visited Nigg to bid for a contract for AI Welders before he finally went to Ardersier. 'By then only a few Americans were still at the yard. After 1975 Brown and Root's partner, Wimpey, took the leading role and an Irishman, Kevin Barry, became managing director.'

Throughout the 1970s and 1980s a stream of structures took to the Cromarty Firth: the 37,600-ton jacket for BP'S Magnus ; Shell's 13,000-ton Fulmar jacket; and, to show the yard's versatility, modules, templates and flare booms. But the work was cyclical. Evan Maclean said when there was a

deadline they just threw labour at it. 'We hired, then when there weren't jobs, people got paid off. But during the peak time in 1983 and 1984 we employed people who had never worked here before and that landed us in problems. A lot were just here for the beer. But you were never really very much in control of your own destiny.' The uncertainty was too much eventually for young Ewan Gillies. 'I got pissed off. We got paid off when we finished our time in 1984. The TLP had gone out and we had only three months to do, so we were on care and maintenance. I was taken back on in 1985 for a Shell contract and I did another two years. Then I just said, "Sod it – I am not going back." They asked me back, but no.' He now works for himself at Kishorn.

Like everywhere else in the industry the financial culture in the yards was changing in the mid-1980s, most noticeably after the big slump. Union organiser Jimmy Gray said he thought both yards were feeling the pinch from the lack of early national planning. 'There were too many yards competing. They became more price sensitive. In the early days, you built the jackets and then hammered in your bill. Then oil companies became less willing to carry on like that – they began to look abroad.' The steel for the hull of the idiosyncratic Hutton TLP came from Japan, where a lot of the work was done. 'It was so big and problematical,' said Tom Clement. 'We had a lot of reworking to do. It was low-cost and when it came back it was poor quality.' The customer, Conoco, was equally unhappy. Former vice-president Harry Sager said there was serious trouble with the metallurgy, which involved very thin but very strong steel. The welding was critical. 'We had bought the very finest Japanese steel but when the inspectors X-rayed the welds they found cracking.

Plate 93.

The folk who helped to build the North Sea giants ... staff at HiFab from a twenty-year period up to 1992.

That was a tense time. Eventually the welds were ground out by hand and replaced. This took a year while the TLP just sat there, the oil price rising, tempers rising – and so were the costs. Hutton probably cost us a couple of hundred million more than it should have done.' Former HiFab public relations officer Bill Shannon admitted, 'You couldn't really say anything about that contract – you had to take it on the chin, but it made Nigg look at itself in a different way.' One result was the construction of new halls, the UK's largest covered facilities, built for topside and subsea work.

But another problem with the Hutton TLP hit the headlines in a dispute the newspapers christened 'the orange-juice strike'. Inside the huge tubular hull the temperatures were incredibly high. 'Horrendous conditions,' said Jimmy Gray. 'Initially they gave the men orange juice. Then they told them they weren't getting any. The strike lasted eight to ten weeks.' Bill said that everyone was asking for the free juice. 'Nigg had been very good at issuing perks, but when they changed to fixed contracts all that had to go.' He was left with dozens of 4-litre containers of concentrated orange juice. 'All the youth clubs and old folks' homes in the area had free juice for months.'

The 'orange-juice strike' was only one of the disruptions to the yard over the years, ironic for a company that originally sought a location free of unions. Unlike Ardersier, Nigg had more than one union and the boiler-makers, who were in the majority, had the upper hand. Tom Clement said, 'We eventually realised if they asked for more money we had to pay it. There was one strike in 1974/75 when they were out for four/five weeks and we got a call from Downing Street, "Pay up. This is of importance to the UK economy." That was Forties. In those days labour was cost reimbursable. The guys' pay went on the markup on any profit. Then the contracts changed to totally fixed price so when we tried to change the terms and conditions there were a number of strikes.' Evan claimed the yards weren't any worse than anywhere else. 'They were always very high profile. We had a row just before we finished the last project at Nigg in 2000 for Elf and we had a bad press. People saw there was nothing visible coming along behind – so they started seeing life a bit differently.'

Eddie Campbell, who spent twenty-five years at Ardersier, said, 'We had gone through all the ups and downs. If there had been some Government intervention like the Norwegians, who kept all their work for their own yards, it might have been different.' Jimmy Gray maintains that all the politicians were interested in was getting the oil out. 'They really weren't interested in the manufacturing side. Then there was the BARMAC period. When the management said they were going for a joint venture, we were quite concerned. I think they got off on the wrong foot and we never quite got over

it. There was a lack of trust. We had been rivals for twenty-odd years – two
different cultures.' There were also industrial disputes. Frank Peacock said
they wanted to upgrade the dock. So the yard closed and work moved to
Ardersier. 'The uproar was just unbelievable. They thought we would never
reopen. Yet Nigg was the most successful and would have continued.'

The joint group became the largest manufacturing employer in Scotland –
5,500 people – and the most profitable fabricator in the industry. They built a
number of structures, including BP's Andrew jacket and Elf's Elgin before
finally demerging in 2001. John Wood, who had become responsible for
business development and business strategy by the mid-1990s, said, 'The
BARMAC initiative was good but it was the first sign things were declining.
We lost BP's Clair and Shell's Goldeneye contracts. These yards, big animals,
the volume of work wasn't there to justify them.' So the yard, now renamed
KBR Caledonia, has only a caretaker staff, who have been actively seeking a
new role for the site.

The vast sites on the two firths are now sadly deserted and forlorn. The
Ardersier site has been bought by a local consortium who plan to develop it
for housing and leisure. Next door to Nigg, Canadian oil company Talisman
Energy have a service base, while there is a thriving oil installation repair and
maintenance base at Invergordon which employs 250 people and has a
healthy forecast of more rig work. But the real giants are gone. 'It is a shame
really,' said Jimmy Gray, now an Inverness town councillor and chairman of
the Firth Port Authority. 'I think there will be a lot of people with a lot of
regrets these kind of opportunities are no longer here in this area.'

Just like World War II

The two yards made a massive impact on their respective communities,
injecting annually £60 million of new money into the local economies,
increasing during the BARMAC period to £80 million.

To their credit, the councils in Ross and Cromarty, Inverness and Moray
and Nairn were determined to maintain planned control of this bonanza
which was suddenly making demands on their communities. Councillor
Torquil Nicolson, the chairman of Ross and Cromarty's planning committee,
said with some trepidation that they were faced with an enormous task. 'It is
impossible to do this in a hurry . . . otherwise we will land in the same state
as last century following the Industrial Revolution.' Fortunately the Scottish
Office were equally intent on protection and a civil servant arrived to
coordinate the councils' housing strategy. 'We got a lot of support from the

government,' said Ross and Cromarty planning consultant Howard Brindley. 'It was seen as particularly important that the oil industry would be allowed to develop. It was almost like World War II when they built airfields in the Highlands, everyone pulling together for the good of the region.' One of the greatest legacies of the industry was the transformation of the great north road, the A9, the ribbon of highway running from Perth to Wick across a series of strategic bridges. Unlike the network of trunk roads in the North-East's oil region, because of the presence of the fabrication yards, it got priority.

New homes for the newcomers began to appear in key areas in Easter Ross and Moray. At Alness, a few miles south of Nigg, the population doubled in three years to more than 3,500. The incomers had a young demographic profile, revealed in the expansion in the local schools. All the pressures led to overheating in the business and service world. 'So we had to set up labour camps,' said Howard, 'and moor accommodation ships in the Firth.' The two liners, the *Highland Queen* and the *Hermes*, held 300 men. They rapidly gained a raffish reputation. Bill Shannon said there were stories about prostitution, but added, 'I don't think it was ever as bad as was suggested.' But John Wood told how 'ladies of the night' used to board the boats and disappear for a week. 'One of the buildings on the site was converted to a police cell. Before they took the liners away, they had to dredge out the beer cans.'

During the peak employment periods, local hotels and boarding houses had to absorb the overspill. The area was buzzing, according to Liz Whiteford from Invergordon, who now lives in a farmhouse high above the empty yard. She worked at HiFab as a senior secretary ending up before her marriage as office manager. 'Everybody you knew worked there. It was just constant traffic, and an abiding memory is the amount of buses. People were flying in by helicopter; the ferry between Cromarty village and Nigg was introduced to take people to work.' Liz is now the unofficial archivist for the yard. 'It is part of our industrial heritage. The greatest number of people I have ever seen in Nigg has either been to watch the floatouts or when cruise ships come into Invergordon.'

The same was happening on the other side of the firth, especially in nearby Nairn, where new housing estates were created and the hotels, bars and rooming houses did a roaring trade. McDermotts built a camp on the site, while the Americans were put up in a nearby hotel. Ian Bain, local newspaper editor, saw the changes when he returned for holidays. 'Nairn was said to have one of the highest number, of liquor licenses per capita in Scotland, but most only operated half the year. That winter shutdown ended with oil and the hotels and bars benefited from the subbies.' That was the local term for the incomers – subcontractors. He said at one time there was bad feeling between locals and the 'Hey Jimmies' from Glasgow who brought other attitudes. The effect of the new spending power was quite striking: new cars and a different attitude to housing. Ronnie Sharp said before oil few people bought their own homes. 'From 1978 that changed. My mortgage interest was 13.5 per cent. Yet I never defaulted. That tells you the money you could earn.'

Inevitably, there was a clash of values and social problems emerged, according to Liz Whiteford. 'The new estates didn't have amenities so inevitably young people got up to mischief. For the young wives their menfolk were working long hours and that would have been difficult. More income led to more drink – a Highland disease. Now there is an established drugs culture, but I don't know if you can blame that on the oil industry.' Freda Dick, Duncan's wife, knew of a number of broken marriages in the Nairn area. 'Money had a lot to do with it. People were coming in who weren't able to handle it.'

Now that it is all over some parts of the area are still trying to recover. 'Certainly,' Liz Whiteford said, 'The shops suffered horrendously, probably Invergordon more so, and there are more charity shops. Alness used to have boarded-up shops but they have worked very hard to rebuild the high street.' Nairn is another town that has suffered. Ronnie Sharp said there was time when shops in Nairn shared in the oil revenue. Once the big redundancies came and people were on the social, you saw a lot of empty shops.' Many villages enjoyed large increases in population because of Nigg. 'Now there is nothing there at all.'

Yet Howard Brindley believes the seismic impact of the yards was a good thing. 'If someone asked if we would look at a large industry coming in again, I wouldn't turn against it.' It is also obvious Inverness has benefited. Brindley's fellow council planner Chris Clarige, Inverness area officer, thinks the vibrancy of the expanding Highland city stems from the oil culture. 'The locals were able to do something here without having to go away.' Another important benefit was that young people learned new skills and the best of them were actively encouraged by both yards to broaden their experiences overseas. Ken MacDonald, now an international oil consultant, kept meeting 'graduates' from the yards in executive positions. When the yards eventually ran down Highlands and Islands Enterprise commissioned a database on the workforce. There are still 2,500 on that register, all willing to return.

[12] A Kingdom for Oil

Underground the Wellesley was like a great city; a city which, with its outlying suburbs, covered more than twenty-five square miles . . . In other years it would have been accepted that the children would follow their fathers down the Wellesley. That is no longer possible and in the case of most pits, the immediate – and natural – mining response would be, 'An' a good thing, tae!'

Charles Brister, 1967

Britain's newest energy industry has now staked a claim for a manufacturing site on the Fife shores of the Firth of Forth at Buckhaven and Methil, where men have sought sources of fuel for hundreds of years. First there was Wellesley Colliery – recalled with wry fondness by one of its former miners and celebrated local writer, the late Charles Brister – the second biggest colliery in Scotland, established by the ruling lairds, the Wemyss family; it was followed by a sporadic series of companies who built structures for the North Sea oil and gas industry; now there are plans to establish an industrial park concentrating on renewable energy.

The chequered nature of industrial enterprises is an old story to the region called the Kingdom; apart from the loss of its many pits, 13,000 jobs were lost at the once-strategic naval dockyards at Rosyth; Fife's sunrise electronics industry, some defence-related, has been enduring more troughs than peaks. In the Levenmouth area alone, which encompasses Methil, the once-thriving docks, a big employer, virtually closed when they lost the region's coal output; and there have been other casualties in engineering. The oil and gas industry in Fife, which at its peak employed 8,500 people directly and indirectly, is now represented by the last remaining fabrication yard in Scotland, at Burntisland – which also has a foothold in the Methil facilities – and the huge Shell and ExxonMobil gas processing plants at Mossmorran.

The Kingdom's thirty-year involvement with oil began with scouting parties from a number of companies, among them the Fred Olsen Group and a Dutch company who expressed a fleeting interest in the site of the Seafield Colliery. But the most persistent interest was being shown by a subsidiary of British Steel, Redpath Dorman Long (RDL).

Giants above the city of coal

The first choice for RDL was the Tentsmuir area between the Tay Bridge and Tayport and they approached Dundee City Council, who they thought was the appropriate authority. 'Somebody from Dundee actually phoned me and said there was a chap looking for an oil platform construction site.' said Bill Taylor, then depute director of planning for Fife County Council with responsibility for economic planning. At his home in Balmullo, with its panoramic picture window that overlooks the coastal sweep of RAF Leuchars and the famous ancient golf links at St Andrews, he described what happened next. 'Well, I told the chap from British Steel there was no possibility of leasing that site, but I showed him Methil, Dunbarnie Links and the south side of Kirkcaldy. He was particularly taken with the colliery area and it progressed from there.'

The application for the redevelopment of the land – returned to the Wemyss estate after mining operations ceased – was given the go-ahead in 1972. The first gigantic task was to reclaim space from the sea, flattening out 136 acres with what ultimately amounted to a million tons of rock being laid to a depth of about three metres. The site had to be continually topped up to sustain the increasing weight of the yard's massive cranes. The original colliery offices, which still overlook the Forth, were utilised as drawing offices, administration and workshops.

The fabricators arrived with an order, a jacket for Shell's first North Sea find, the Auk field, followed by three structures for Brent. Bill Taylor said British Steel were basically seizing an opportunity to use their product. 'But they didn't do awfully well for a start.' The yard plunged into difficulties from the first day. They were hampered by three problems: the inexperience and the lack of knowledge shared by both the designers and the construction engineers, who did not mesh; and the recalcitrance of the unions. A young engineer from Manchester, Peter Holt, had followed the Brent C project from Holland, where the main structure was being built. Like everyone else, the platform business was new to him. 'People had to learn how to build these jackets but those two learning curves by design and construction didn't bode well for a good contractual relationship. I think all the UK yards were

Plate 94.

Fife's economic planning director during the oil yard boom, Bill Taylor in a more environmentally friendly part of the Kingdom.

inexperienced together.' Then there were the unions. 'Those were the days of high industrial relations activities on the yards and all orders suffered union troubles. On Brent C we had a nine-week strike.'

The company had obviously sought a workforce with marine construction experience and that meant taking men from the UK shipyards, recruiting from Dundee's Robb Caledon, from Clydeside and from the north of England; other workers came from the Western Isles. The shipyard men carried with them historical baggage and a tangle of different unions for each trade, dominated by the boilermakers. Peter said that demarcation – who does what – was one of the main causes of conflict. 'While we were trying to change work practices in a new industry, the men felt pressured into a greater pace of work. We were all learning.' But the yard had a bad image, reflected in media stories about men sunbathing on the roofs in the yard and arriving in coaches with beer on board. A young boilermaker, John MacDougall, from Burntisland, was on his first term at the yard. He had served his time at Rosyth dockyards and had worked at Longannet Power Station. He was astonished at what he found at Methil. He paints a vivid picture of life inside the yard: 'That was the first time I had seen really rigorous trade union debate. The only time you went on strike at the power station was when somebody died and you came off as a mark of respect. The nature of the oil industry meant bringing in high skills from outside, a whole different range of passions from Dundee and from Red Clydeside – very militant, the Bears as they were called – and you got thrown in amongst these people.

'There was a union meeting once a month discussing all sorts of work conditions. They started off as good conditions but they were taken to the extremes, by sheer opportunists. I was a passive trade unionist and I didn't like what I heard. There would be about a thousand workers in the canteen. Talk about no-smoking policies and you had all these tough guys who wouldn't think twice about starting a brawl. They would say, "We have heard the report back, but to teach the management a lesson we move a half-day token strike." I thought the guys standing to second were never going to stop getting up. A very, very oppressive situation. That meant a strike once a month. Well, I was getting fed up of all this. I thought, "This place will never survive like this."' John was eventually paid off when the orders dried up.

'RDL were regarded very much as the poor relations,' said Bill Taylor, 'the awkward squad – the ones who were always getting it wrong, overtime, design faults.' Something had to change – and the transformation came with new management and a new attitude by the unions. Engineer Syd Fudge, now an authoritative figure in the UK oil and gas industry, entered the scene. A brisk confident man, Syd, despite his broad English accent, was born in

Plate 95.

The Redpath Dorman Long yard at Methil in Fife. (*Fife Council Museum*)

Dunoon. He had been director of operations for RDL's structural engineering division at their Teeside fabrication yard in 1976. The chairman of RDL, David Waterstone, knew he had two choices: either shut Methil or do something about it. He formed a joint venture with the Dutch company De Groot and the former Scottish Development Agency, with a minority stake held by Edinburgh investment house Ivory and Sime. The company became Redpath de Groot Caledonia (RGC) Methil. Jaap De Groot put in a Dutch team. 'They asked me to join them as operations director,' said Syd, who took over as managing director in 1979. 'The yard was in serious trouble. They had contracts but they were grossly over-designed. The temporary works involved became phenomenal. Their system of launching the structures using two barges was unbelievably costly. They lost a lot of money on Brent A and that was one of the big issues.' There were also industrial relations problems. 'Basically the yard had got it itself into a place where nobody wanted to go. It had a very poor reputation.'

Plate 96.

RGC managing director Syd Fudge (second right) with a group of political visitors to Methil in the 1970s, Donald Dewar, MP for Glasgow Govan, Fife Convener Councillor Bert Gough, Dr Peter Dyer and Henry McLeish, MP for Central Fife.
(*Fife Council Museum*)

Peter Holt believes a Dutchman played a large part in turning the yard around, particularly in dealing with the unions. He was a construction manager called Jan Schaeffer. Syd Fudge described him as a 'really wild' character. 'Nobody particularly liked him but they respected him tremendously.' Peter said Schaeffer was very hard. 'In the shipyards people tended eventually to give in to the unions. Well, he refused so strikes lasted nine, ten or eleven weeks.' John MacDougall, who had been rehired, had a high regard for the volatile Dutchman. 'Jan was brilliant – the first day he arrived he brought a discipline to the shop floor. He was tough, but what most impressed me was his efficiency. The place needed something like that. Jan was very temperamental but we became good friends before he died.'

Peter Holt said that the workforce were actually earning good money, 'So they eventually saw sense and realised the rate of pay at Methil was far higher than in the shipyards or at Rosyth. The unions were all amalgamating while the younger workers had mortgages and families, more incentives to work. The old hard shipyard workers were eventually being phased out.' According to Syd, 'Once they saw which way was up and worked out they would have a job in future, they knew they had to adopt a very different way of life. We had two good shop stewards at that time – one of them "Jock" MacDougall.' The boilermaker was now a union official. 'I remember Syd once told me, "MacDougall, you are walking on eggs", but I said, "I will tell you what you need to know, not what you want to know." John had finally had enough of being dragged into a downward spiral by the Bears. One meeting I said to this boy next to me, "This is absolutely ridiculous. If these guys want to go on strike we all know where they are going – down to the boozer. Why don't we just let them go and we will go back to work. That way everybody is happy." He said, "Move that and I will second you. Go on you have nothing to lose." "Aye, maybe my neck." But I stood up. "Let's call a spade a spade. I move the guys who want to can go to the pub. Anybody else who wants to go back to work, fine." The boy seconded it. Then one of the Bears stood up and moved for a half-day token. It was seconded. My motion was overwhelmingly

Plate 97.

The years of industrial warfare at Methil – a protest march. (*Fife Council Museum*)

carried. Later I was asked if I fancied standing as a shop stewards' convener. "We can't carry on like this." I wasn't keen but I did and I was elected.' He recalled his first meeting with management. 'I said, "This is the deal. You give me the honest truth and I will try to get the best deal in return for what the workforce are putting in. If I think that is not happening I will come and tell you." We never had a strike for five years after that.' John became joint chairman of the national inter-union liaison committee and he was involved negotiations over Nigg's infamous 'orange-juice strike'. He took voluntary redundancy in 1982. He was already a Fife councillor and became leader of the council. He is now the Labour MP for Central Fife.

Just after he started at Methil in 1979 Syd Fudge was approached by the Offshore Supplies Office, the Government body which promotes fair commercial opportunities in the UK oil and gas markets, with a remit to encourage the use of UK companies. 'They were having great difficulty with the French, UIE Cherbourg, who were undercutting prices and taking UK work. They said the only way to get work to Methil was to bring in the technology and management skills of an experienced yard. So I formed a joint venture with UIE. Supported by their management, we began to build structures. The trade-off was they built components in Cherbourg. That introduced French credibility into the equation and a number of customers like Total.' Syd put in a new management team and brought in Dutch engineers. The industry had started to pick up after a trough and a number of big projects were coming on stream. One of them was Mobil's Beryl B. 'That was what turned the yard around and also kicked off the investment phase. We bought new cranes and built what I call the big cathedral [the huge shed that still dominates the area]. Generally from then on it was a reasonably prosperous yard employing quite a number of people – 500–600 – for quite a long period.'

In Syd's time at Methil the yard was never as big as Nigg or Ardersier, their biggest competitors, but they completed as many contracts. 'To be very frank although we were all in the UK, we were in a different economic area in Fife. I couldn't prove it but I am absolutely convinced they got better support. For example, a lot of their training costs were heavily subsidised. That is no criticism of Fife Region, who couldn't get the help to give us.' But the Government wasn't always biased in favour of the Highland yards. When the yard was bidding for Beryl B, Shell and Esso were setting up the processing plants at Mossmorran above Dalgety Bay. Bill Taylor said, 'We got into a quite significant battle with the Highlands who said we wouldn't get the welders because of competition for skilled workers from Mossmorran. We worked very closely with Syd and opened a register of skilled people and

potential suppliers and discovered 6,500 were interested in working in
Mossmorran – of whom 150 were coded welders. So we were able to rebut
claims of a skills shortage. A group saw Hamish Gray, energy minister, and
just as they were starting to put the Fife case, he said, "Relax – it is going to
Methil." And he was a Highland MP!' Those were the days when
governments were anxious to keep the UK work in house and it was not
unknown for fabricators to be given discreet advice about changing their bids.

The Methil yard also had a formidable ally in the form of Sir Ian
MacGregor, the chairman of British Steel. 'He was very committed,' said Syd.
'He told Mobil BS would underwrite the project. He also allowed us to invest
£10 million so we were able to present a very different yard to the market

place.' They then built small jackets for the Morecambe Bay development, for the Southern Gas basins and for Total A and B.

They also began exporting their expertise. Just before Syd left, in 1984, they produced some jackets in Brazil. They also built the only offshore structure for South Africa. Syd remembered, 'At that time apartheid was still very much in force, so it was quite a difficult job to do. To be fair to Fife Region, the chairman said, "I am not going to do anything that will take food out of bairns' mouths." We did about £10 or £15 million of fabrication work here and shipped it out to South Africa. That took me to when I left the yard. It was then bought by Trafalgar House, a subsidiary of the Cunard Line.' Syd went on to run the offshore operations for the company from an office in Scott Lithgow's shipyard, also owned by Trafalgar. The yard eventually shut down.

Syd later became chairman of the Offshore Module Contractors Association and currently holds a number of non-executive directorships. Looking back, he believes that what the fabricators had to learn was not the actual engineering. 'The real issue was how to handle all these big bits and pieces. It was as much a lifting technology as it was construction. Nobody had moved a 23,000-tonne structure before. It was a feat – quite an engineering feat.' One particularly fraught moment remains in Syd's memories about Methil. 'We were loading out Total B on to the barge, using low-friction material on the skids on which these structures were pushed out by big hydraulic rams. We decided, in our wisdom, to set it on a slight incline. What we didn't take into account was the Scottish weather – it had rained for about twenty-four hours – and there was also grease on the skidways. The jacket was about halfway on when it ran free – 18,000 tonnes off like a jet, the Dutchman after it, yelling. Holy Hell, the barge went "Doying!" The jacket fell beyond the end of the runways on the barge. Then at just the right height, a bracing member across the bottom legs caught the barge wheelhouse, otherwise the whole thing would have gone rear end into the Forth. We were very lucky nobody was injured and there was no serious damage.'

Over the twelve years Methil was owned by Trafalgar the yard prospered. Peter Holt pointed out, 'We built something like half a million tonnes of structures here.' But the technology was changing. 'The base structures went from 22,000 tonnes down to 10,000. Which gave two added advantages – there was less steel, therefore less work and a much simpler design. Also they became liftable by offshore vessels. The 10,000-tonne structures were bogied on – wheeled on. We just drove them on like little kids' toys. Marvellous to see that, 3,000 pairs of axles and as many wheels – all linked and all operated by remote control by a guy just walking ahead.'

The yard had three specific workshops. 'We actually had two sets of workers, berth people and shop people and the two never actually mixed – people skilled at making the nodes [jacket joints] and people skilled at working at heights.' There was a training school where welders had to qualify to the industry's high standards. The welds for the node sections had to be 100 per cent perfect. The pieces couldn't be rotated so the welder had to work in all sorts of positions to get into the nooks and crannies. 'The node sections were very thick – 100 mm – involving lots of passes so you needed patience to clean them all out. We put a lot of qualified welders into the marketplace over the years – at the peak we probably employed 400 or 500 welders.' They also trained apprentices. 'That's where we sought our future workers – among the apprentices. Apprenticeships stopped towards the end. The union rule in the case of redundancies was last in first out. Admittedly near the end there wasn't a demand for apprentices.'

In 1996 the yard was bought by the Norwegian group Kvaerner. Peter,

Plate 99.

Multi-contract work at RGC, demonstrating the versatility and capacity of the yard during the peak periods.
(*Fife Council Museum*)

who was general manager, was appointed vice president in 1998. 'Which was good – but not in a dying business,' he added wryly. Methil, in full flow, despite its rocky start, was considered to be the busiest fabrication yard in the UK. The three companies that owned the yard over the years between them completed, for a wide range of oil and gas operators, seventy-two contracts, thirty-four of them jackets, others modules, decks, piles and assorted oilfield structures. Peter said 'Nobody touched us when we had 2,500 to 3,000 of a workforce – all building four different projects on the site – for Marathon, Amoco, British Gas and Shell. I really enjoyed it as an engineer. Armada, which we built for British Gas – that was one of my jobs – when you saw that finished, all lit up and working – it was a tremendous achievement.'

A band of local firms grew up around the yard. 'We tended to sub-contract smaller fabrications to reduce costs. When the work stopped some companies who hadn't been smart enough to see it coming failed, although we never encouraged them to be totally reliant.' By the end of the 1990s, Peter admitted it was becoming harder and harder. 'This site was just too big. We couldn't survive on one job every now and then. We needed a million man hours a year to make the place viable and there just wasn't that in the business.' Kvaerner began to sell off its UK fabrication interests. The end for the yard, which was calculated to have pumped £120 million a year into the Levenmouth area, came in 2003.

Peter's job now is to market the site, on behalf of Enterprise Fife and Fife Council, who bought the land from Wemyss Estate. He currently has 7 companies working on 30 of the 130 acres. The former yard boss loves his adopted area. 'I live in a house in the country where we brought up our family. Like a lot of people who came here to work, we chose to settle.' His contract with Kvaerner is now up but he may now stay on to help Scottish Enterprise develop the site. It is perhaps fitting that one of Peter's customers for the facilities in the yard is Burntisland Fabricators (BiFAB), who built part of the structure for the Buzzard field at Methil. As the only fabricator now left in Scotland, they picked up the gauntlet Kvaerner had to drop.

The last fabrication yard

Plate 100.
The old shipyard at Burntisland in Fife – two vessels on the stocks.
(*Fife Council Museum*)

To swim against the tide in a merciless trade like oil and gas when you are the sole survivor in Scotland of a lost onshore industry sector asks a great deal of a management team. Apart from the basic ability to keep afloat they need strength of will, skill, belief, courage, vision – all these and probably a fair measure of good fortune. John Robertson of BiFAB and his colleagues must

Plate 101.

The vessel that sank Burntisland Shipbuilders, the cargo liner, *Ohrmazd* – built for a Pakistan steamship company. (*Fife Council Museum*)

possess a combination of all these qualities to have taken over a construction yard their employers believed had no future. 'We saw, however,' said John, 'the market was in fact heading in our direction.' And so far, in four years, BiFab have taken sizeable steps towards proving that confident projection.

The site is virtually in the shadow of the Forth bridges, on the shore of the ancient Royal Burgh of Burntisland, a resort which lies where the line of the Forth begins to curve up the coast. It has had a varied and fitful career. Some 310 ships were built there in the 50 years from the end of World War 1. But the third-last contract, for a cargo liner, the *Ohrmazd*, built for a Pakistan steamship company, was to be the downfall of the little yard. Contractual wrangles led to the shipbuilders facing financial penalties that were beyond them. They built two more ships, then, in 1969, the yard went into liquidation, throwing 870 men out of work.

When the offshore oil industry began to burgeon, the Fife yard appeared to be eminently attractive for oil-related construction. British Shipbuilders subsidiary Robb Caledon were first on the scene to carry out prefabrication work for their shipyards. Then in 1973 they formed Buntisland Fabricators. Local man Jackie Phimister knew all about the shipyard. He had served his apprenticeship there as a hammer boy in the blacksmiths' shop. He also worked in the pits and at the Methil yard. 'I did a test for a welder at Burntisland Fabricators and worked there for five or six years. They tried to pay us the same wages as the shipyards but we were in the oil industry and we

Plate 102.

Jackie Phimister (right), boilermaker and welder who worked at the Burntisland site in most of its phases, with a mate, Kenny Waddell.

wanted the same as Methil. We used to get extra money for heat, for working oot in the cauld, working in confined spaces – just pennies, a tanner for this, a shilling for that. It put your rate up but all we wanted was the same money as RDL. So we were on strike a lot of times.' This happened on a contract for an American company. 'Eventually the Yanks got fed up, took all the contracts and paid us double the wages. In six weeks, we went from twelve weeks behind to up to date. Once we got the money we got the job finished on time. The oil company wrote a real nasty letter afterwards saying they would never build anything in Scotland again.'

Jackie believed the welders had the toughest job in the fabrication yards. 'You wouldn't be allowed to put a dog in conditions welders were working in. It was 150 degrees Fahrenheit, you couldn't put your hand on the job. You had to cover it with thermal blankets. You were lying there all day and it was maybe not a massive temperature but it was a high heat. You could fry eggs on it. I have seen us at Methil coming oot lashing o' sweat and made to staun' until the gaffer says, "Right you can go to the hut." They didnae bother aboot your health. Most of the welders my age are all knackered.' The fabrication yard went out of business and the men were paid off.

Under denationalisation, Forth Ports then acquired the yard but it lay dormant for a number of years. It was opened up again in 1983 by a company called Subsea Technology and then closed when the market declined. Next came Hall Russell, the Aberdeen shipbuilding company, who had

BURNTISLAND

Shipyard Journal

HALL RUSSELL

Crown Copyright reserved

Vol. 20   No. 4

CONTENTS

Influence of Foreign Contemporary Ship Design

BRITISH shipyards loaded, as never before, with export orders. . . . British ship-owners hesitant : that is a picture of the present state of affairs. Nevertheless, in view of the wide variety of ships now building for foreign owners' account and the knowledge of their requirements, it seems impossible for the shipbuilding industry to go through such a period without taking on a freshness of outlook on ship design and construction. Ship-owning is an individualist business. The requirements of no two owners are alike ; the requirements of no two nations are the same. Yet, a cross-section, cut nationally, reveals that there are certain essential characteristics found in all the ships, whatever their type, which fly the same flag, whatever their size. This is inevitable because nations, like any group of individuals, have their own foibles. Furthermore, the owners in any one nation, according to their individuality or enterprise, do not always choose common spheres of trading, so their

Plate 103.

The short-lived influence of Hall Russells, the Aberdeen shipyard, on the Fife fabrication industry.

historical connections with the shipyard, sharing a parent company. They didn't last either. The yard was then bought by a French company. Jackie said, 'They really sabotaged the yard. When we went back in they had cut all the cables, there was no power. They were stripping it down and selling it.' The yard fell into disrepair.

A Swedish company, Consafe Ltd, who had a queue of orders, saw the possibilities and took a lease on the yard from the Port Authority in 1990. At that time, the offshore industry was on the upswing. Up in Angus, at the busy Montrose oil service base, Consafe operated a fabrication unit which made specialist accommodation modules. Their main base, Consafe Engineering in Aberdeen, had been restricted so they had expanded down the coast to a more spacious quayside assembly facility. Then the same problem of lack of room became apparent at Montrose. They decided to investigate the deserted yard at Burntisland. The UK managing director, Jim McMillan, had taken over Consafe in 1986 when the parent group collapsed. His deputy was John Robertson, an engineer from Elgin, who had learned the oil business at Speyside Engineering when the company carried out contracts at Ardersier.

Plate 104.

Burntisland Fabricators
under the management
of Swedish company
Consafe.

Jim McMillan worked from the same Moray firm. 'We came down here to look at the site,' said John, 'with the intent of moving the Burntisland buildings up to Montrose but that wasn't feasible. We ended up striking a deal with Forth Ports and set up the yard. We also had operations in the States and the Caspian Sea.'

In a company brochure Jim McMillan described what they found at the 135,000-square-metre premises. 'The yard itself was very run-down and the birds had taken over the place. The roofs, walls and floors of the old shipyard plating shed were in a terrible state and all the electrics had been stripped out; [it] was really ready for demolition.' The renewal of the buildings was one priority but another was to widen the dock gates for barges. Supported by Fife Council, Fife Enterprise and some EC grants, a financial package was organised. The original workforce was estimated at 250 but in actuality it grew to 3 times the number – many of them drawn from a local pool of labour.

For the next eight years Consafe prospered. The original dockside crane was restored and overhauled, the huge assembly hall repaired. The yard specialised in 5,000-ton structures and the orders flowed in from companies like Shell, BP and Chevron, as well as subsea projects. In one contract, for a manifold assembly, the company did the design as well as fabrication, working with new material which was difficult to weld. Welders had to be specially trained. Consafe and Alcan – the aluminium company – were then the town's biggest employers, the fabrication yard's staff peaking at 550. Among them were former workers from the original shipyard.

In 1998 the Consafe group was sold to another Swedish company, Prosafe, who operated the yard for a further three years until the demand for their products started to decline and there was no longer synergy with the rest of their business. They closed Montrose first and then Burntisland. That was when John Robertson stepped in. 'The management team who had worked the facility since 1990 took a view on what else had been happening in Scotland and said "No, there is a future for this yard." We took an option to go forward with a management buyout. In 2001 we were successful and we started Burntisland Fabrications Ltd [BiFab].' With the demise of Alcan in 2005, the yard is now the biggest employer in the area.

John said he believes in the industry. 'We have a good quality labour force in this area; the yard can offer a diversification of products and while the larger yards were struggling, ours was the right size. If any yard was going to survive it would be BiFab.' Another factor was that modules and topsides were decreasing considerably in size compared to the earlier structures: the total weight of the topsides is now nearer 5,000 tonnes rather than 20,000. 'With the overheads of the larger facilities, unless you are building five of these at one time – which wasn't going to happen – they would be struggling to survive.' And none of the other yards did survive. 'We recognised as part of our business plan that diversification is key. Oil and gas is still important, but we saw the need to diversify. Marine and harbour work is one area, pharmaceutical modulisation and alternative energy are others.' BiFab offer a wide range of products from subsea to minimum facility platforms. They have already completed a number of contracts in their short life including link spans for a bridge at Rosyth ferry base.

But the biggest job they've tackled so far – for the Buzzard field – was too large for Burntisland alone. Undeterred, John and his team leased the Kvaerner yard at Methil and completed the 4,400-ton wellhead module there in 2005. That success has obviously widened the company's scope. They won a contract from Talisman to build two jackets for the proposed Beatrice Offshore wind farm, which will produce renewable energy from the centre of the oil field nearest to mainland Scotland, off Brora in Easter Ross. The jackets will be built at Methil, while John is confident he can fill the gap at

Burntisland with something else. The multimillion-pound energy park concept is seen as another potential source of work. 'Fife Council and Scottish Enterprise Fife are investing heavily and we like what they are doing in renewables and see potential there. We would like to keep both yards going in the meantime and take a view on things maybe in two or three years. We have taken a chance with Methil. So far that has worked and we have managed to get another job because of that,' said John. He added, 'But we must also be prepared to cut back whenever we need to because you have to conserve and stay alive to survive the gaps.'

He thinks the UK should still be putting a lot more focus on its manufacturing base. 'We tend to lean too much towards finance and tourism. There are still real opportunities here and we have got to keep fighting. Other countries seem to do it better. Norway, for example, has schemes where if you employ somebody and you are downmanning, the government picks up 80 per cent of their wages for two years.'

John firmly believes the Scottish Executive and Scottish Enterprise should be doing more. 'The drive has got to come from them. If there is only one

Plate 105.

The huge well-head module for the Buzzard field built by BiFab of Burntisland at its second site at Methil. (*BiFab*)

yard left I see our company as the main strategic asset for Scotland at this moment in time. But to be perfectly honest if I decided to say tomorrow, "Right, we are chucking it", there wouldn't even be a reaction. They would just say, "Fine, that is it – there are no facilities in Scotland now."'

And that would be a tragedy. The BiFab facility is the end of an incredible thirty-year era in the history of Scottish industry that saw the rapid rise and fall of the coastal ring of massive oil fabrication yards, created from nothing and from no comparable engineering tradition. The men of the yards – more than 20,000 of them – brought new skills to the country and built giants that are still producing enormous wealth for the UK. Like the miners and the shipyard workers they should be remembered.

The Fife gas project

It all really began in 1976 with a little German 'fixer' from Düsseldorf who was hunting for a location for a petrochemical plant in Scotland. He was convinced Mossmorran, in Fife, where there had once been an open-cast coalmine, was the ideal site. He met up with some trade unionists in Edinburgh who invited members of Dunfermline council to meet him.

'Herr Schmidt was not the developer,' said Les Woods, former provost of the Fife town. 'He had a grant from the German government but they were chasing him up for it.' The Fife planning director, Bill Taylor met him. 'He was looking for the site for a couple of major German chemical companies. The industry in Germany had vast amounts of production capacity at the time. We did a bit of checking on Herr Schmidt and his credentials didn't stack up. He actually ended up in prison. But his visit prompted us to look more closely at Mossmorran and add it to the regional economic development report as a credible site.' Les Wood said the German simply disappeared. 'But he got a lot of publicity and it put Mossmorran into the public eye.'

About the same time, Fife planners had a confidential approach from Esso. Esso had been advised by the Scottish Office, who had seen the region's report on potential industrial locations, to look at Mossmorran. The American oil company and their exploration partners, Shell, were on the verge of a public inquiry at Peterhead into their plans for a petrochemical plant in the Buchan port to process gas from Brent. Bill Taylor said Esso were not convinced Peterhead was the most suitable location for their planned ethylene cracker. The public inquiry went into recess while the ability of the port to handle the required size of oil tankers was investigated. By then, in 1977, the two oil companies had positively switched their interest southwards down the coast to

Fife. The Peterhead inquiry was abandoned and planning applications, first from Shell Expro and later from Essochem Olefins Inc., were lodged.

The Mossmorran location itself, which was within Kirkcaldy District but also impinged on Dunfermline and Cowdenbeath, was not the principal attraction; the important factor was its proximity to Braefoot Bay, 4.5 miles away on the Firth of Forth. The inlet, between the villages of Dalgety Bay and Aberdour, was the ideal site for a marine terminal and tanker mooring. It was to be the end of the line in an extraordinary 416-mile journey for the gas flowing from the Brent field via St Fergus, down through Scotland and then from Mossmorran by pipeline to Braefoot Bay. But the prospect of a terminal in the heart of a picturesque residential area was also to provoke many vociferous campaigners against the project. A planning consultant later said that the 'real weight of objections was not against the site but the location of the marine terminal'. There were three planning applications: one for a natural gas liquids plant by Shell and for the Braefoot terminal, one for an ethylene cracker by Esso, and the other for related downstream development. Esso took the options for the land. 'They didn't want to apply for the linked development,' said Bill Taylor. 'They said they weren't ready. But the council were pretty insistent.' There were a large number of objections, 400 in all, mainly from the two villages. So a public planning inquiry was held.

Bill Taylor said the big issue was safety. 'The Flixborough disaster was still in the public memory, and the whole question of petrochemical plants and safety was predominant at that time. The geography was that you had one community hungry for jobs and another community who were concerned about land.' He said the diehard opposition was from Aberdour; Dalgety Bay eased off as time went on. Les Woods said that the village residents were very articulate; 'They were very middle class, incomers, many commuted to Edinburgh for work.' Fife's councillors took a very different view. 'Most of them came from mining areas, they had seen the dereliction from the closed pits and the high unemployment.' At the inquiry, which began in Dunfermline in 1977, the regional convener, Sir George Sharp, outlined the grim reality of unemployment in the area. 'Over the past 20 years, Fife has lost 20,000 jobs. Unemployment in West Central Fife is 22.1 per cent compared to the regional average of 8.4 per cent. There are 11,000 people out of work – and that is greater than the population of Cowdenbeath.' He placed a great deal of emphasis on the prospect of downstream development – the manufacture of a wide range of products from ethylene by ancillary industries around the plants – and stated, 'The development is not only essential for the long-term development of the region but of the United Kingdom.'

Oil-company experts stressed that special safety precautions would be taken but the objectors concentrated on fears of an explosion. A member of the Aberdour–Dalgety Bay joint action group, DJ Rahash, told the inquiry, 'I think there is a significant hazard of an explosion or fire of an open flammable cloud that may develop as the result of leakage from or fracture of equipment on the site. Such an incident could cause many deaths and much damage.' The inquiry report was in the hands of the Scottish Secretary – at that time Labour's Bruce Millan – by the autumn. But while he was considering his decision, the action group produced new evidence based on fears that radio frequencies from nearby television transmitters could set off an explosion. They applied to the Court of Session for an extension to allow them to present their evidence. In court an engineer from the Massachusetts Institute of Technology, speaking on behalf of the objectors, raised the spectre of 'a fireball engulfing the north side of Edinburgh'. Bill Taylor said the Scottish Office found themselves on a treadmill they couldn't come off. 'They had agreed if new issues emerged they would consult on them.' The Health and Safety Executive investigated the claims. Finally, in 1979, after eighteen months, a new Scottish Secretary, the Conservative George Younger, approved the applications. After a two and a half year fight, the objections finally petered out. Construction on the 650 acres of moorland and at Braefoot Bay could begin.

The basic operation involves the Shell plant purifying the natural gas liquids separated at St Fergus from methane piped ashore from a variety of fields. The resultant constituents include ethane, which is sent 'across the fence' as feedstock to the Esso (now ExxonMobil) plant and to Grangemouth. There, it is heated with steam until it 'cracks' down to ethylene and hydrogen. The purified ethylene is either distributed via the UK ethylene grid to the chemical plants in the North-West of England or exported by tanker from Braefoot Bay. Because of the sensitive nature of the enterprise and its locations, Mr Younger imposed fifty planning conditions on the companies: seven related to safety, fifteen covered air and water pollution controls and nine concentrated on visual impacts. In a paper given to an international conference in London in 1980, on oil and the environment, JF Taylor of Shell UK Exploration and Production wrote, 'Of fundamental importance to neighbouring communities, safety has been a paramount consideration in design of both fractionation and international safety code requirements. The whole design is based on a fail-safe philosophy providing assurance of maximum safety whatever the malfunction.' These precautions included unique dual containment tanks partially embedded in the hillside and surrounded by a rock and earth embankment (a berm); the gasoline storage tanks are protected by a bund which can hold the tank capacity in case of any breach. A double

security fence and a comprehensive fire detection and fire-fighting system are also in place.

Another of the big issues at the inquiry was that the propane and butane had to be moved to the terminal in a frozen state through cryogenic pipe – the world's only fully refrigerated long-distance pipeline, installed at a cost of £31 million. Stuart Dalglish, a senior authorised electrician in the Shell plant, explained: 'The Company hired an independent consultancy, Arthur D Little, who recommended a unique system. The propane product is refrigerated to minus 44 degrees and butane to minus six degrees and sent down a pipe system that zigzags all the way to the bay. This would have produced vapour, while the line's thermal cycle – warming up and cooling down – would have softened the pipe and made it dangerous. The consultant's proposal was to keep the cooled product circulating through the pipes until it was needed to fill a tanker.'

Four thousand workmen originally moved on to the three sites in 1979; the huge complex was completed five years later. It was a massive invasion

Plate 106.

The massive ExxonMobil ethylene cracker (left) and Shell's gas processing plant at Mossmorran in Fife. (*Shell UK*)

that required the construction of temporary accomodation. The majority of workers, who came from the Central Belt, were, in oil industry parlance, 'travellers', commuting from home. Some fifty double-decker buses used to appear daily. Stuart Dalglish, originally from Glasgow, joined Shell at Mossmorran in 1983 after working at Rosyth Naval Dockyards. 'They were still nine months then from completion. Of the workforce, the biggest percentage came from outside.' The construction of the complex array of tubes, pipes and huge tanks required experienced boilermakers, welders and fitters. 'They couldn't get enough people locally with the necessary skills as they found out when they advertised at Cowdenbeath job centre.'

Stuart was one of an original group of sixteen recruits who trained for nine months, partly at a centre in Aberdeen and partly on assignment at the plant itself. 'Only four were local and when the plant came on-line in 1984 there was quite a high number of contract staff who were full time.' There are now 450 staff directly employed between both plants, which have since been extended and modified; about 60 per cent are from a wide local area.

When Shell brought in a third of its modules in 1992, the Fife Natural Gas Plant was processing 12,000 tonnes of gas per day, increasing two years later to 15,000 tonnes. The Fife Ethylene Plant, which was commissioned in 1985 at a cost of £435 million, was originally designed to handle 500,000 tonnes every year. Capacity has since increased by 60 per cent. The £54 million berth at Braefoot, which is owned and operated by Shell, can handle 35,000-ton tankers in a 24-hour operation while the Forth Ports Authority administer strict traffic controls: historic Incholm Island is used as a 'roundabout' by the vessels.

The downstream manufacturing sector, which the councillors hoped would be based around the site, failed to materialise. Bill Taylor said that on the plus side both companies have a very good record and the scale of the plants has been bigger than intended. 'But,' he added, 'I suppose the one thing that is disappointing is that the downstream jobs didn't emerge although at one stage one or two companies expressed an interest.' The global petro-chemical industry had in fact changed as Middle East countries started to add value to their own gas products and it became more cost effective for the oil companies to manufacture nearer to the main markets in Belgium and Holland.

The MP for Central Fife, John MacDougall, said the companies weren't to blame because they couldn't fulfil their original promise. He was the region's convener before going to Westminster. 'They have always worked well with the local community, and it hasn't been the environmental disaster everybody feared – the system was built to a higher standard than Cape Canaveral.' One of the council's planning conditions was the establishment of a liaison committee, involving the companies. The main issue raised was over flaring. An ExxonMobile company spokesman said, 'I think most people now understand that it is not a danger, but they don't like it. The majority of complaints are about light pollution when we flare – which is very irregular now.'

Mossmorran now takes gas from many more fields than the declining Brent, as well as from the SAGE plant at St Fergus. It was originally estimated the complex would be returned to a greenfield site in 2009 but the Government's gas agreement with Norway has changed that. The cross-border deal allows Shell and Esso to build a pipeline from Statfjord to transport gas to St Fergus, and then to Mossmorran for processing. 'That now adds a considerable dimension to the future timescale,' says Bill Taylor. 'Otherwise it would have been into an eight-year decline.'

The huge Scottish Gas Project was estimated in 1999 to have injected more than £35 million into the economy annually with every job supporting 2.1 more jobs outside the complex. The companies also backed a number of community projects. When the pipeline to the marine terminal was built it crossed a right of way, so Shell built an underpass. Said Stuart Dalglish, 'In conjunction with Aberdour Golf Club they also recreated the eighth and ninth holes. It actually improved the course.'

The main employer now in Fife is a thriving tourist industry. The promising IT sector recently suffered a series of shocks, with the loss of hundreds of jobs. The only sizeable industrial survivor apart from Mossmorran and Burntisland is the engineering group Babcock, which took over the Rosyth naval dockyards and is preparing to help build sections of the next generation of British aircraft carriers.

[13] Treasure Islands

Place in the sun

At the time they called it the David and Goliath deal; an agreement struck by an isolated community of fishermen and crofters 'clinging to a rock' in the North Sea, who confronted international oil over the operation of a massive terminal and wrung out financial agreements unique in the industry, in order to control their own destiny. Only one other island community was to win similar concessions for the good of their people.

'For a long time in the 1970s and the 1980s,' smiled Alastair Cooper, Shetland Islands' Council head of development resources, 'there was an inbuilt bias against the council by the senior executives in the oil industry. They felt they had been taken to the cleaners by this local authority. Having to make payments to a community wasn't a normal thing. It took a long while before that generation grew out. Some carried that chip on their shoulders up to the higher echelons of BP and Shell.' He added, 'I suspect some of the other

Plate 107.

A foretaste of things to come – the first sighting of international oil – the storage base for the Anglo-American Oil Company in Lerwick in the 1930s. (*Shetland Museum*)

companies said, "You were outsmarted by a bunch of folk clinging to a rock up there in the North Sea." One disgruntled leading oilman told a Shetland councillor, "We thought the Arabs were bad to deal with – you are worse." The councillor replied, "I will take that as a compliment then."'

Today there are many who say that, in hindsight, because of the billions of pounds that companies have earned from the oil and gas flowing through the islands' terminal at Sullom Voe, the council should have fought for more. Yet, by any standards, what these fiercely independent and determined men of the 1970s achieved for the future benefit of their people was remarkable. Put simply, they took absolute control of their own land through pioneering planning legislation; and they negotiated deals for a levy on every ton of oil reaching the terminal, for an annual fee and for the revenue from all the port's services. There were also the added benefits of rates and rents paid by the industry. Invested shrewdly over three decades that money grew to a treasure trove of many hundreds of millions to be distributed for the good of the community.

It was all very different at the end of the 1960s and the beginning of the 1970s, when Shetlanders became aware of great activity 100 or so miles east of their islands. Linked by relays of supply boats from Lerwick Harbour, a number of big oil companies, among them Shell and Chevron, had begun exploring the blocks bought in what was to be the fertile east of Shetland Basin, in the northern North Sea. The first oil-related vessel arrived in 1971 and by the end of the 1977 a total of 1,817 vessels, including research and standby ships, used the port. The main early cargo was drilling mud (barites). It was obvious Shetland would be the landfall for any hydrocarbons found. But there were also visitors seeking land for service bases, for a refinery and for a tanker and pipeline terminal and processing plant. Sandy Cluness, current council convener, was a councillor at the time. He said, 'Strictly speaking, with modern technology and floating production platforms, oil would not have made it to Shetland at all. But at that time the technology was about pipelines to the nearest land . . . The island of Unst was nearest, but it was felt Sullom Voe was a better bet.' The great fiord, whose name in Old Norse means 'place in the sun', had already been 'invaded' in World War II by the RAF, who used it as a flying-boat base, adding an airstrip alongside at Scatsta.

Sandy well remembers the atmosphere. 'It was really a question of fear – a feeling of doom. We saw what was happening in Alaska, where local communities had been changed dramatically by the oil companies. But we thought oil would only be here for twenty years, a huge upheaval to affect the local way of life, and then it would all be gone.' There were two camps: those prepared to welcome the new industry, and those concerned at the threat of a flood of incomers and the effects on the islands' traditional pursuits. The Shetland economy – based on fishing, crafting and knitwear – had begun to prosper again after cyclical dips in the 1950s and 1960s. Fishing, in particular, was on the rise. But depopulation had continued since World War II and the census figure of 17,000 inhabitants in 1969 was hovering dangerously near unsustainability. What concerned the authorities was not so much the numbers but the quality of those young people who left, most of whom never returned. A former provost of the old Lerwick Town Council, Bill Smith, said, 'There was one county councillor who wished they could build a fence right round Shetland from Muckle Flugga to Fair Isle.' To Andrew Williamson, then curator of the Shetland Museum and a member of the growing and partisan Shetland Movement, such invasions were not new. 'Since away back, we have been used as a colony. Never part of England or Scotland, so when anything of any value turned up, then they were interested. We were in a nice strategic position in case of war, otherwise for Scotland and the Scottish government – the place could sink and nobody would care.'

Early in 1972, however, the council realised they would have to start formulating a policy. Adding urgency was the fact that speculators were busy tying up land around Sullom Voe – 20,000 acres had been purchased or were under options. First in were the French company Total Oil Marine, and Nordport, subsidiary of a consortium of Scottish banks and investment houses called North Sea Assets. The man who was to provide the ideas and the drive in formulating local policy was the council's new general manager, Ian Clark. Then only thirty-two, he was originally treasurer to Zetland County Council (as it was before local government reform). Even today there are mixed opinions about Clark and his achievements. Some have never forgiven him for an alleged promise the oil deal would mean no more council rates – which didn't happen. Others still regard him as the saviour of the islands. 'Some people won't agree with me,' said Bill Smith, 'but we have a lot to thank Ian Clark for. I was always very impressed with his skilful negotiating abilities – not necessarily in connection with oil. Sometimes it was almost brinkmanship; he was a diligent and hard worker entirely in the interests of the local community.' Clark and the council, led by the tough, shrewd, former headmaster George Blance (Dodie Wullie), realised they needed greater powers than normal planning legislation allowed.

The late Edward Thomason, former council convener, tells in his book *Island Challenge* (Lerwick, 1997) how he consulted a former school friend, an engineer working for Esso Petroleum in London, about the challenges his native Shetland faced from his industry. John Manson had left in the 1940s

Plate 108.

Forging an agreement – the architects of Shetland's successful negotiations with the oil companies' Sullom Voe partnership, council convener George K Blance (seated) and the general manager, Ian Clark. (*Dennis Coutts*)

for college in Glasgow and joined Esso after service in World War II. His particular expertise in planning cross-country oil and gas pipelines throughout England offered the council a valuable insight. 'I wrote Edward a long letter setting out what I thought the oil companies might be planning, mostly about legislation. He was keen to know what powers they would have, and having sat on some committees in London I was aware of these things. But I hadn't really appreciated the differences between Scots and English law.'

In 1972, when the council had begun preparing the legislation, he returned to the islands for a relative's funeral. He was asked to address the councillors. 'They offered me a job to liaise with the companies.' He certainly didn't take it for the salary, half of what Esso paid him, but he had always planned to return home. 'There wasn't a day when I wouldn't look out of my office window and wonder if the sun was shining on Shetland and if the ships were going in and out of Lerwick harbour. I used to tell the councillors the oil companies wanted to do things as cheaply as they could, but safely and with the least interference possible. Their attitude would be, "We know what we are doing – just keep out of it."' John is another great admirer of Clark. 'He was not an easy man to work with, but he was the one with the ideas, although he was always careful to take the councillors with him.'

Over that year, as service firms sought space for bases – including British European Airways and Bristow Helicopters at the airfield at Sumburgh – the debate raged back and forth throughout the islands: embrace the industry, or reject it. Shell had already dropped a broad hint they were looking for a pipeline landfall. Then they announced the discovery of the giant field Brent. Finally, at a council meeting in November, the islanders took the momentous decision: they would promote a Provisional Order in Parliament for the authority to acquire land for development and to exercise legal powers over their harbours. The terms were again subject to intense criticism from a wide range of Shetland interests and the greatest concern surrounded the council's intent to use compulsory purchase of land. There was now no question of turning the industry away but the council wanted the means to control development for the good of Shetland and to take it out of the hands of outside speculators. Nordport's plans to build a terminal at Graven alongside the voe had been rejected, while an American company's proposals for an oil refinery never progressed.

The councillors knew they held an almost unbeatable hand: the economy was reasonably buoyant with more or less full employment. 'There was nobody hungry,' said Alastair Cooper. 'So we were able to fight back and say "OK, you can come – but at our price."' More significantly, other than loading at sea – which Shell also threatened to do – there was really nowhere else for the oil companies to go. 'There are not many places round the UK with thirty metres of water alongside the shore to take a large crude carrier into port. Sullom Voe can actually absorb a bigger ship than Scapa Flow in Orkney.' There were other noises off stage: the Labour Government wanted the process speeded up and the outbreak of an Arab–Israeli war disrupted oil production and prices. Sandy Cluness said, 'To the oil companies we were a nuisance. I would imagine we were that to central-government civil servants as well. They were anxious to get this oil ashore as quickly as possible and get the money into central government coffers.'

The Order became a Private Bill and was submitted to Parliament. The council told the interested oil parties about their plans. There were thirty-one who eventually formed a partnership, with BP chosen as operator. Their general reaction was: Shetland wouldn't complete the long and difficult road to legislation. Shell, in fact, told the Scottish Office the council did not have the necessary expertise to control the terminal group. Alastair Cooper wasn't aware at any time that the Government were directing things. 'We got many a push and a shove and at times they didn't hold with what we did.' Scottish Office thinking, according to Government archive documents, was that a normal development structure plan would have been sufficient. Bill Smith claims, 'Central government were most reluctant to hand over those kinds of powers, especially to a very small authority. Overall they would have wanted to be in control.' The next issue, which figured largely in the county council elections in 1973, said Sandy Cluness, 'was whether the developments would be best left to private enterprise in the shape of Nordport, or to the community. The elections were won by the pro-community group of which I was a member.'

Presenting the Bill for its Second Reading, the supportive Liberal MP for Orkney and Shetland, Jo Grimond, told the Commons it would 'enable representatives of the community in good time to take control of developments the ultimate shape of which is very difficult to foresee'. There were a lot of difficulties getting the Act through, according to Alastair Coooper, 'But we had a lot of friends in the House of Lords who actually drove the thing through.' Despite a long and hard passage the Zetland County Council Act became law in 1974. Shetland had been given the basic tools. They could now control the oil developments. There was one other highly important power: the legal right to establish a reserve fund for any ensuing revenues. Alastair Cooper said the Act was regarded as pioneering legislation. 'But in actual fact if you go back – the business of taxing the oil industry – a similar type of agreement was struck by Anglesey [the Welsh island site of a Shell marine terminal]. They probably didn't get as much as we did.'

Plate 109.

Oil traffic in Lerwick

harbour. (*Dennis Coutts*)

Attention now focused fully on Sullom Voe, where the council had commissioned a survey. The compulsory purchase orders were carried out. Originally they were for 9,700 acres in the district of Graven, but the Bill had been amended and it was reduced to 2,760 acres. That included a stretch of desolate peat and heather at Calbeck Ness – the actual site of the terminal – and part of Laxobigging Farm, owned by Bertie Johnson and his wife. Their hillside home now overlooks the sprawling industrial complex squatting on land that was once theirs. 'Nobody really approached us from the council. We just got notification from their parliamentary advisors all our land was under a compulsory purchase order. We were annoyed. We had just developed the land for farming from the mess of rubble left from the wartime. We had about 800 acres – all sheep. I suppose the price was in line with the price of development, but you were heavily hit by tax. The order covered the house and we were told there could be no more development of the farm. So that just tied us up. You could see it from their point of view, but it just seemed kind of harsh – something you weren't accustomed to.' Bertie said the whole village of Graven was involved. 'This place had already seen a takeover by the Government, but that was wartime. It was more the uncertainty that was the problem: what was going to happen to the people? Graven was very much concerned.' The villagers were among the petitioners against the Bill. The retired farmer was philosophical: 'It was thirty years ago and you just put it behind you.' But he remembered the disruption. 'So many men, so much traffic. They had to build a new road through the land, all that heavy machinery. You had a job to get across the road at times. It wasn't convenient for us with the gathering of the sheep.'

Well before the first peat sods were cut the David and Goliath struggle had been fully engaged. The cut and thrust manoeuvres as the council fought the companies are too complex to detail in this brief historical account. They have been well documented in several books, including Jim Nicolson's *Shetland and Oil* (London 1975), and, the most acute critical analysis, Dr Jonathan Wills' *A Place in the Sun: Shetland and Oil* (Edinburgh 1991). The memories of some of those involved, however, are worth recalling. What emerges, even now, is the sheer mettle of Clark and the council in the face of tremendous pressures, overtly from the oilmen and covertly from the Government, who were never involved in the direct discussions. Sometimes, according to documents from the 1974 files of the Scottish Oil Task Force, a committee of civil sevants and local authority representatives set up to expedite the development of the industry onshore, the pressures from St Andrews House were anything but subtle; the civil servants were obviously fearful the oil companies might turn away from Shetland. Their main concern was the council's determination to squeeze out revenues with a 'through-put charge', as compensation for the industry's intrusion into the area. This, the document said, 'could create an unwelcome precedent'. The Scottish Secretary later met Shetland's convener, an encounter the taskforce described as 'essentially an exercise in bluff'. The objective 'ideally was to persuade the county council to accept a substantially reduced sum based on charges for the operation of the terminal rather than the price of oil'. The bluff didn't work. A joint industry and council body was set up, the Sullom Voe Association.

'Those were extremely interesting times,' Bill Smith said. 'I thought we were privileged to be in the council when these changes and challenges were being met. I am not sure the general public were aware of the drama being played out.' Florence Grains, now a councillor, was on Whiteness community council. 'We had a council with no knowledge of that sort of dealings and I think they did exceptionally well. Hindsight is a great thing and some people think they didn't get enough, but they deserve all credit for what they did.' John Manson was very impressed. 'I had been in discussions with other councils about pipeline routes. Very few of those councillors were of the calibre of Shetlanders. The oil companies were quite taken aback at this little council holding out for their pound of flesh. I wouldn't have missed it for all the tea in China.'

The present chief executive of the Shetland Islands' Council, Morgan

Goodlad, watched the progress of the negotiations from his job abroad. 'I have nothing but tremendous admiration for the council. But as a Shetlander I wasn't surprised; that was the kind of thing Shetlanders would do. They have always had their feet on the ground and a passion for actual development in the islands. So when something like that came along they actually embraced it.' Ian Clark left Shetland in 1976 to become executive director of the British National Oil Corporation – later Britoil. He is now retired. But he and what was then Shetland Islands Council left a remarkable legacy: two sources of revenue from Sullom Voe. Firstly, there was a disturbance agreement, signed in 1974, based on a pipeline capacity fee, a minimum annual payment and the famous index-linked penny per long ton (2,240 pounds) of oil. The second source, settled in 1978, is the revenue from the council-controlled Sullom Voe port. Other financial benefits are derived in rental and through a massive rates bill from the operators. The oil companies discovered they had to lease the land on which they built the terminal from the council. The first structure at the voe was a jetty to take in construction materials. All the harbour facilities were built by the council, with the terminal operators repaying the costs annually.

It was twenty-year-old Marabelle Murray's uncle who persuaded her to seek work at Sullom Voe in 1975. He was the postmaster at Mossbank, near the site. 'I wasn't very keen. I had heard stories about these wild men. I worked in Lerwick and this meant I could stay at home. I became a secretary with the first civil engineering contractors, TMJ, from Northern Ireland. They were building a rough road and I began basically in a hut, no electricity, only generators. There was a pioneer accommodation camp, with shared shower

Plate 110.
The distinctive entrance sign for the Sullom Voe Terminal; the wall built by Peter Manson (left) from Brae. He helped construct the two huge accommodation villages – and still works at the terminal.
(*Nigel Martin*)

blocks, canteen and bar – very rough and ready.' Marabelle's mother was a chambermaid. Miller Construction, from Edinburgh, were building the big camp at Firth and shared the accommodation with TMJ. The work was tough on the men, Marabelle said. 'It was six weeks up here and a long weekend at home. Twelve-hour shifts but sometimes they would work through the night. They really were hard, hard grafters. That was just the type of them, here for the big money. Most of them were Irish.' Herbie Clements, a self-employed joiner, came with TMJ from Omagh in Northern Ireland. 'I had already spent six weeks working on Flotta and I only went to Shetland for three weeks.' He is still there, running a boarding house in Brae with his partner Kathleen. His guests are mostly from the terminal. 'What made me stay here was peace of mind and no bother. The Shetland people are easy to get on with – nobody cares about your religion.' Herbie worked as a joiner at the terminal until the 1990s before moving to the plant's small ambulance service. 'We had one death while they were building the jetty – a local man – he was crushed. There

Plate 111.

Toft 'village', the largest of the two accommodation camps built over the hill from Sullom Voe.
(*Nigel Martin*)

was nothing we could do.' The Sullom Voe Hotel had the only bar in the area. 'The place made a bomb,' said Marabelle, who went on to work for Foster Wheeler, the terminal's main contractors. 'You could go in there any night and they were knee-deep at the bar.' There was occasional trouble but, Marabelle said, if they misbehaved their accommodation was withdrawn. 'That was their job and everything gone.'

When the huge camps at Firth and Toft were completed an army of 7,000 strangers, with their trucks, cranes and heavy machinery and thousands of tons of imported sand, cement and steel, descended on the quiet windswept hill. For the next seven years the folk around the voe were overwhelmed by an invasion on a scale last seen in wartime. Herbie watched the daily flood of transport. 'There were more than 300 buses going from the camps to the terminal, plus the mini-buses from Lerwick delivering the bus drivers. It was amazing.' Commuters from the settlements and from islands like Yell contributed to the rush hours. Marabelle had to arrange bookings for flights and accommodation. 'One Christmas was like an evacuation, 6,000, 7,000 people going home and then coming back at New Year. We always reckoned it was the biggest movement of people since the Berlin airlift.' Marabelle Jack, as she is now, married and with family, is still employed at the terminal.

Peter Manson was a bricklayer in Brae when the first construction company arrived. He helped install the bases for the first two sheds, later working on staff houses being built by BP. 'I went up to Toft on a February morning in 1977. It was cold and snowing and the hill was guttery. Miller had the contract to drive in the piles. In some places the peat was six or seven metres deep. That was my job for four or five months. Then they assembled the blocks – all prefabricated and brought from the mainland.' The camps were epics in themselves. Toft held 4,900 and Firth, 2,500, but at one point more rooms were needed and two accommodation ships – one the *Rangitira* from Kishorn – were moored in the voe. Toft had seven blocks of single rooms and three big centres, two bars, snooker rooms, gymnasium and cinemas. One block was reserved for the chambermaids and canteen women. The terminal itself had twenty-eight canteens.

Pat Wall, from Birmingham, whose husband, Peter, worked in the laboratory at Sullom Voe, applied for a job in 1979. 'It was as a receptionist with BP. I was also offered a job as chambermaid. I took that because the wages were higher.' The girls had to gain the respect of the men. 'I was quite young and although we had a laugh and a joke I got through to them pretty quick I was not available. So I got on well with them. A lot had "girl friends" in Lerwick although most were married. In the early days they were a bit wild. Saturday was half day and they all came back to the bars. We knocked off as well and spent the rest of the afternoon out of the way in what we called the cupboard.' Peter Manson, who still works at Sullom, used to visit the centres. 'They had two or three cabarets every week, star entertainment – Rod Stewart one week.' He scoffed at lurid newspaper stories about life in the camps. 'They said guys were drinking pints of whisky and there were fights – rubbish. They were just normal bars. It was a good time. If I could put the clock back I would – it was good crack.' Pat remembers the food. 'Fresh strawberries and fresh salmon, T-bone steaks – absolutely out of this world.' She said the majority of her fellow workers were Shetlanders. 'The men worked on the crofts while the women came to the camps. The money, the company, the life those places brought to the island.' And the wages were good. Marabelle's mother, who had worked in knitwear, was later employed in the canteens. 'Compared to what she had before,' said Marabelle, 'it was unbelievable.' They made a lot more than I did on staff.' Herbie said back home he had been doing well earning £80 a week. At Sullom he could clear £1,400 for six weeks with a 'Shetland allowance' of £150 a week.

Scattered around the area were clusters of new estates built for the permanent staff. Pat and her husband lived in a company house in Firth for seven years until Peter transferred offshore. Sandy Cluness was involved in planning the new housing. 'We wanted to limit the environmental damage, concentrating all the houses in one area, Brae, 2,000, 3,000 people. But we decided to spread the load. I am not sure that was the best idea. We now have eighty empty houses at Mossbank.' Pat Wall talked about the changes at Firth before she and her husband left Shetland in 1989. 'They started to bring in transient people – a lot from down south – problem families from the West of Scotland. Life there went down very quickly.' The two giant camps were dismantled in 1987 and 1990. 'I helped put them up and take them down again,' said Peter Manson, 'Only the centres are left – the sheep use them.'

It took 25,000 people to complete the massive complex of harbour and terminal. It was a civil engineering feat to match any in the history of the North Sea. The partnership of oil operators had been forced by the council to co-operate in one common facility, which eventually cost £1.2 billion, a far cry from Shell's original estimate of £20 million. At one time the largest oil and liquefied gas plant in Europe, it covers 1,000 acres, with processing plants, storage tanks, power station and fire-fighting systems. By the late 1970s the main pipelines from Brent and Ninian were in place, and the first oil from Ninian, east of Shetland, arrived in 1978. Sullom Voe was inaugurated by the Queen in 1981. 'When the first vessel went out in 1978,' laughed Alastair Cooper, 'everybody thought it was oil she was carrying – a Shell tanker, the *Donovania*. But it was dirty water used to clean out the pipes.'

The real cargo comes from twenty-four oilfields, which hit a peak throughput of 1.5 million barrels per day in 1985; the 7 billion barrel mark was achieved in 2001. Current output is under 0.5 million barrels, including oil from the new frontier west of Shetland, shipped by tanker from BP's Schiehallion and down a new pipeline from the neighbouring giant Clair field, first discovered in the 1970s. Alastair was involved in settling the port's operational dues and tariffs with the oil companies. The harbour, tugs, pilots and pollution control are owned by the council. 'Of course, the oil people wanted it for far less – tough negotiations. We got other payments for disturbance, for the cost of the jetties and we charged all construction traffic coming in. We came into profitability by the early 1980s and recovered all debts.' Alastair, who was the harbour finance officer for twelve years, was also involved in the mid-1990s when the rentals and the payments had to be renegotiated to match the downturn in the terminal's output.

Jim Dickson, who was born in Shetland, became oil pollution control and safety officer at Sullom Voe port in 1981. He had worked for BP and as marine superintendent for Chevron's Ninian field. He is now general manager and harbour master at the Shetland Ports and Harbour Authority. 'When the

Plate 112.

The alternative accommodation – two cruise liners moored at the jetty during the peak years of construction. (*Nigel Martin*)

Plate 113.

Landfall for the pipelines from the West of Shetland oil and gas fields.

(*Shetland Museum*)

Plate 114.

The Royal seal of approval on the Shetland oil development.

(*Nigel Martin*)

terminal was at its maximum we dealt with 800 tankers a year. You often had eleven, twelve ships waiting offshore. Now, with a quarter of peak production, we are lucky if we have 250 vessels. This is because of the run-down of Brent and Ninian – now all called Brent. So you can imagine the harbour income has decreased.' The harbour, which is entirely financed by shipping, generates money into the general reserve fund. 'We make a profit directly and indirectly from an equalisation account set up when shipping was at its busiest. That bolsters the harbour accounts when the volume of shipping comes down.'

Shetland, which lies in a sensitive marine environment, is protected within a 20-mile international maritime organisation (IMO) zone and ships cannot approach until they are ready to be brought into harbour. In the early days, spotter planes ensured the tankers were behaving properly and not discharging dirty ballast water. Now all vessels are fitted with automatic identification systems so they can be tracked. The standard vessels are measured by capacity: 1 million barrels, 130,000 tonnes and 2 million, double the tonnage, 260,000 tonnes. As well as the oil Sullom also processes gas piped to the terminal and enriched before being sent to the Magnus field to enhance further extraction of oil. The excess is exported to St Fergus. Other gas, extracted from Brent crude, is separated, some used to drive the power station, the rest liquefied and shipped out at 10,000 cubic feet a month.

Drewie Laurenson, former chief engineer on the port's tugs, had previously been sailing deep sea and then working on supply boats. He tells of one potentially dangerous incident. 'One morning at three o'clock, I got a rude awakening. The pilots were shouting to get the engines going. It must have been a Force 12. A tanker had broken her moorings and was drifting across the Voe. Four tugs went out. Before she hit the side we got hold of her and towed her straight out. That was lucky. She was empty. After that if the wind was up to a certain strength we used two tugs to push up all night to hold the tankers to the jetties.' The one significant oil pollution incident which captured world headlines was when the Esso Bernicia oil tanker hit a jetty and ruptured a fuel tank causing a large oil spill. 'With hindsight,' said Alastair Cooper, 'that was one of the best things that could have happened. The industry was in the spotlight with a small vulnerable community. We ended up with quite significant oil spill kit paid for and manned by the industry. They had become more aware of the risks involved.' He said the oil companies had not been enamoured with the environmental people. 'But we drove a hard bargain and were fortunate in being looked after by the Sullom Oil Terminal Environmental Advisory Group, set up by the late Prof. George Dunnet, of Aberdeen University. Today the industry recognises the importance of high

Plate 115.

(*Overleaf*) The full panoramic vista of what was once Europe's biggest oil and gas terminal – Sullom Voe in all its glory. (*Dennis Coutts*)

standards.' Between the port and the terminal, which have both cut staff in recent years, there are 1,100 employees; more than half are local.

Shetland has other oil-related centres – the main one being Shetland Base Services. There is also Sumburgh airport, and the airfields at Tingwall, Scatsta and Unst. The main air terminal has enjoyed busy spells but had to endure fallow periods when it was by-passed by the giant Chinook helicopters. In 1971 there were 46,994 passengers, rising to a peak of more than 0.5 million in 1978 and 1981; the latest figure for 2005 is 116,090.

But the Sullom Voe complex has always been the main money spinner, feeding millions in revenue, rates and rents into the reserve fund, which over thirty years have been invested shrewdly, with the interest streamed into a number of charitable trusts. These have been the catalysts for the financial and social transformation of the islands. They have paid for the remarkable leisure centres strung throughout the community, the enviable network of fine roads, the new schools and the senior citizen's residential care homes. Despite this veritable outpouring of money, the reserve fund stands at approximately £400 million. Apart from the financial obligations left over from the flurry of new housing at the start of the oil era, Shetland is debt-free, the only Scottish local authority able to claim that. But there are concerns about the viability of some enterprises they have supported, such as salmon farming. There is also a belief that it is time to start pacing new investments and give the diminishing funds a chance to recover.

These northerly isles today have a buoyancy and a spark about them that comes from the bright new infrastructure and from the people's belief in their own ability to look after themselves without having to leave the islands. The migration trend has been reversed: the population is back up to 25,000, 30 per cent of whom have no ties to the island. But many are exiles who have returned. Morgan Goodlad is an example. He went to the mainland for qualifications and spent twenty years away from home. He came back as principal of Scalloway College before joining the council. 'Before oil there was little chance of any jobs here except as ministers or teachers, or with the council. Now there are opportunities.' The chief executive recalls talk of oil ruining the basic cultures. 'The very opposite has happened, the cultures are now stronger than when I left. One of the things I noticed was that we actually have more confidence and we have done a tremendous amount of things – different from what you would expect from a small local authority.' Organising the Tall Ships Race for one and the highly successful International Island Games for another. The council has also invested in the fishing industry, buying quotas for future generations. Alastair Cooper said the pelagic industry is on a high. 'The fish are back and the fishermen are making a lot of money with a new fleet operated by young men.' Farming is not so prosperous. He is a crofter in his spare time, tending 100 ewes. 'There is no real incentive for those finding it ever harder to make a living.' What is exercising the authorities, however, is the future of Sullom Voe. Once projected to last until 1997, that has since been extended by another twenty-five years, with hopes resting on securing the contract for the second Clair field and on other prospects in the west.

There are few Shetlanders who would argue oil has not been good for the community or that the council have not fulfilled the terms of the key clause in the Act which covered the reserve fund: that it could be applied to anything which was in the interests of the Shetland islands inhabitants. They have done that – probably more effectively than any other community in Scotland.

Andrew Williamson had a cousin who wrote a prophetic play in the 1930s about finding a massive coal mine in Shetland. Andrew said, 'What a change it made, nightclubs in the hills, pubs – and all the hard times forgotten. When oil came, it wasn't that different.'

Just a little dot

The legendary international 'wheeler-dealer' oilman, Dr Armand Hammer, chairman of the Occidental Corporation, exploded at the report from his European vice president, Robert S MacAllister. 'For God's sake, where is this damned place? It is just a little dot – I can hardly see it on the map. Just go and buy the whole goddamned island.'

The dot in question was Flotta (population eighty), one of the Orkney Isles, in Scapa Flow and the site where the oil company planned to build a terminal to receive the hydrocarbons from their Piper and Claymore fields. Hammer's lieutenant, so the story goes, told his boss the islands' council wanted Occidental to pay for the construction of the plant, the harbour and all the support services. But the council would own and maintain control of the port. 'This ain't Libya where we can buy a heap of sand and do what we damn' well like with it,' McAllister said, 'There are things called planning rules in the United Kingdom.' The doctor's further reaction is not recorded but amazingly the company did pay all the bills – and bought not the whole island but nearly 17 per cent of it.

Like Shetland, the determined councillors dug in when the oilmen came calling in 1972. Occidental had struck hydrocarbons in the Moray Firth licensing area and they were looking for a suitable landfall. 'I knew they had a few areas in mind,' said George Marwick, then vice convener of Orkney County Council; after local government reform, he became first convener of the new council. 'But they chose Flotta in Scapa Flow, a wonderful natural harbour that served this country in two world wars, deep water close into shore and a sheltered harbour for tankers.' At that point the islands' economy, based principally on agriculture, was stable; there was little unemployment among the 17,000 inhabitants and there was a fear any big demand for labour would be harmful. Like Shetland, the council knew they had no protection under existing legislation and they decided to seek greater powers through the Orkney County Council Act, which came into force in 1974. By then Occidental had bought up around 395 acres on the Golta peninsula at £1,500 per acre; one farmer alone made £250,000, attracting national media headlines such as 'Treasure Island'. The negotiations over building and operating the plants began.

They were tough times, according to George Marwick, 'but we had to be strong and firm even though we were a small local authority. The general manager, Graeme Lapsley, and myself drove the discussions.' They also had dialogues with Shetland. 'I remember we went in tandem at that time,' said Graeme Lapsley. 'But to be honest they were difficult to deal with.' He was an Edinburgh lawyer who had arrived in Orkney at the age of forty-five expecting a quiet life. 'It was anything but. I enjoyed it, though sometimes the Occidental guys were hard to negotiate with and they would grumble, but once you got to know them, they were all right. Dr Hammer now, he just said his piece and that was that. We didn't fear them – even if we were small. There was never any threat they would go elsewhere. We got everything we wanted eventually – and an awful lot of money at the same time.'

Under the Act, which was several months behind Shetland, they acquired powers to control Flotta and all the other island harbours. They were also able to use compulsory purchase like Shetland, but didn't; Occidental sold them the Flotta land as part of the agreements. Orkney chose a different route from their northern neighbours, described by Graeme Lapsley at a 1980 international conference on oil and the environment in Edinburgh. 'Shetland exercises control . . . by participation on a large scale. Shetland has licensed and constructed the terminal facilities at Sullom Voe, requiring very large sums of money, whereas Orkney has proceeded on a course of control by license and agreement involving a minimum capital investment, bearing in mind the small population available to carry such debts' (eds. William J. Cairns and Patrick M. Rogers, *Onshore Impacts of Offshore Oil*, London, 1981). This air of quiet, careful but determined decision-making was characteristic of the council during the negotiations, but it was not without outside political interference, according to Marwick. 'I had everybody under the sun wanting to get involved. Not the Scottish Office, but Whitehall. They were always wanting meetings about issues they thought didn't comply with existing regulations. But I held them off – I was conscious I was batting for Orkney.' The council also came under heavy pressure during the devolution debates of the late 1970s, but, unlike Shetland, the islands were content to be administered from London and voted against Scottish autonomy.

What they won from Occidental was the leaseback of the Flotta ground the terminal was built on and licences for all the marine works, including two single-point mooring towers, a jetty and the incoming pipeline. There were two other important financial agreements: the first was a disturbance allowance from the throughput of crude oil. 'It was originally called royalties,' laughed George Marwick, 'but the Americans didn't like that word so we came up with disturbance – it came to the same thing.' The oil company also agreed to pay all harbour running costs, and an additional levy on extra oil and liquid petroleum gas exported through the port. Occidental operated the terminal but Orkney controlled the harbours, lighthouses, towage and pilotage.

The revenues from these agreements were banked in a reserve account which fed into three separate funds: development, community facilities and leisure and recreation. 'I think we did jolly well,' said the former convener, now lord lieutenant of the county. 'We set up the oil fund initially to ensure that after twenty years we would be left with a legacy which could restore Flotta and also provide a good standard of life and employment for those who work at the terminal.' Apart from the rent for the land, Occidental agreed to pay the disturbance throughput tariff of 2.5 pence per barrel or 19p per tonne – a charge which brought in about £2.5 million annually. These revenues stopped in 2000. There were also compound harbour charges, which varied, and which are now paid into the strategic reserve fund, currently worth more than £100 million. The interest on the total sum, now about £4 million annually, is spread between various council committees. The council also agreed to set aside £16.5 million to decommission the terminal.

At first the people of Flotta were afraid the massive construction project would overwhelm their tiny community, as about 1,200 construction workers – the majority 'travellers' from all parts of the UK – descended on the island in 1974. There were protests mainly centring round fear of pollution and the possibility Flotta Community Council wouldn't benefit fully from any revenues. But Orkney Council had given the go-ahead to Occidental and their consortium partners, who included the Scottish company Thomson North Sea. The task of building the massive £410 million oil and gas storage and processing plant began. Most of the building material had to be shipped in, but for a time Flotta folk had to cope with heavy traffic to and from a stone quarry. The whole project took seven years to complete, by which time the

Plate 116.

Three of the four jetties in operation as tankers feed on the oil piped to Shetland from a cluster of North Sea fields.
(*Nigel Martin*)

islanders had learned to live with the 'Bears', as the construction workers were called, who were housed in two camps. The locals even occasionally enjoyed entertainment in the social clubs. Residential accommodation was also installed and the decline in the population was reversed, with more youngsters attending the island school. The island also gained an emergency airstrip and much improved roads. From the start Occidental recruited locally: 80 per cent of the terminal's first 276 employees and 160 contractors came from Orkney.

The staff of Flotta's port authority, which has its control room and offices seven miles away at the head of the 50 square miles of deep water in Scapa Flow, were also predominantly local; a number had been at sea. Captain Bob Sclater was serving with P&O when he applied to Occidental. He turned down a boatmaster's post at the terminal and became a marine officer at Orkney Harbours, eventually gaining a pilot's licence. 'It was a chance to get a job at home, and there were others like me.'

By 1976, the terminal, with its array of huge storage tanks, liquid petroleum gas plant, jetty and single-point moorings 2 miles offshore, was ready to receive from Piper, a two-day trip down the 130-mile long, 30-inch wide pipeline. Flotta was commissioned in January 1977 by the Energy Secretary, Tony Benn, accompanied by Dr Hammer. The first tanker, the 70,000-ton *Dolabella*, left one of the single point mooring buoys (SPMs) with its cargo of crude, heading for Shellhaven in the Thames. Claymore then came on stream followed by Texaco Tartan and other third-party business in 1981, with Flotta accepting oil from eleven fields. In the first year, there were 121

Plate 117.
Breaking the ground on
the 'dot on the map' –
the start of three years
of construction at Flotta
terminal.

Plate 118.
Everything arrives by sea
for the construction of the
terminal – except for sand
and stones from the
island's quarry.

tankers, rising to a peak of 223 in 1987. By 2004 2.35 billion barrels of crude oil had passed through the terminal, generating some 6,600 tanker movements. The plant also produced 50 million barrels of propane gas in that period – all contributing significantly to the total UK oil and gas output.

The port and all harbour operations, including Kirkwall, were controlled by six pilots twenty-four hours a day at first, but as traffic built up, a further nine pilots were employed. 'We had one big scanner and a couple of old 16-inch. Decca radars watching the Flow,' said Bob Sclater. 'Then we put a remote scanner on South Ronaldsay to monitor the Pentland Firth.' Towage was handled by two tugs until a third vessel was added. 'It was a hard job. Scapa Flow can be a dirty place to take a ship in the middle of winter. There is a lot of windage on a big tanker and although the Flow is sheltered it is not protected from the wind. You can get rough seas.' Bob became deputy director and then director in 1989 of Orkney Harbours. 'We had regular meetings with the terminal managers to ensure everything was running smoothly. We all worked well together. It was all new to us and we were all

Plate 119.

(*Opposite*). The huge plant dominated by storage tanks begins to rise and spread on the little island in historic Scapa Flow.

Plate 120.

Energy Minister Tony Benn and the chairman of Occidental, Dr Armand Hammer (left) commission the Flotta Terminal. (*Orkney Islands Council*)

young – in our thirties – growing up with it. There are still some of them there yet, turnover has been very small.' He retired in 1998 and is now an islands councillor.

When construction started on the terminal in 1974, Mike Budge was a nine-year-old schoolboy in Kirkwall. His father worked away from home on Flotta and two cousins, one an oil movements operator and the other a lab technician, were also employed at the terminal. 'So I guess it was always something at the back of my mind.' It was probably inevitable he would apply to join Occidental when he left school. He went to Leith Nautical College for two and a half years, returning regularly to Flotta for work experience before qualifying as an instrument technician and starting work back home.

In 1988, disaster struck the heart of the Flotta pipeline system – the Piper Alpha platform was destroyed in a series of explosions which killed 167 men. Mike said, 'The first indications were a drop in flow through the pipeline. Then there was a phone call from the harbour who had heard on the marine radio channel from the platform's standby boat – a fire had broken out on Piper. Our control room operator couldn't contact the platform but managed to get through to Claymore, who provided brief details. Later that night they were told to depressure the main oil line to the platforms.' One Orcadian died and another was badly burned. 'Like the offshore community, I guess there was a feeling of being stunned at what had happened.' Bob Sclater said it was a big blow to the islands. 'Throughput dropped quite considerably. People were worried about what was going to happen. Was this the end of oil in Orkney?' He had the unwelcome task of flying out to the field to oversee the stricken accommodation unit being lifted from the seabed. 'That was an awful experience, seeing it lifted out of the North Sea.' The unit, with its tragic 'cargo' of victims, landed on the terminal's jetty to be investigated.

The plant was shut down for about a year while Occidental worked to restore production. The community were assured the terminal would not close. But under huge public pressure the Americans decided in 1991 to withdraw from the North Sea. 'As far as I was concerned,' said Bob Sclater, 'Oxy were a very good company in their day. What isn't generally known is that they paid for part of the conversion of the grammar school into the new council headquarters.'

French operators Elf took over the assets and the terminal in 1991. Piper Bravo came on stream in 1993. Mike, who had been re-employed, says, 'I guess it was a new era, a European oil company, as opposed to the old American approach, and new regulations following the Cullen Report.' Elf brought in improved technology and training, recruiting new personnel, but also implementing a redundancy programme to reduce the overall manpower.

Plate 121.
Captain Bob Sclater, former director of Orkney Harbours.

Plate 122.
Joint manager of Flotta Oil Terminal, Mike Budge, first Orcadian in the post. (*Talisman Energy*)

Plate 123.

The Flotta processing

plant. (*Talisman Energy*)

They also launched an offshore exploration drive to avoid a decline in production forecast for 1997. Peak employment at the terminal was in 1992, with approximately 280 Elf employees and 120 long-term contractors. By the late 1990s, just prior to selling the assets, that had been reduced to about 125 with 60 contractors. A major development was a modification to handle crude oil by tanker from fields like BP's Foinaven, west of Shetland; a contract won in competition with their rival islanders. The *Petrotroll* delivered the first shipment.

Because of the sensitive nature of Scapa Flow, which is environmentally protected, pollution control has always been an important feature of the terminal's marine operations. Bob Sclater was the control officer for the whole area and maintains that a reasonable plan was in place. During the first twenty years there were thirty-three spills, most of them minor. 'The two biggest were in 1987, the bigger one involved forty-five barrels of oil; we spent two weeks cleaning up the shorelines. After that we drew up a new plan and began to monitor the situation ourselves.' A fund was set up out of the harbour charges to purchase their own equipment, including a high-speed pollution control vessel. When the authorities approved the addition of tanker-to-tanker transfer to Flotta's operational facilities there was some criticism from environmentalists, but Bob said there had been no problems with the system. There were two fatalities at Flotta during construction, one a diver, but the terminal has since consistently won awards for safety and environmental protection.

THE KLONDYKERS

Plate 124.

The import tanker from the Foinaven field, Petrotrym, feeds oil to the terminal.

(*Talisman Energy*)

Plate 125.

The terminal's friendly neighbours, seals, bask on the loading hoses of the Alpha SPM.

(*Talisman Energy*)

In the year 2000 the fast-growing independent oil company Talisman bought over the Flotta system. Mike Budge, who had gained a degree at the Open University in 2000, became maintenance team leader, then terminal superintendent in the next few years. At the age of thirty-eight he is now one of the joint managers, the first Orcadian to make it so high up at Flotta. 'The new company introduced a different philosophy, outsourcing employment to contractors. They have also begun a big capital investment programme to renew some areas of the terminal.' Mike said the vision for Talisman is to maximise recovery from existing reservoirs, and, a new development for the company after winning blocks in a recent licensing round, to explore further around the fields. 'This is the first time we have stepped up to the frontier. I believe that if Talisman had not taken over, the future of the terminal would have been in doubt.'

Like Shetland, the oil and marine revenues can only be used for the benefit of the people and in effect the council's policy is to finance any project that would not normally attract funding from the Scottish Executive. One major development has been the new library, but the money has also flowed into local concerns such as the rapidly growing jewellery and craft industry and fish farming; oil cash has also funded herring and canning factories and new fishing boats.

Said Bob, 'Because of the knock-on effect of the terminal – which with the harbour is a major employer – the work created, new houses being built and bought, new cars, holidays abroad, you ask anybody on Orkney and they will definitely say the oil coming to Flotta was of great benefit to the islands.'

The first convener, George Marwick, looked back over the past thirty years. 'What we did stood the test of time. Maybe we didn't get as much as Shetland. They had a throughput four times that of Flotta – but *pro rata* I always felt we did better in the long run.'

Plate 126.

The onshore oil development that brought boom times to the islands of Orkney. (*Orkney Islands Council*)

[14] Married to Oil

You have to be a particular kind of person to be married to somebody who works offshore, because if you can't change a light bulb then you are totally lost. Guys who work with my husband – their wives are on the phone all the time in absolute bits and sometimes the men have to quit the job because the wives can't cope.

Most of my brother's friends are involved in the oil industry and they are on two marriages – and heading for their third. It is unbelievable. Especially when there is family involved – that must be pretty tough.

The managing director was speaking at the annual dinner and dance. He said, 'It is really important to the guys working offshore that they don't get bothered with problems at home.' I thought, 'Excuse me – thanks very much – I work as well!'

When he comes home it's like party time. The family all come round for lunch or we go out. It's nice. I like the way we live now. Some people don't like it and I know a lot of people who can't do it – but I think the majority have learned to live with it now.

Oil wives

Behind the 25,000 oilmen who labour offshore, there are thousands of women 'on the beach' – wives and partners – also married to oil, who bear the responsibility of maintaining home, hearth and family in arguably the most pressurised marital relationships in Britain's industrial society. Comparisons can be made with the fishing industry, the military services or the Merchant Navy, but the contract oil women have entered with their menfolk is unique.

The distinctive on-off system enshrined in North Sea employment since the early days to maintain the twenty-four/seven demands of the industry, is mirrored by an idiosyncratic on-off lifestyle burdened with its own catalogue of problems. With the majority of offshore work contracted out to specialist companies, the most common difficulties centre around the uncertainties of the shift patterns and call-outs for contractors trying to meet the demands of the installation operators.

Aberdeen girl Pat Allen had worked in the oil industry since she was eighteen but she admitted she knew nothing about offshore when her husband, originally a watchmaker, went to work for an oil service company. 'What was hard was that there was no work pattern. If they were needed then they were away. It could be two days, a week, ten days – they were so busy. We were just married. He would get home and phone me at work. "I am here, I will meet you for dinner." When we got back there would be a note pinned on the door, "Check in six o'clock tomorrow morning."'

That is also a fact of life for Laura Gibson, whose husband has gone offshore at home and abroad for nearly twenty years. An oil industry accountant, she has been inured to the life from the very beginning. But the uncertainty has an effect. 'We have no routine because my husband is on call. It is a pain in the backside. He cannot plan anything. You can't say you would like to go to a concert next week. Birthdays, Christmas, New Year – you just can't plan. He goes offshore when they are ready for him – or more frequently he goes before they are ready and paints containers and does maintenance. It can be for any length of time. The longest was just over three weeks for this particular job.'

The circumstances were different for Pauline Baxter but the effect was the same. In 1976 her husband, who worked for an American drilling company, was spending more time in Aberdeen and offshore than he was at home. The problem was that home was in Portland in Dorset. 'He was in the Merchant Navy when we were married and I was accustomed to him being away. But the kicker came one day when he got home at four in the afternoon after five days trying to get off Shell's Brent Delta. They had been fogbound in Shetland and then Aberdeen. He had only been home twelve hours when he was told to be on the next flight up from Heathrow. This was when we decided it was no good because it was having an effect on our marriage.' The Baxters based themselves in Aberdeen. 'Unlike [when he was in] the Merchant Navy I never knew when he was coming home or how long he would be away. He is an engineer and he had to wait on the rig for other people to finish. He could be up for forty-eight to seventy-two hours sometimes before he could come home.'

In the past few years, since the debilitating effects of two recessions, more and more oil workers travel beyond the North Sea to seek work in Russia,

South America and Africa. This has meant longer spells away from home –
and from their families. Linda Joseph's husband, Grant, a motor mechanic, is
originally from New Zealand. He is a driller with Transocean in Nigeria. 'He
was two on two off – but now it is a month away and a month at home.
Sometimes six weeks. He is standing in as a toolpusher [in charge of drilling
operations] just now – after starting as a roustabout [rig labourer]. I prefer
two and two. A month is such a long time on your own. After three weeks it
is difficult. He spends two days travelling and then he's away two days early –
so you lose too much time. He usually spends the week on the computer
organising his return trip and keeping in contact with the rig – so he loses that
time as well. It is a bit of a nightmare.'

Some wives, however, differ in their standpoints about the divided
lifestyle. Christine Smith from Newcastle had no experience of what it would
be like. Her husband has been offshore more or less all his working life since
the early 1970s. She met him when he returned to the North-East of England
shipyards. When shipbuilding deteriorated he went back offshore. 'At first I
didn't want him to go away. Then it was a case of needs must, there was no
work otherwise.' He is currently employed in Baku. 'We prefer to live this way
– six weeks on and two weeks off. When he was at McNulties or William
Press at home – it was seven days a week – twelve-hour shifts – he would just
come home, eat, sleep and back to work. I actually see more of him over all.
The time he is here is quality time and we have the money to enjoy it.'

The peculiar nature of a relationship where the couple are together for only
half of the year necessarily inflicts strains. It certainly loads responsibility on
the woman at home. Caroline Hay-Crawford is a busy young mother whose
husband, Andrew, is a welder working in the North Sea. She has two university
degrees and is employed fulltime by Aberdeenshire Council on a Government
child care initiative. She was well aware of what it meant to become an oil
wife. 'I have to arrange everything. Childcare for example. I have to go away
sometimes in my job and it is a nightmare. My daughter has started school and
that is another change I had to think about. My husband is very good when he
comes home. He 's built an extension to our house, he cleans and does all the
cooking. I have no problems when he is at home. But when he is away you are
totally responsible for everything. I don't really phone him unless there is an
emergency or a crisis – and I had a lot of crises when we were building our
house. I was just tearing my hair out. I was trying to get on with my work each
day and I had to come home to problems. That was a very stressful time.'

Christine said she felt that everything seemed to happen when her
husband was away. 'I always paid the bills so there was no pressure there. It
was more things going wrong in the house. One time something happened to

the car and he wasn't here.' Laura thinks her husband would disagree with her contention that she is actually quite capable on her own. 'If I play the daft female when he is here, he will do things but I organise all the holidays, all the running of the house, the bills and so on. If something goes wrong I can sort it out, finding a plumber or a joiner. We work quite well doing it this way. I quite like my own company, but then he is away for a couple of days and it is great to have him home again. You are all excited. Absences do make the heart grow fonder. And it is worthwhile now we have our son.'

Linda, who has a flexitime job with people with learning disabilities, said she had grown used to the life. 'But every time he goes away it gets harder and harder. It never gets any easier. Maybe because I am getting older. I am okay after two or three days when he is away, I kind of settle and I say well, that's it, I will just get on with it. My answer is to work constantly.'

Home and away husbands can be difficult to live with, according to Pat Allen. 'The situation can cause problems. Not particularly for Dave and myself, but I have spoken to other women in similar circumstances. They find they are dealing with everything, the kids and the house, whatever happens. When the husband comes back again, then they deal with it. I can see that can cause a lot of conflict. The wives can find it a bit irritating going back to being the little woman at home.'

Linda said the absent husbands missed so much. 'It is always the same, birthdays, anniversaries you never seem to be able to time it right. They are always away and that is the hard part. People say it's all right for me – Grant's away and making good money. But he worked his way up to get there and I tell them, "You don't have to put up with everything that comes with it." He is home for a month but that is not a holiday. He has stuff to catch up with in the house and the garden. We also help my elderly mum and dad. Grant spends all his time with the family, like in the summer months we go up to the caravan. We also have four grandchildren to look after.'

The presumption that offshore workers are paid fabulous wages, compared to traditional pursuits onshore, has prevailed since the start of the North Sea oil industry. While that may have been the case at some stages – particularly during the high-rolling days – and is still certainly true of the higher echelons of the business, the money the men make is not always commensurate with the amount of work they actually do. Gil Lonie's husband is an assistant driller in Baku. They got together in their teens in the 1970s. 'We were young, with money to spend, and that was why he went offshore. We weren't really thinking long term, it was just a case of grabbing what was on the go at the time and enjoying ourselves.' Caroline's husband served his time as a welder in the 1970s when there was lots of work offshore. 'The money was very very good for what they did then. It is not as good now. Nowadays for what he is doing it is not poor, probably about average. It is certainly not fantastic for twelve hour shifts. In the last ten years, the cost of living has gone up but wages haven't. That was after the oil slump. He gets his fortnight off but while thirty to forty grand sounds a lot of money, with a mortgage and commitments I don't feel we could live on that, have a holiday and run a car. We wouldn't be comfortable.' As an accountant Laura likes to budget. 'My husband gets his basic salary, then he gets his day rate. He can be really busy for weeks on end then he is home for six weeks, in what was meant to be a really busy time. So you never know what money is coming at the end of the week or the end of the month.'

There have been a number of studies on the effects of the on-off lifestyle on the families of oil workers. Some children learn to accept the absence of their fathers – others don't. Laura has seen the result in oil industry children at school. 'One boy in particular – you can see the lack of his father has made a big difference in him. His mother sometimes is at the end of her tether. She doesn't work but she has two children and she is just exhausted. He is not getting the discipline he needs and this comes out in his conduct in the school playground.'

Caroline Hay-Crawford didn't think her daughter really understood the situation. 'She knows he goes away and comes back. But at special times she will say, "Why is my daddy not here?" Christmas, New Year – they get one or the other. So sometimes she has to realise he won't be home at Christmas and that is not easy either.' Caroline, who is in her early forties, said the lifestyle has influenced her decision about whether or not to have more children. 'I am the one who would have to cope. Andrew isn't around half of the time – but he doesn't have a problem with that. He realises that it is me who will have to deal with it.' Christine has a grownup family. 'We also have grandchildren. The oldest, who is three, has grown up with her granda going away and she just accepts it. He just goes away in the aeroplane and then he comes back. She thinks that is normal.' Eileen Young's husband, who is an engineer, is currently on his second spell offshore. While he was offshore in supply boats, Eileen had her second child. She had been working but it became practically hopeless to continue. 'It was just a case of dad's in, dad's out. No change. There was never any problem. He has always lived his own life, when he comes home he bowls. So Dad's here, he comes and goes. They all look up to him and he gets respect. He has always been able to supply them more or less whatever they want. If they don't get it from me, they can try and wangle it off him.' Gil Lonie's family have similarly become used to the life. 'They'd be counting the days. It is a bit harder with the month. That is longer for the kids. The fortnight passes quicker. If there is any discipline to be done I do it at the time.'

Pauline Baxter kept telling her two children, 'Wait until Daddy comes home, and they would think, "Why wait till Daddy comes home? We don't know when he is coming home."' She didn't bring the family from Dorset at first. 'We had been told the job would be only for six to nine months and you can't move children for such a short period, plus the fact our parents were there and we would have been taking them [the children] away from family and friends.' She said it was extremely distressing. 'When I think about it now, I wonder why we did it. It was like my arms had been cut off. But my husband was the breadwinner and I had been brought up to go where your husband's job takes you. The children used to come up on holidays, until one time I was down there my son asked to come back with me. So he came with my daughter in the summer. They didn't like it initially, being away from their friends, and they found it difficult to make new ones.' Both now regard Aberdeen as home and have found jobs in the oil industry.

Despite the imposition of a legislated modern safety regime, which emerged from the recriminations of the Piper Alpha disaster, offshore work is still regarded as one of the most dangerous occupations in British industry. The wives are well aware of that. 'Yes, I am afraid for him,' said Christine. 'Even now, when I think of all the travelling he has to do, the state of the world and what can happen. I used to be bothered about helicopters and he would tell us little things over the years, incidents and things that would worry you.' The Piper Alpha situation heightened awareness of the risk for Caroline. 'You always worry – it is a high-risk environment he works in – helicopter crashes, gas leaks – but I am really quite busy and I don't have time to think about it or dwell on it. He is now an offshore safety rep and he doesn't worry himself. It is just part of the job and he accepts it.'

Eileen Young was more concerned when her husband was working in supply boats. 'One of his friends was out all winter and the whole side of the boat was stoved in. That was really bad. Then when there was fog they had to lie off rigs and they couldn't get back to port, especially in June, which was always very bad. The supply boats were good in one respect; they came into Aberdeen. But, you did worry. I never really found out about the horrible things that had happened until afterwards.'

As is apparent, most oil women are long-suffering, but phlegmatic and understanding about the sacrifices both partners have to make. They have forged a life out of difficult circumstances. Other wives and partners – and offshore workers themselves – are not so tolerant. There are no statistics at present but anecdotal evidence suggests that there is a high incidence of often multiple divorces and the severing of relationships. At one time in the late

1990s Aberdeen had a higher divorce rate than anywhere else in the UK: 7.5 per cent compared to a national average of 6.4 per cent. Some of the women's situations are more extreme than others, and women have had to endure extreme treatment from their men which they blame on the pressures of the oil lifestyle. One divorcee, who wishes to remain anonymous, described what happened to her. 'I worked as a stewardess offshore and I went for the money, which was much more than I had been getting onshore – something like £700 a trip in the 1980s. The life was all right, but it was twelve-hour shifts and it took me about a week and a half to recuperate. I met my first husband offshore, but there was no funny business. I did share a cabin with a lassie who was away with the head chef. But I was told, "We had this with two other women and we are not putting up with it again." I said I wasn't like that. Those men were married. But I suppose you would get that in any kind of environment.' She and her husband worked together for a time then she stopped and became a housewife in a remote country village. 'I found that quite hard because I didn't drive a car and I had a daughter. I had to depend on him, but he was tight with money and he would accuse you of all kinds of stuff – in fact he got really heavy. I was quite restricted in relationships. He was really possessive, a control freak. He had been married before. I couldn't wait for him to go away and I dreaded him coming home. It made me really ill and I had bouts of depression.' The marriage lasted eight years. 'He eventually went off with somebody else. It was a messy divorce.' But it wasn't over. A series of violent incidents followed before she was left alone. 'The Child Support Agency had to actually take money from him. He doesn't have any contact with us.'

She totally believes the industry imposes a strain on a relationship. 'Money, mental cruelty – the job played a part. Offshore life can be hard. You are restricted and programmed: have your breakfast, do the job, then try to wind down in the evening. You are there fourteen days regardless. It's not like working in an office, close the door and you leave it behind. You don't, not offshore.' She then entered another relationship with a former boyfriend who proposed to her, but they have since parted. 'He had kids from a previous marriage and he wanted to spend time with them.'

That is an extreme case, but it nevertheless illustrates a number of issues in oil industry relationships. Since the beginning, the tough and sometimes dangerous nature of the North Sea – especially under the early American influence – fostered a macho society; hard drinking and hard living were a common feature once the men hit the beach. One woman, known only as Mary, knows all about this particular situation. 'My first husband was totally different from my present partner. Maybe the first day or two he spent with the family, then he changed and it was straight into the pub. I used to think:

two weeks away, is that it? My husband now meets up with the guys when they land and have a couple of drinks. I pick him up and thats it. Then all his time is spent with the family.' Another wife said a lot of the guys were quite a bit younger than her man. 'They are still at the going out and getting bladdered stage. Although he still does that, it's not quite as much as before.'

Some of the wives told stories that were humorous but retained an edge of bitterness towards their errant menfolk. Some offshore workers deliberately mislead their women about either the extent of their trips offshore or the exact day or time they are due home. One wife said, 'My husband often used to come home and not tell me. I once found his bag in the garden. He had come home when I was out and then gone straight back out again to the pub.' And another wife: 'One time he was expected on the Saturday. We had planned to go out for a meal but he never arrived. I went out and came home about midnight and there was a phone call. "Where are you darling?" "I am offshore." Just as he said that I heard a police car going past. There are not many of those offshore.'

The women admit that onshore the man with time on his hands and with nothing to occupy the empty hours is subject to temptation. 'He was very young when he worked abroad. So what does a young man with a lot of money in his pocket do all by himself because most of his onshore pals are at work? He goes to the pub and that is what he did. Fortunately he was sensible and still put aside savings. But he could tell you every bar in our town that opens at nine or ten in the morning. Because that is how he used to spend his time.' Another woman said she could understand why so many marriages fail. 'It is very difficult. Some women maybe get too independent. When their husbands come home they are in the way. My husband is really very good he always has a little project – so he gets himself involved. Some guys I know just sit on the sofa and watch television and that must be very, very frustrating.'

Communication was certainly a difficulty in the early days. Pauline Baxter's husband worked on a pipe-laying barge. 'I used to write to him every day. The secretary in the office was insistent all the wives wrote to their men even if they couldn't post it for four or five days. Then the mail would go to the office in Great Yarmouth and then out to the barge on the supply boats. I used to number them.' She was able to make contact by ship-to-shore radio when they moved to Aberdeen, but she tells a harrowing tale of one attempt from the little fishing village of Portlethen where they had made their home. 'They were all brand new houses built for incoming oil workers by the Scottish Special Housing Association, but there were no telephones and everyone was screaming for them. I can remember going to a phone box to book a call using the telephone credit card my husband's company had given him. This was at three in the afternoon. The operator said to return at half six. I got to the phone box at twenty past. There was a crowd of boys and one was on the phone. I said I was expecting a call and he said, "I wonder if this is your call. I have just been speaking to somebody from the radio station." They had heard the telephone ringing and answered it. The line was so bad but I told the operator she had put the call through early but she said the line was fading and they had to get it through when they could. I just managed to say, "Hello, how are you." And of course everybody at his end could hear what was being said. It wasn't very private. Those were communications in 1977.' Even today the oil wives have problems keeping in touch. Linda Josephs' husband is in Nigeria. 'There have been phone calls two or three times a week. We email now and we are trying to set up a webcam. But if the rig is moving we get no communication. Once there was nothing for ten days. It is a nightmare, because I keep getting phone calls with questions I can't answer.'

The general public tend to regard the weeks offshore workers spend at home as 'holidays'. That is far from the case, as Caroline Hay-Crawford explained. 'You don't get two weeks really because of travel and you can't go on a package holiday. You either have to lose a day or use up some of your actual holidays. Contract people are different because they are self-employed. My husband is staff. So you tend to go away on holiday for a week or ten days.' Linda: 'I have had to go on my own – that was when it was two on and two off. Someone had to stand in to give him an extra week and then he had to do an extra week to pay him back. It was either that or taking a whole month off, unpaid. When we went to New Zealand, for example, the time off was unpaid.' Laura Gibson said when her husband was at home he was meant to work in the company yard. 'In some companies you don't own your life, when you are at home you are meant to be in every day – seven days a week – unless you get a holiday.'

The oil unions have been fighting for a European working-time directive to be applied to offshore workers, giving them four weeks' paid leave. The oil operators have always maintained they should be able to take vacations during their spells onshore. However, after balloting their staff, independent company Talisman are changing the shift pattern to two on and three off. One of the reasons is to retain and attract skilled workers. It is an example of how firms can iron out the kind of difficulties oil families face.

Because of social problems arising from the unique nature of the industry most of the women feel strongly about the responsibilities of firms, who are, after all, the instigators of the fractured working structure. Some companies, generally the larger ones, make allowances for the wellbeing of their staff – and their families. But a number of wives said the majority didn't. 'Companies don't do enough to help wives and I think they should. If only from the point of view that if your husband's home life is happy – he will be a happier and a safer worker. There is no network whatsoever in his company to support the wives.' Sometimes the support and assistance can be unofficial. Jean Gaffney worked for Conoco in both Dundee and Aberdeen. She used to hear about the problems when the men came to the base to be measured for protective clothing. 'A lot of the guys had moved up from southern waters. Some of them relocated. Others didn't and just commuted. The wives were living all over the UK.' But Conoco did try to keep the women involved. 'There were annual dinner dances and the wives were encouraged to participate as much as possible. We used to run trips offshore so they could see their husbands' work environment. Those were very popular.' A number of other companies did the same thing. Jean said the main difficulties arose from the isolation of the wives. 'I used to get phone calls because communication wasn't as good as it is now. They would be wanting to speak to their husbands or boyfriends. It was always an emergency, but it wasn't really. When there was a real emergency offshore you obviously got a lot of calls. But I was always amazed at how many wives didn't know the platforms their men were on.'

Caroline thinks companies should take more responsibility in helping wives. 'They don't do enough if they want people to go and work out there. They say they are well remunerated but that is another thing. What they are doing is making women single parents for half the year. They refuse to recognise that I have to arrange childcare. There is pressure to pay for it, but it is just the hassle of having to do that. In normal family life the other parent can help. I just feel they could do more. They have these huge profits and it is their responsibility to make sure these things are in place. If I have a problem, the company wouldn't be interested. There is no liaison with the families and I think that is general in the industry.'

Laura Gibson agreed that contractors should do more. 'Wives may have to get their husbands home in an emergency. If there were a company support network that might not be necessary. I know the secretaries and if I was stuck I would know who to phone. But there should be scope within the human resources department for those kind of problems. The oil operators may have things like that – but the contractors – it is all down to cost.'

Another wife said that at first every Christmas the wives were given a great big bunch of flowers. 'There was a card signed by the manager to say thanks very much for putting up with us during the year. It didn't cost much but it was a nice touch. Making sure that the husband's slippers are warming for him when he comes in. Then one year it changed to bottles of wine which was fine, but then never again.'

[15] Tall Tales and Legendary Folk

The free-spending high-living era onshore, when oilmen of all nationalities hit the beach round the coastline of Scotland, has spawned a fund of anecdotes and incidents – some funny, some bizarre, some totally disastrous – only equalled by the tall tales that emerged from the giant fabrication yards where thousands of workers created a brand-new industry. Whether it was a service base or a terminal, the industry rapidly established a reputation for working hard and playing hard and for producing larger-than-life characters – especially amongst the early Americans.

'Clive took a dive'

Frank Peacock, an engineer from the Clyde shipyards, eventually worked in both Ardersier and Nigg. His first experience of the Americans' eccentric lifestyle and management methods came when he was sent to Highland Fabrications (HiFab) from his Inverness firm, AI Welders, to bid for some work. 'I remember going into the boardroom – we were in suits and ties, typical British industry. The room was full of guys with their feet up, no ties and every so often they would get up in the middle of the meeting and walk about as they talked and drank coffee. We were thinking, "What is going on here?" And there was this guy spitting in his cup and we thought, "What is his problem? I bet he's a tuberculosis case that one." But he was chewing tobacco.'

Frank's former colleague Evan MacLean said, 'That guy was a bit of an institution, Lawrence Welsh. He became operations manager. We had a construction manager who had an office in the yard. Lawrence always carried around a plastic cup to spit into. There was a bin in the manager's office and if Lawrence didn't have a cup he used to spit in the bin. But the office had been done up with a new carpet. Lawrence came in, chewing away, and he went to spit in the bin – but there was no bin. "Where's the goddam bin?" "I leave it outside the secretary's office." So Lawrence spits in the corner and says, "You'd better get it back in."'

Some of the other American imports at Nigg were a constant source of amusement for the Scots. Bill Shannon, the former director of public relations at the yard, tells many a story, complete with plausible Deep South accent and colourful industrial language. 'An interesting guy was Wolf Pabst, a German American, very intimidating wee man. The rumour was he used to sleep with a radio under his pillow to keep in communication. Anybody talking too long on it, he would get, "Hey, shut up, you are talking too much." One day a manager got plastered at lunchtime. This was in the middle of a big lift, eight cranes hoisting this great 1,000-ton module and radio silence had been imposed on the whole yard. This American – absolutely blazing – picked up the radio. "Come in there, Zulu." "Shut up, man," but he carried on. "Come in Zulu." "Will you shut up!" "Hey, you all can't tell me to shut up. You can't talk to me like that." So he was fired and I said to Wolf afterwards, "You fired Clive." He said, "Clive took a dive."'

Evan MacLean had another radio communications story. 'Just before the Americans left there was a welding superintendent who always had this thing going with electrical maintenance – they had the call sign Tango. Well, he was getting no reply and it went all the way to, "Come in, Tango 5." Still no reply. So he ends up saying, "Can anybody give me a Tango?" This wag comes on and starts singing "Tarrara rat ta ta – tarrara rat ta ta!"'

Tom Clement, the last manager at the Nigg yard, remembered Pabst as a bit of a dictator. 'I was at a planning meeting which was about getting a structure ready. One American said, "I doubt if we are going to make it in time." He was on the next plane home. Wolf fired him for "negative thoughts".' Bill Shannon edited the staff magazine, *HiFab News*. 'Wolf never liked it, but it was a PR thing. He said, "What is this you are writing here? You are writing the truth. We don't want the truth. You just tell it like it is."'

For the first *HiFab News* Bill commissioned a cartoon on the christening of the first rig. 'Glenmorangie Distillery had given us twenty-four bottles of their best whisky. So, one of the Yanks smashed two bottles on the jacket. We had this cartoon of a couple of Glasgow welders looking up at the rig and saying, "See thae Yanks – utter nutters. When the wifie cuts the tape maybe ra rig'll break and no tha boattle." I had to show it to the managing director, Herb Nelson, for approval. He said "Ah didn't quite get this one, Bill" So I explained. He looked at me and said, "Do you think that is f-n funny?" But Herb was a lovely guy.'

Another Wolf Pabst story came from John Wood, a civil engineer who was one of the first people on the Nigg site. 'The local Institute of Civil Engineers wanted to see the biggest project going on in the Highlands. So one Saturday morning we showed them around and then brought them to meet Wolf. Using a model, he described the whole process. "When we tow it out to the North Sea, then we upright it. The engineers tell me it will take maybe about 30 seconds to go from horizontal to vertical. Because of that momentum we have these flotation balls to stop it turning turtle." One engineer put his hand up and said, "Why do you have to do it so quickly?" Wolf turned to him – actually he hadn't a clue why – but he said, "Well, if you are going to make a f— up, you may as well make it a fast one." The two cranes at the dock were named Big Wolf and Little Wolf after him.'

Americans have left lasting impressions in other areas of the onshore business. The US firm Conoco operated a base at Dundee, where one manager was notorious for his dubious staff relations. Jack Livingstone, from Fife, who set up the base, said, 'Bob Bodie was an obnoxious sod. One time he was giving one of my lads hell. I said to the lad, "Go into his office and before he opens his mouth tell him to 'F-off and shut his face." Well, he did that and Bodie stormed out of the room. Two minutes later he walked back in and said, "Why the hell did I go out of the room? It's my bloody room."'

So life with the Americans was never dull, but sometimes it could be dangerous. Eddie Campbell, a local Easter Ross man, worked in both Nigg and Ardersier, but started off in the latter. Most of the Americans were billeted at a hotel near Nairn. Eddie recalled that one time hotel staff called in the police. 'One of the new arrivals had brought his six-gun with him and left it on his bed when he went to work in the morning. The maid had found it. There was a big panic to find him at the yard. He got sent home and was never seen again.'

McCabe's Castle

But the incomers weren't the only memorable characters; the industry attracted a number of the home-grown variety, according to Bill Shannon. The one who made the headlines in the national newspapers was Jim McCabe of 'McCabe's Castle', one of a cluster of World War II pillboxes abandoned on the hill above Nigg. 'McCabe was a qualified engineer who worked at the yard. He invited me to dinner and I asked what was on the menu and he said, "porpoise". He had picked up a dead one off the beach and he was going to serve it to me for my dinner.' His 'castle' was on land where they wanted to build a tank farm. 'But they couldn't get him to move, which was when he attracted the newspapers. So they got him pissed one day and blew up his castle.'

McCabe had an equally strange friend. 'Tex was a scruffy-looking character, devoted to his dog. He always said he and the dog were going to die together. Well, the dog did pass away and I met Tex in the pub. I said to him, "There's a story that you ate your dog – did you really do that?" He said, "Aye, man." He put his hand in his pocket and came out with a paw!'

Over at Ardersier, new recruit Jimmy Gray recalled being introduced to the high life on the soaring structures that became the platform jackets. 'The first time I went up was with a guy who thought he was a hen. Seriously. One of two brothers from Nairn. The other one thought he was a dog. Called them Willie the Hen and Johnny the Dog. The hen used to strut about the scaffolding going, "Cluck, cluck!" He could speak to you in hen. I thought, "Oh hey, what have we got here?"'

All the BP storemen at Dundee were Transport and General Workers' Union members. One day one of the men was loading fuel onto a supply vessel, which meant standing at the jetty to make sure it was pumped on. 'But one of the local stalwarts,' said Howard Price, who was operations manager at the time, 'set a chair into a container to make himself comfortable as he watched the fuel loading. I went out and found him fast asleep. So I called the chairman of the union shop. "Look at Potted Hough (the guy's nickname). That's not playing the game. What are you going to do about it?" He said, "We'll get a crane, lift up the container and swing it out over the bloody river – and then wake him up."'

United we fall

John MacDougall was a shop steward at the oil fabrication yard at Methil in Fife. 'There was a dispute involving this guy who had refused to work in a smoke-filled area. He said the extraction system wasn't powerful enough. I said, "So what is the solution?" He said, "I am not going in there unless I get more money." I said, "You condemn the management on health and safety but I get more support from them than I get from you. I can ask for stronger extraction fans and I'll have a better chance of them backing me on that, than I have in convincing them you are quite happy to sell your health for more money."'

On the other side of the coin, a national strike had been called. All the managements had agreed to it and so had all the trade unions. John said, 'I told a meeting of the men about the call for a day's strike. Somebody said, "Can I just propose we take the afternoon off?" But I said, "The management are in agreement." And I am trying to explain. "There is nothing wrong with this. You are not going to lose contracts or anything." "No, but I am losing half a day." I had to accept the motion and I seconded it. No amendments. So a half-day strike it was.'

The chancers

Jackie Phimister was a welder in a number of yards in Fife. He worked at the original Burntisland Fabricators in the 1970s. 'There was a management team building barns on the side with the steel ordered for a module. One job up at Westfield they built a barn for a farmer who was a Coal Board tenant. When they inspected the barn they asked who had built it, and that is when it all came out. The foreman had to carry the can and got sacked. But they built a few. Another time we were doing a welding job at Rosyth dockyards and five miles of welding cable had been ordered. Well, it wasn't all used but it never came back. A guy told me he loaded a container with tools for that job and they never came back either.'

The repartee

The construction of Conoco's innovative Hutton TLP was a joint operation at both Ardersier and Nigg yards. Tom Clement said that at Nigg subcontract work had been done by Japanese firms. 'When we got it there were faults which we had to repair. So some Japanese workers were sent over. One of the local guys said to one of them, "You buggered that up, didn't you?" The inscrutable response was, "Other shift."'

One of the former Ardersier workers, Ken MacDonald, remembered a girl who used to work in a bar in Nairn and applied for a job as a welder. 'She didn't get it, so she went to the media. The McDermott personnel man made the classic statement, "She never got the job because she had too high an IQ." Well, the welders were going to go on strike over that.'

There is still a legendary hotel at the ferry terminal on the Cromarty Firth, which blossomed into the biggest pub in the Highlands in the halcyon days of the Nigg yard. Bill Shannon recalls seeing men packed ten-deep at the bar. 'The story goes that when the men got their bonus cheques – as much as £1,000 – this guy said to the owner. "Hey, Peter would you cash my cheque?" Peter just took the cheque and said, "No problem." The guy was a wee bit miffed the owner hadn't expressed any astonishment at the size of the cheque. "Hey, Peter, see if I win the pools, Ah'm gonnae come back an buy this poxy pub." Peter said, "You come back here, son, when you win the pools and I'll cash your cheque."'

At your service

In the onshore offices of the oil-related companies the staff were constantly kept amused by the antics of some of the offshore characters who came under their charge. Phyllis Thomson worked for a time for a Norwegian diving company in Aberdeen and she was responsible for ensuring the smooth crew changeovers. 'A vessel couldn't get out because of the weather. The men were staying in the Gloucester Hotel in Union Street. I got a message a boat was coming in so the crew change would be at Aberdeen harbour – not far from the hotel. So I had to get them together. Now, this was a week before Christmas and they were all out shopping. So I phoned and got one of the diving superintendents. Totally mad, but a super guy. He said, "Dinna worry. Come down to the Gloucester and I will help you find them." His idea of finding them was to get two placards on which he wrote, "Would the crew of the DSV Arctic Seal, please follow me." Well, I walked around Marks and Spencers with this placard. I was well known there. My head was down at my feet. Then I was in Littlewoods, British Home Stores until eventually we got them all together – probably about thirteen – got the crew change done and the vessel left.'

Local girl Jean Gaffney was one of the first employees at Conoco's Dundee base, and she moved to Aberdeen when the company left Tayside. 'It was really silly money in those days. We used to be called out all hours for breakdown equipment but one weekend I was brought in specially. The offshore guys wanted me to buy greenfly insecticide. They were having a sunflower competition offshore and they wanted the insecticide choppered out the next day. Another time they ordered brand new covers, duvets, even though they had ones that had never been used. Never even laundered, they were just sent back onshore. So they were handed out to the staff. I still have one of the single duvets.'

BP Dundee had an experience with the law – in the form of the local constabulary and Customs and Excise. 'Two new "Bobbies" arrived when I was standing in as base manager,' said Dave Thomas. 'They had come to arrest me. "Your vehicles are not permitted to drive on the jetties." I asked them what they were talking about. "The exhausts are not in the right place – they should be up in the air." One of them showed me this old Dundee byelaw from when it was a jute port. The vehicles had to have special exhausts fitted. Nobody had bothered to change the byelaw. So they tried to shut the base down. I went to see the port authorities and the two policemen were moved within two hours.'

One of the supply ships contracted to Conoco was the *Polar 901*, which was built in the Gulf for the North Sea. It had everything on it including a refrigerator to keep the meat fresh in case the vessel was held up. Howard Price, BP's Dundee manager, said all the dockers putting the meat on board seemed to be wearing big jackets with big poachers' pockets. 'It was unbelievable, you've never seen anything like the size of these boys coming off the boats.'

Disasters and triumphs

Ken MacDonald, who supervised the construction of the Hutton field topsides, described the launch as the most embarrassing in the Ardersier yard's history. 'The topside was built the wrong way round. It was one of the few topsides that was symmetrical. But what was embarrassing was that the McDermott derrick barge – the biggest of the time – didn't have the capability to lift it off – they had to go to their rivals, Hereema, and ask them to lift it. The guy responsible who took the rap for that was forever given the nickname "Wrong Way Ron". He eventually went to Australia to re-invent his career.'

But the biggest disaster to strike the Moray Firth yard was the rise and fall of a giant crane, built at the yard and the biggest of its kind. The former finance director, Phil McBride said, 'The company ran a competition for a name and the prize was a trip to Argentina for the World Cup – the famous Ally McLeod team. A lad in accounts won the draw with the name Nessie. There were probably 300 Nessie entries.' But the 400-foot 110-ton crane never really operated. 'It could lift 2,000 tons and what they reckon happened was that during the first lift, the craneman dragged his boom too far back. The 200-ton spreader bar, which was about 200 feet long, came off the top of the module it was lifting, and the boom swung back. Unfortunately there were heavy gales and the crane was blown down. The driver was unhurt but he later had a mental breakdown and went back to Germany. He died not long after.'

Bill Shannon records an unusual solution to a technical hitch at Nigg when one of the platforms was going out. 'They opened the dock gates and as it was going through the wires, the hawsers holding it were supposed to be severed by explosive devices. Bang, bang, bang, but apparently one didn't go off. So they didn't know what to do. The wire was about 400 or 500 feet up.

So they got a local farmer to come out with his gun. He was bobbing up and down in a boat and the rig was bobbing up and down but he hit the explosive with his second shot. Bang it went, cutting the hawser and out went the platform. Some shot.'

Love for sale

In the rumbustious peak years of Peterhead as an oil port, Phyllis Thomson used to visit a friend in the town. 'I remember going to a hotel bar with this lassie and I had a new pair of shoes. But I had forgotten to take the prices from the soles. I was sitting there with my feet up when she muttered, "Get your shoes off!" She then hurriedly ripped the labels off. "Don't you know that's the way the prostitutes advertise their charges." Well, I was mortified. I remember the price was something like £9.99. I said to my husband Dave later, "I wonder if I would have got discount for cash?"'

[16] Energy City

Ile toon, boom city
Houston o' the North –
Sombreros instead o' bonnets?
Black gowd instead o' siller?

Ken Morrice, 1991

The appetite of the oil and gas industry over the past thirty years for resources – people, land and property – in Scotland has been voracious and insidious. With its dependence on a massive onshore life-support system, its influence has penetrated almost every crevice of society, with the greatest impact on Aberdeen, the city which now flies the flag of Europe's Energy Capital.

The difficulty is to distinguish and disentangle its effects – beneficial or detrimental – from those of the postwar modernisation which has defined the whole United Kingdom in the latter part of the twentieth century and the beginning of the twenty-first. While it is true to say television may have had the greater cultural impact in a previously remote region, oil has enforced and accelerated change in hundreds of different ways which would never have reached a pre-discovery stagnant North-East economy resigned to limited industrial and commercial growth. Virtually all of the 900 new companies set up in Aberdeen since 1970 have been related to, or are offshoots of, the North Sea oil industry; the clusters of science-park software companies are a prime example. Given the established policy of successive governments to continue to guide new industry towards the Central Belt, it would be fair to assume that without oil the new IT firms would not have found their way to the North-East. The industry transformed a backwater into one of the richest and fastest-growing areas in the country. While the benefits of these changes are in many cases debatable and have not reached everyone, they are unarguably manifest. Virtually every family in Greater Aberdeen has relatives or acquaintances who work in oil, and even non oil-related commercial concerns have been affected in one way or another. Not everyone has been a winner; some have been losers. What has happened over the past three decades to the community that attracted the greatest concentration of oil people, that was chosen above all others in the UK to be the onshore heartbeat of North Sea oil, the changes – good and bad – across a wide swathe of society in employment, wages, wealth, family life and the social scene, are all worth closer analysis.

A hostile welcome

> 'It would be extremely inadvisable for your company to consider coming to the city of Aberdeen. Industrial sites in the town are already full and labour is unavailable.' [*]

This extraordinary warning was sent out by Aberdeen Chamber of Commerce to prospective incoming inquirers at a crucial stage, when onshore development was beginning to penetrate the city, in 1974. The local business organisation was perfectly correct in its assertions: there was insufficient space allotted within Aberdeen's boundaries at that time for new industry, and, with one of the lowest unemployment rates in Scotland at 3.3 per cent, there was a severe shortage of skilled workers. But for the North-East's authorities, who were striving to attract any new enterprises, it was the wrong message to send while the city was still in direct contention with other areas as the choice for an oil base. Unlike the Chamber, the local councils were fully prepared to make space available, and a workforce could be – and was – procured, if not from the region, from elsewhere in Scotland and the United Kingdom. Fortunately for the city, the international oil industry 'aye gangs it's ain gait': they paid no heed and came anyway. But it took some time before Aberdeen's business community – still clinging to the 'Cosy Corner' mentality – responded. Local businessman Derek Marnoch was working in his family fish firm. He later became a highly successful chief executive of the Chamber, joining in 1983. 'The Chamber's attitide in the 1970s was: don't bother us and we won't bother you. Very few of the locals saw oil as an opportunity. They saw it as a threat, and nationally, a lot of UK companies saw it as short-term and it was going to run out.' The Harbour Board's general manager,

---

[*] Letter from Aberdeen Chamber of Commerce *c.* 1974. The author was shown a copy of this missive by an oil executive at the time. Also quoted by Guy Arnold in *Britain's Oil*, (London 1978).

Norman Beattie, was not surprised by the letter. 'The business people didn't want to see anyone coming in from outside. They didn't want to change their old-fashioned habits. I remember coming back from a trade mission to Scandinavia and Germany with a number of contacts. I was told to drop them. "This is Aberdeen. We don't want any foreigners here."'

The collective hostility of local commerce to any disruption of 'Cosy Corner' was understandable, however. There had been scant business expansion in the late 1960s and the firms were protecting an historical low-wage culture, which was below average across a range of industries. In reality, they were caught in a dichotomy of interests. There were those – almost all in the traditional industries – who feared competition and there were those who were alert to the new opportunities the incomers were likely to represent. In *Aberdeen Manufacturing Industry* (Aberdeen, 1983), a study made more than thirteen years after oil was discovered, J.M. Begg and S. McDowall described the resultant dual economy, true of the region as a whole: 'It has two main components: one relatively dynamic, growing and related to oil activity; the other with no, or weak, links with oil, relatively sluggish in performance and linked to a manufacturing base which is contracting in both output and employment terms.'

At the beginning, the indigenous non-oil companies had good reason to be apprehensive. Over eight years from 1971 they lost skilled and unskilled staff lured by higher wages. A survey in 1981 noted the average wage increase was 10 per cent above the norm. A probably apocryphal story concerns the Aberdeen typist who thought the 'twelve' in wages she was offered verbally by an oil company was insufficient. She was thinking of more than £12 per week. The offer in fact was for £1,200 a year. The large companies were hardest hit: textiles and engineering, where there was a strong marine tradition, all suffered. By 1977, of the 267 engineering manufacturers in Grampian 58 were involved in oil-related work and 23 in oil fabrication. The worst affected were the paper and board mills. A former mill graphic artist, Alan Morrice, recalls the disappearance of a whole shift of machine operators, 'They just upped and left for more money. That happened to a lot of places in the early days.' The exodus wasn't confined to manufacturing: the service and public sectors felt the effect. Tom Carter, former finance director for Grampian Region, lost essential female staff in his department's computer section. 'The turnover in operators one year in the 1970s was 100 per cent. It was disastrous – they took at least six months to train.' The 1970s and early 1980s were therefore hard times for the paper and textile mills and the food processing industry, who only survived in this remote area because their low-wage culture compensated for high transport costs and poor road links. Oil disturbed the balance.

Local employers must have felt they were under siege and not solely by the oil industry. The wage freezes of the Heath Government of the 1970s made it illegal for established firms to increase pay levels, whereas new companies could. Some North-East businesses were fined for breaking this code. Then, in the 1980s, the region lost Government development aid and European funding. Grampian Region's convener, Sandy Mutch, was concerned about the effect on the traditional sector. 'An estimated £15 million per annum of financial assistance will be lost to non-oil industries.' In a general submission on regional aid policy the local authorities told the Scottish Office in 1979 that although oil had brought 4,800 new jobs since 1971, non-oil manufacturing employment had fallen by 6,000 as a result of a contraction particularly in food processing, paper and packaging, and textiles. All of these industries, the mills and the three traditional indigenous pursuits, fishing, farming and forestry, were undergoing great changes that had nothing to do with North Sea oil. Apart from losing labour, the only direct effect for the fishing industry was that the newcomers were 'squatting' uninvited over waters North-East fishermen regarded as their birthright. They eventually resolved the territorial issue through a mutual consultative group and an oil debris compensation fund. But fishing was at a crucial juncture, crippled by loss of fishing grounds, high fuel costs and later by European fisheries conservation policies. The battles over quotas and numbers of boats in a now devastated industry rage on. A related business, the city's last shipyard, Hall Russell, should have been ideally placed to serve the new marine industry. The yard, which also had an interest in Burntisland Fabricators in Fife, underwent several metamorphoses while competing for orders for naval and oil-related vessels and, ultimately, for offshore structures and modules. When the oil standby-vessel fleet was scheduled to be replaced in 1990, the yard should have profited, but it couldn't compete with subsidised foreign shipyards and closed less than two years later. The other shipyard, John Lewis and Son, had been bought in the 1970s by the John Wood Group and converted to an offshore repair and maintenance base. In some city businesses the controlling incumbents had inherited the family firms but not their predecessors' driving ambition – 'short sleeves to shirt sleeves in a generation'. 'There was no culture of enterprise. No real entrepreneurial spirit,' claims Sir Ian Wood. Derek Marnoch said that for many family firms, selling out was the easy option rather than expanding: 'They were able to release their capital and retire.' The attitude puzzled entrepreneur Jimmy Simpson, as he informed a seminar in 1974. 'Our American colleagues are far too polite publicly to knock the performance of UK or specifically Scottish companies, but I find the apathy a wee bit distressing. People ask me: "How do you get into this business?" There is nothing particularly magic about it. It's the same as any other business: you have a service, you have a product, you feel it might be of use to this giant in our midst. And then you get out there and sell it. After all, it's not terribly difficult.'

A number of family firms, of course, were to break away from the 'shirtsleeve syndrome', among them the food manufacturers Baxters of Fochabers and Walkers of Aberlour. Others demonstrated there was still entrepreneurial vigour left: the huge national meat-processing group, Grampian Country Foods; FirstGroup, which grew from a management buy-out of Aberdeen's small municipal transport department to one of the UK's biggest public transport organisations; and the remarkable Stewart Milne Construction Group, a private house-building revolution led by a former rural plumber and electrician. While the embracing of opportunities in oil and gas by other local businessmen was a slow process, the new industry's juggernaut was already in motion.

A wealth of opportunity

The most immediate effect came from what the authorities had been striving for since the late 1960s: new employment. However, it came in unimaginable numbers where previously 100 fresh jobs would have been a cause for celebration. The figures more or less mirrored the pattern offshore. During peak production in 1985, total oil employment was 52,000 – a fifth of the working population in Greater Aberdeen. Of these, 30,800 worked onshore, the highest number on record. A hidden benefit was that a further 20,000 people were estimated to be involved at the 'soft goods' end of the market – the service sector. And they still are. There were even higher levels in 1991, when employment on- and offshore achieved a balance of 27,000 each for a total of 54,000, while 1992's total of 52,500 reflected upsurges in exploration. In both cases onshore numbers dropped below 30,000 and never recovered. Thereafter total employment has been gradually reducing, reflecting tighter financial controls and the development of less labour-intensive new technology. The onshore figure for 1999 was 21,500 out of the total employment of 40,000, but the decline appears to have been halted by an upsurge in oil activity and there has been a total increase in oil jobs.

The unemployment figures – the recognised barometer of economic health – illustrate the beneficial impact of the industry. Since the development of the oil industry – except for considerable blips in 1985 (8.6 per cent) and 1987 (11.2 per cent) caused by the world oil price debacles – Grampian Region has had one of the lowest unemployment rates in the country, around 48 to 57 per cent of the Scottish average. Since 1990, when the figure was 3 per cent, that rate went from 40 per cent to 55 per cent by 1995; compatible Grampian statistics are no longer available but the current rates for those claiming unemployment in Aberdeen are running at 1.6 per cent – half the mean Scottish figure

A remarkable consequence was that the historical migratory exodus of people went into reverse from an annual loss of 11,000 – 13,000 in 1971 to a gain of between 17,000 – 20,000 in the 1980s. Interestingly, the 2001 census showed a decline in the city's population of 0.2 per cent to 212,195, compared to a 2.3 per cent decline in that of Scotland as a whole. The reason is most likely to be the massive 20.1 per cent increase in neighbouring Aberdeenshire, the largest rise of all other areas in Scotland. The combined population of city and shire increased by 9.4 per cent – a good indicator of the healthy state of the local economy. The transformation can be accounted for by an increase in commuters. A shortage of land forced most new building deeper into Aberdeenshire and the old Kincardine area. Many rural residents work and spend some of their incomes in the city, but the new families have also rejuvenated schools, services and social activities in their adopted communities. Unfortunately, they have introduced the blight of rush-hour gridlock to the city's five gateways.

The hard economic benefits of new, continuous and lucrative employment have been manifested in dramatic changes in wage scales, and a flood of new revenues from sales, services and business taxes, all of which are reflected in the stunning growth in the gross domestic product (GDP) per head of population. At times it has soared far above that of other Scottish regions and most of the UK, outside London and the South-East. The stagnant pre-oil low-wage regime was driven up into the higher brackets to the extreme chagrin of local employers. Currently, average male gross weekly earnings in the Aberdeen employment area continue to be the highest in the country. Although the salaries of offshore workers domiciled elsewhere are never spent in the area, and the revenues of the externally-owned and multinational companies fly over the Border and overseas, the regional economy was, and still is, stimulated by greatly increased domestic expenditure as well as the mighty spending capability of the industry itself. The palpable effect can be seen in the comparative performance of the region, as recorded in the *Office for National Statistics 1999 Economic Trends* (Edinburgh). The GDP in 1991 was £5,893 million, 29 per cent higher than 1989 and 60 per cent higher than 1987. This was greater than the equivalent Scottish increases of 16 and 40 per cent. The most recent estimate by Mackay Consultants for the *Economic Review for*

North-East Scotland 2005 Update (Aberdeen) was that the area had a GDP of £8,300 million. The importance of the industry to the area is shown by Mackay in a fall in economic output in 2003, directly reflecting a decline in activity offshore. The combined non-oil industries contributed £5,303.9 million. The final value of oil and gas to the region is found in a recent calculation of its economic input: in 1991 it was £1,206.6 million.

Such affluence has radically altered life in the urban and rural communities and there are a number of indicators, among them the continuing boom in private-sector housing, which sent prices soaring in the 1970s and has not abated. There are other indicators: Aberdeen had the highest percentage of car-owning households in Scotland in 1991, at 60 per cent, compared to Edinburgh (53) and Glasgow (34). The figures for two cars per household were Aberdeen (17.06 per cent), Edinburgh (13.5 per cent) and Glasgow (6.52 per cent). In comparison, in 1966, only 56 per cent of North-East households owned cars (Aberdeen 36.30), reflecting the greater need for cars in a predominantly rural area. While the increase in car ownership is a universal UK phenomenon, the comparison in figures with Scotland's two larger cities during the peak oil years is quite marked.

A further sign of affluence was the appearance in the late 1970s of national jewellery concerns, their windows sporting the heavy gold watches, chains and bracelets beloved of the new oil workers. The overall effect on

Plate 127.

(Boxtree Creative)

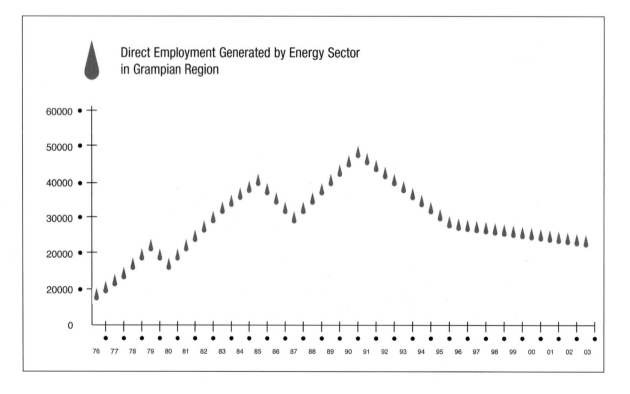

Direct Employment Generated by Energy Sector in Grampian Region

Aberdeen's retail facilities, and the choice and range of new shops, is less clear. In the mid-1970s, as was said earlier, Aberdeen was found to be lagging behind the rest of the country. There was no doubt by the 1980s, with the UK market in a depressed state, Aberdeen had the attraction of the fastest-growing disposable income per head in Scotland. There was an increased demand for prime shop space, with more up-market shopping malls being added to the array of central retail attractions. Yet Aberdeen still does not have the status-symbol stores seen in other major Scottish shopping centres which its purported wealth should attract. And this despite the fact that in 1994, over the peak festive shopping period, nearly £6 million – an all-time UK record – was dispensed from one central bank's hole-in-the-wall machines. There are still too many empty shops and units in the retail centres, while Union Street's former grey grandeur is shabby, unbefitting a wealthy energy capital.

Other signs of the financial lures for entrepreneurs can be found in the expansion of the city's social scene and night life (see Chapter 2 for comparison). The growth of an eclectic choice of exotic eating places – with prices to match – from 5 (excluding hotels) in the 1960s to more than a 150 in the 1990s, speaks volumes. Among them are 92 American, Chinese, Thai, Vietnamese, French, Italian, Indian, Greek, Mexican and Turkish restaurants. There has also been an influx of pubs serving meals, new hotels and travel

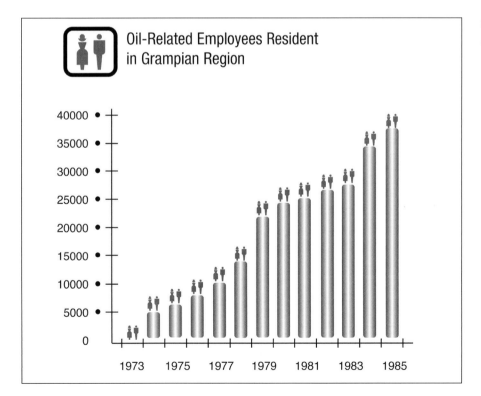

Plate 128.

(*Boxtree Creative*)

lodges – 6 built in a 7-year period in the 1980s. Not to mention casinos, a new entertainment enclave of bowling alley, cinema, ice rink, eating houses and nightclubs, constructed at the previously sparsely served seafront, 3 cinema complexes and a new film and media centre for specialist movies.

There has been little growth in the live entertainment sector although His Majesty's Theatre, built in 1906, now owned by Aberdeen City Council, was recently extended, while the Lemon Tree, the Arts Centre and the Music Hall provide alternative entertainment. Well rooted in the community before oil, one of the annual cultural highlights is the International Youth Festival. Originally established in the 1960s as a gathering of world youth orchestras, the festival now promotes all the musical and dramatic arts, attracting more than 1,000 young people from dozens of countries. A complex at the Bridge of Don now hosts all the major pop and rock concerts, as well as large conferences and exhibitions. Originally a joint venture by Grampian Regional Council, the organising Spearhead Group and the former Scottish Development Agency, the centre developed from marquees to permanent buildings in 1985, and has since undergone an £18 million reconstruction, complemented by the building of a neighbouring hotel. Since 1975, it has been home to the biennial international oil and gas conference and exhibition Offshore Europe.

In general the city's nightlife has been transformed from rowdy shoreside bars and hotels to a greater sophistication, more deserving of one of the richest and most vibrant centres in the country. One of the most conspicuous developments has been the controversial concentration of new clubs and theme pubs in and around Union Street. For a city where entertainment styles had always lagged several years behind the rest of the UK, the loud and garish

Plate 129.

(Boxtree Creative)

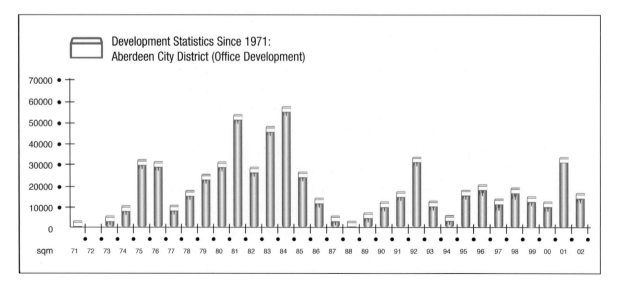

new venues have been a revelation, propelling Aberdeen into the state-of-the-art late twentieth-century and new millennium cultural milieu – to the delight of young people with money to spend and to the exasperation of a police service faced with a new late-night public order phenomenon. Mervyn Jones observed in *The Oil Rush* (London, 1976), 'There were three ways to make money out of the oil boom: own a big house and go into the bed and breakfast business, own a pub or drive a taxi.' For the sheer scale of income generated, owning a pub or a club must take pride of place. After several shrewd Aberdonians amassed small fortunes, the drinks moguls moved in to capitalise on a booming market in the 1980s. There are now 250 licensed premises in the city centre; 88 are pubs; 35 are 'places of entertainment', including 28 nightclubs (some currently closed), and lap-dancing clubs (although Aberdeen has had premises offering striptease since the 1950s); the rest are casinos. Other cities in Scotland – and in the UK generally – have undoubtedly experienced these new city centre phenomena, but the douce and stagnating Granite City of the late 1960s would never have attracted such commercial interest without the latent spending power that came ashore with oil and gas.

On the dark side

This late-night invasion of the city centre by thousands of rowdy clubbers was not welcomed by residents, and it has been a constant source of conflict ever since. One consequence of the greater numbers and the big increase in offers of cheaper alcohol and 'happy hours' has been a noticeable rise in the number of people with alcohol problems. Between 1980 and 1989 the figures doubled, with more than 1 in a 1,000 men diagnosed as dependent – compared to an average national increase of 15 per cent. Sally Wilkins, development officer for the Alcohol Advisory and Counselling Service, claimed in 1993, 'This rise happened in the oil years when there was a lot of money around . . . A lot of entertainment on a Friday and Saturday night is focused around licensed premises, particularly as far as young adults are concerned.'

Another impact in those years was a sharp increase in the level of violent crime recorded by the police. Extra weekend patrols were always on duty in an effort to stem the rise in serious assaults. According to figures issued by the Scottish Executive, in the period from 1979 to 1999 Grampian's crime rate rose by 111 per cent compared to 26 per cent throughout Scotland as a whole. In the same period there was a three-fold increase in violent crime. Within the statistics for serious crimes there are some ominous changes: in

1975 there was 1 case of murder and 1 of attempted murder; by 2000, the numbers had increased to 7 murders, 49 attempted murders and 5 cases of culpable homicide, although the figures were slightly down in 2003. Similarly, the number of serious assaults over the 25-year period increased from 157 to 398. The upward trend in cases of housebreaking was also significant: 3,989 in 1975 and 7,751 in 2000.

In a 1978 BP booklet an unidentified American oilman praised the pristine nature of Aberdeen life. 'You've got to live in places like Los Angeles or Houston to appreciate what you have here. Like being able to go out for a walk at night without fear of an attack, and leaving your front door unlocked. If you have a young family it is also nice to know that drug-taking is practically unknown among school kids.' That idyllic state might have pertained in 1978, but it is doubtful if that same oilman – if he has remained in the area – still feels the same. Certainly not about drugs. The North-East now has an unenviable reputation for the abuse of hard drugs. The number of drug offences recorded in the Grampian police region has increased from a total of 49 in 1974 to 3,263 in 2002/3. As yet no one has actually studied the possible correlation between the development of the oil industry, the resultant increase in affluence and the growth in the use of illegal substances in the region, although there has been evidence of a growing trend of drug abuse among offshore workers. The issue, however, is complex and multi-factorial. The social span of users indicates strongly that drug abuse recognises neither class nor economic barriers – it is no less an affliction of poverty than it is a by-product of wealth, hence the crime figures. An analysis of specific city-centre crime in 1999 revealed that drug addicts were responsible for 79 per cent of robberies, 65 per cent of car crimes and 92 per cent of house-breakings. There was a feeling among police officers that the perception of readily available expenditure in Aberdeen's greatly expanded new social scene and the cultural acceptability of performance-enhancing chemicals can only have encouraged external drug traffickers to target the area. The 2000 annual report by HM Chief Inspector of Constabulary in Scotland stated, 'There is a belief that drug dealers facing near-saturated markets in Newcastle, Sunderland and Liverpool have turned towards the relatively more affluent North-East of Scotland.' In fact in 2002/3, Merseyside was the main source of heroin, while crack cocaine was being couriered from London and the West Midlands. Detective Inspector Alan Smith, head of Grampian's drug squad in 1997, told the Scottish Police Federation he accepted the problem was related, to a degree, to Aberdeen's oil-related wealth, but he was more inclined to concentrate on the club scene. 'Associated to this is the inevitable abuse of so-called recreational drugs such as amphetamines, cocaine and, more typically,

Ecstasy. My understanding and belief is that too many relatively new heroin addicts spoken to by my squad cite this arena as the breeding ground for experimentation with heroin.' According to Grampian Health Board, the area was significantly different from the rest of Scotland in that 28 per cent of addicts were working compared with 11 per cent nationally. This suggested that wealth was masking the real level of abuse in the middle classes. This class of addict doesn't have to commit crimes to buy drugs and is more aware of how to avoid overdosing. There are highly successful periodic joint Customs and Excise and police operations in and around the area. In 1999/2000, drugs worth £8.2 million were seized by police and customs in the North-East. The figure for 2002/3 was £6.2 million.

One facet of Aberdeen's 'underworld' that police say has thrived is prostitution. There is anecdotal evidence of an off-street trade in women in the first flush of the oil industry, but former CID boss George Souden talks of 'more sophisticated types' operating in hotels near the harbour. The number of street girls traditionally prevalent in a seaport and market town increased with the arrival of oil. Police noted the occasional short-term visits of women from other part of the UK, but there does not appear to have been any evidence of organised vice on a troublesome scale. George Souden explained: 'In the early days you had young lassies turning up from Leeds and the north of England, students, young housewives and the like. They'd heard of guys with money to burn. I remember in 1979, a coloured man – a pimp – came up to Aberdeen with his team. He was just testing the waters before bringing his girls up. I sent for him that Saturday night and told him, "On your bike, there is nothing for you here." Give him his due, he didn't give us any trouble and we never saw him again. That just needed a start and we would have had a real problem.' There are now believed to be at least 140 prostitutes operating in the city. The council administer a 'management zone' at the harbour where the women are given regular health checks and offered a needle exchange.

There are other shadows across Europe's energy capital, those of problems of homelessness and discernible pockets of poverty, both urban and rural. A city council report in 1995 warned, 'The image of Grampian as one of the most prosperous parts of the UK has tended to disguise the fact that not everyone has participated equally in the high growth rates that have been a feature of the local economy. Many areas have not benefited from the "oil premium" and have standards of living below the Scottish average.' The number of people without homes, or sleeping rough in Aberdeen appears to vary. Researchers in a 1997 survey by Robert Gordon University, commissioned by Aberdeen City Council and Aberdeen Single Homeless Forum, talked to 144 single homeless people and discovered that 77 had slept rough at one time and 50 of them in that year. One facet of the problem has been the shortage of low-rent homes since the introduction of the policy of selling council houses. It was estimated that of 7,000 households who were in need of accommodation, 93 per cent could not afford to buy or rent in the private sector. The 1995 report said the fact that many areas had not enjoyed the benefits of the 'oil premium' was recognised officially when large parts of the region were made eligible for European structural funding. Measuring what it calls multiple deprivation, the report identified 39,000 households – 36 per cent of the total number – living in the most disadvantaged urban areas. In the rural sectors, 37 per cent of households were located in similarly disadvantaged areas. A further problem was identified by Muriel McIntyre, of Aberdeen Citizens Advice Bureau, in 1997. Half their workload was dealing with debt, which was on the increase. 'Oil boom prosperity is just a myth for many in Aberdeen. There is a great gulf between the haves and the have-nots which is even more evident than anywhere else. There are some marvellously paid jobs but not everyone is able to get them. Without a doubt there are some very low-paid jobs as well.'

A study of the two faces of Aberdeen – one affluent and the other suffering poverty, ill health and unemployment – concluded that the current methodology for allocating funds to deprived areas is flawed: Professor Thomas Lange, of the Grampian Chair in Public Policy at Robert Gordon University, says in the report, 'It is a sad reflection on modern society that we have within Aberdeen, one of the most affluent cities in the country, areas of poverty that are among the worst 10 per cent in Scotland.'

A clash of cultures

With the oil industry, now the region's premier indigenous business, Aberdeen's confident marketing slogan of 'Europe's Energy Capital', justified or not, has given it an instantly recognisable international identity, leading to a series of strong links with other oil-producing countries. The councils are members of organisations formed by countries with common oil and marine interests around the North Sea; they also have links with Canadian oil provinces and, more famously, with the US in the shape of the thriving Grampian-Houston Association, an organisation formed in 1979 to promote cultural exchanges between the two oil towns. But the industry's influence on the city and its folk has been so intrusive that one of the greatest fears from the outset was that it would damage, even destroy, the unique cultural heritage of their region, preserved in the Doric words and the distinctive

Plate 130.

Aberdeen Airport's busiest day – September 17, 1975 – oil company executives in town for Offshore Europe park their aircraft on the aprons.
(*Aberdeen Journals Ltd*)

indigenous music. Both the music and the words have, however, proved to be robust enough to survive the onslaught. While the people continue to demonstrate their ability to adapt to and absorb any intrusive cultural influences, the area's heritage is still being celebrated unabated in traditional music and folk festivals. It is interesting to note in newspaper coverage of the festivals the names of obviously 'foreign' children who have entered traditional music competitions. There has also been a vigorous renaissance in the study of the history, languages and culture of northern Scotland, led by the University of Aberdeen's Elphinstone Institute, established during the quincentennial celebrations. Sheena Blackhall, Fellow in Creative Writing in Scots at Elphinstone, has discovered in local schools that Doric thrives. 'As always the children speak one tongue at school and their ain twang outside it.' The area's bookshops are full of Doric 'dictionaries' and growing numbers of new local histories. So there is a distinct impression that despite concerns about the detrimental impact of oil, interest in the preservation of North-East traditions, has in fact been rekindled and stimulated.

[17] Winners and Losers

Winners . . .

'When it started coming what was very depressing was people saying, "They are just going to use us and abuse us. They are cleverer than we are and they have more money than we have." That's one of the reasons I started getting involved. I thought: come on, hang on a second, we can make this work for us. We can have some influence over this."

So Ian Wood remembers in 1972, at a time when he was an ambitious young Aberdeen businessman who was managing director of a sizeable family firm engaged in the traditional industries of fishing, shipbuilding and marine engineering. He was in the process of growing the company, started by his grandfather and developed by his father, when he became aware of oil. He knew little about it or its potential but his instinct was that it was important he found out. He joined a party of North-East businessmen and council and development agency representatives led by Maitland Mackie, chairman of the North-East Scotland Development Association (NESDA), on a trade mission to the world's oil and gas capital, the Texan city of Houston. He would later describe the experience as 'Damascene', a conversion, a 'mind-blowing revelation' about the industry starting to intrude on his native community.

'Coming back on the plane I started to comprehend this thing was actually huge. I remember talking to my colleagues when I got home. "Look guys, we are not going to service this from within our ship repair company. We have to form new companies and invest in new buildings. We need new management if this is really going to go the way it really might go." I had no real vision. I had just begun to see the unpeeling of the first layer.' What he absorbed in the US would also inform his whole business philosophy and inspire a commercial ethos that would dictate the dramatic progress of his company over the next thirty years.

In 1964 he had been a reluctant entrant to the fishing industry. 'The whole business was old-fashioned – about twenty years behind the times.' At the age of twenty-two, with a first in psychology at Aberdeen, he had been bound for an academic career. When his father fell ill in 1964 he agreed to help out over the summer – and never left. 'The reason I stayed even after a couple of months was that I saw there were so many things I could do to change it.' At the time he joined the family business it had a fleet of 10 trawlers, 100 employees, sales of £550,000 and pre-tax profits of £20,000. Today the Wood Group is an international engineering and service conglomerate, now public, encompasses 30 companies in 30 countries, with a staff of 9,000 and a turnover of more than £600 million. He didn't forget his roots. He has also transformed his father's original small fishing business into a separate organisation with a payroll of 600, generating more than £33 million in sales.

Ian Wood is now firmly established at the top table of the industry's hierarchy, accepted and respected as an equal by the majors, serving on several oil-related Government bodies and knighted for his efforts. He is undoubtedly an exception, but he is also the paradigm of what could and should have been achieved in the North-East. Competing in one of the world's toughest marketplaces, against all the historical obstacles that continued to retard the region in the 1960s, Wood succeeded. But he believes there should have been more like him. 'Today Aberdeen should have at least ten or fifteen sizeable companies who have grown out of the North Sea, companies whose roots are here, whose technology is anchored here providing the long term base for the industry globally. How many are there, just three, the John Wood Group, Balmoral and Ramco? What an opportunity missed.' To that company can also be added the George Craig Group, which began in similar circumstances to Wood, as a small family-owned trawler-owning firm, and is now a multi-million-pound concern with nine divisions which include shipping, catering and leisure, and the service and support company. Others who developed in Aberdeen include the international drilling company Abbott and the original Rigblast engineering firm, and in the financial services sector, Aberdeen Asset Management, who bankrolled many of the emergent companies.

Slowly, by the 1980s, Aberdeen's business world woke up and began to fight their way into the cutthroat cabals in the lower strata of the oil market, mainly in the service sector. Even in those lower leagues there is now an enviable taxation A-list of millionaires, many of them self-made after selling out oil-related enterprises they founded themselves. There are many examples, including a former newspaper van driver who sold his award-winning service company for £10 million; a former roughneck who built a successful business around the invention of a drilling tool and was bought out for £30 million; and a group of doctors who set up a medical support service for the industry and made £7.5 million in a management buy-out. There are many other examples of growth: the ubiquitous taxis – increased from 248 in the 1960s to 1,000 at present, including 125 cabs serving the airport; car rental firms – increased from 2 to 20; haulage and transport companies revelling in the huge increase in freight; the creation of a mini financial service centre outside the traditional cluster of banks and accountants; more building societies and English-style estate agents competing with lawyers and solicitors, who have themselves risen in numbers; employment agencies – increased from 2 to nearly 70; 50 travel agents, up from 3 and prospering from the airport's expanding international links; professional consultancies of every hue and kind – public relations for example, up from 1 to 15; and 40 training agencies augmenting a handful of energy-related Government bodies transplanted into the city. There was also a full range of suppliers of general goods and provisions, 300 of them local companies. At last the North-East business world was being seen to be responding to the widening opportunities.

What has also become noticeable is the adoption of the philosophies of the new industry, transforming the sluggish commercial culture, even in non-oil industries. Maitland Mackie said, 'They had to look to their efficiency and that's been good for them.' A new category of enterprise stimulated by oil and, arguably, the most likely indigenous industry to survive post-oil is the city's growing cluster of e-tech companies, some led by incomers, others locally developed. This in a corner of Scotland where computers had been a late-arriving novelty. Mainly concentrated in modernistic science and technology parks are sixty high-tech firms whose skills honed in the oil fields are an entrée into the wider world, and the sector is still growing. The same kind of rigour in research and development has come to an area Professor Gaskin had forecast as 'of strategic importance' in his 1969 *Survey of the North-East Economy*: the potential inherent in the higher education establishments such as the University of Aberdeen (UA) and the then Robert Gordon's Institute of Technology (RGIT), the agricultural and land research institutes of Rowett and Macaulay, and the aquatic science centres of the Marine Laboratory and Torry Research. The latter no longer exists, and because of their nature neither Rowett nor Macaulay became involved in oil. The Marine Lab has contributed a number of oil-related scientific studies on marine environmental hazards.

The university was another matter. A number of disciplines such as engineering, geology and chemistry should have been ideally placed to play an important role. But many academics felt oil was 'too commercial' and the university 'missed the boat' in the early days. Edinburgh's Heriot Watt cornered the market in petroleum engineering, as did Dundee in petroleum and mineral law, while Strathclyde and Newcastle also attracted oil work. One of the significant and honourable exceptions is Professor Alex Kemp, of King's College, who has forged a reputation as a petroleum economist of international repute, with an unrivalled expertise in North Sea and energy-related taxation. He co-founded a financial and economic services company, Aupec. UA did eventually become more heavily involved. One important development was the joint venture in 1977 with Shell, Esso and BP to found an offshore medical centre (OMS), which is now owned by the American Aon Corporation. To date UA has an oil and gas centre, and five chairs and lectureships endowed by oil companies. From 1999 to 2000, some sixty energy organisations contributed more than £4 million through a spread of activities and more than thirty consultancies.

In comparison RGIT, founded in 1903, was initially more business-orientated and generally grasped the unmatched opportunity better. Under its director, Dr Peter Clarke, it grew with the industry, offering qualifications in a broad sweep of related subjects. The institute was incorporated as a university (RGU) in 1992, recognition thought to have been influenced by its North Sea work. The old RGIT's most celebrated innovation was the offshore survival centre, which has trained hundreds of thousands of oil workers at a peak rate of 27,000 students a year, latterly down to 18,000 on shorter courses. The centre has two divisions, survival and health, and is internationally recognised as a world leader, pioneering many of the modern techniques and equipment, including helicopter ditching and survival tank. The possession of an RGIT survival-training certificate is obligatory for working offshore under UKOOA guidelines. The centre is now owned by RGIT Montrose, a subsidiary of the oil service company Petrofac. A more recent feature of RGU is the Offshore Management Centre, a knowledge base for training and development. The city also houses Scotland's largest further education establishment, Aberdeen College, which provides qualifications in engineering, computing and business. Generally, the area's educational establishments are now responding well.

Gateways to the North Sea

The packed industrial estates and business parks, which ring the city and extend beyond, replete with hundreds of oil support firms and road networks busy with vans, trucks and lorries where only farmland existed before, are substantial manifestations of the city's success as a major international energy capital. But two other service centres that did exist pre-oil have been spectacular winners in the past three decades: the region's gateways to the offshore world, Aberdeen Harbour and Aberdeen Airport. Neither has had an easy passage but both have established themselves as strategically and economically important.

When the first little oil survey boats arrived in the mid-1960s they found a medium-sized harbour at a commercial crossroads, as a former general manager, John Turner, relates in his historical account, *Scotland's North Sea Gateway* (Aberdeen, 1986). The 860-year-old harbour, recognised as Britain's oldest business, was Scotland's largest fishing port, the third-largest in the UK, but landings and vessel movements had begun to fall. The 80-year-old fish market was badly in need of redevelopment, and, while the Northern Isles ferries still ran from the harbour, the short sea and ocean trade had declined. The prospects looked bleak. Then, into the 1970s the numbers of busy supply boats in the area began to increase. To meet the demands of an overwhelming onrush of companies the board urgently needed to create more space, but, above all, they needed to provide 24-hour access to the Upper and Victoria commercial docks, then limited by dock gates.

But an even greater dilemma, reported here for the first time, was that the Harbour Board were on the verge of insolvency. Their plight – described in the official papers of the Scottish Industry Department (SID) – was first admitted in 1971 to the Department of Energy (DoE). The harbour had to find £124,000 to cover two bills: one for £64,000 for dredging work, the other, £60,000, to refund overpaid dues in fish transactions. Their solution was a loan of £300,000 from the DoE for capital works. But the department first wanted them to be more realistic with their information and in their commercial activities. They were also asked not to make their situation public and not to give details to the Aberdeen MPs. Although the civil servants were aware Aberdeen could anticipate lucrative new business in servicing oil vessels, they maintained a rugged scepticism about its lasting value. After much discussion, the Harbour Board were given £336,000 in grants and loans to bail them out. Two years later they returned seeking even larger funds to carry out the restructuring and expansion of the port, estimated to cost in excess of £1 million. The berths were becoming overcrowded. Captain Niall McNab, who was marine master for P&O in the port, said they preferred Dundee. 'In Aberdeen you tended to get moved in the middle of the night to change berths. You could hardly get a night's sleep. That didn't happen at Dundee or Montrose.'

Aberdeen had already lost one very lucrative contract when BP, deterred by the non-tidal nature of the harbour, took their business to Dundee. Spurred on by Maitland Mackie and NESDA, the Harbour Board were determined not to let any more customers slip away. Negotiations for the redevelopment finance were protracted, reaching the newspapers, as the DoE and the Treasury demanded firmer information about potential trade. 'It was very frustrating,' recalls Norman Beattie, harbour chief executive at that time. 'They produced every possible objection. They could not visualise the port's role in the oil industry. What they thought was going to happen was tankers unloading oil and that was all. Also the National Ports Council, who had to be consulted, wouldn't allow any scheme unless it would make 13.3 per cent profit. We couldn't guarantee that at that time.'

A survey commissioned by the Harbour Board from the Economist Intelligence Unit predicted that 'A steep rise in trade is unlikely, but there will be a gradual growth.' The explosive increase in traffic proved just how unreliable that forecast was. The board were urged by NESDA to determine what the oil firms really required. Malcolm Bruce, now Liberal Democrat MP for Gordon, who was with the agency, was asked to talk to them. 'All it took was a few phone calls and the companies were happy to provide estimates.' These were submitted and after thirteen months of negotiations a loan of £1.25 million was granted. The transformation of the small struggling port into a vibrant modern harbour capable of handling the bulk of the oil business could go ahead. Norman Beattie said they followed a totally different strategy from Dundee, who gave BP a whole stretch of quay. 'I told the oil companies they would only be allowed to lease a smaller area and to look for storage areas away from the harbour. That way we were able to squeeze in more companies.' There remained one final troublesome vestige of the past: the labour situation. Aberdeen had a history of industrial strife. The stevedores, run by Aberdeen Fishing Vessel Owners Association, operated

Plate 131.

Some of the giant multi-purpose oil supply and service vessels which now dominate the port's traffic. (*Allan Montgomery*)

under the National Dock Labour scheme. It took a year of discussions before they agreed to provide twenty-four-hour cover – but for oilrigs only.

Once the dock gates were removed, the Harbour Board, galvanised by the oil revenues, launched a remarkable lengthy programme of reconstruction. Norman Beattie, who retired in 1978 after forty years with the board, had tried to lease spare land owned by the town council on the Hall Russell shipyard site, but was refused. 'But once the shipyards went the harbour were able to take over the land. That was a great help to the oil industry.' Given the space, the companies built their own facilities: seven marine bases, including one run by the Wood Group to service other firms. Docks were widened and deepened, a number of new quays and a repair dock were constructed, and a variety of new port facilities were introduced to control the maximum of seventy vessel movements a day. The supply-boat sector has flourished spectacularly from the early, more primitive, craft to the gigantic customised ocean-going vessels, packed with new technology and fitted with heli-decks; the annual traffic multiplied from 1,233 in 1972 to more than 5,000 in the 1990s, and it was still breaking records in 2005. The harbour, guided by Barclay Braithwaite, initially harbour engineer and then chief executive officer after John Turner, progressed through an ambitious £15 million expansion programme. This was almost eclipsed in 1994 by one single project, the huge Telford Dock, built at a cost of £12 million, increasing the port's capacity by 10 per cent. Oil revenues of £150 million were reinvested in upgrading the facilities as the port was virtually rebuilt. It continues to thrive, with more investment projected. There are now over 6 km of quays and more than a dozen deep-water berths, one costing £10 million. Some 400 oil-related vessels use the harbour every month – 100,000 in total since 1964.

Meanwhile non-oil customers also prospered. Three roll-on roll-off ferries to Orkney and Scandinavia were introduced as well as improved services to Shetland. A new fish market was eventually built although the industry has continued to decline. At its peak, Aberdeen Harbour, which contributes around £100 million to the local economy, reputedly handled a greater tonnage of offshore traffic than any other port in the world.

In early 1972, Shell Expro employee Bernard Rollingson landed at Dyce Airport, just outside the city. 'The airport was quite basic and the arrival/departure building was an old Nissen hut. It had one counter in it. One end was the bar, the other end was the ticket and seat sales. The same bloke did both jobs.' Like Mr Rollingson, the first advance guard of the oil industry found what was basically a modest terminus, as aviation journalist James Ferguson said in his book *The Story of Aberdeen Airport* (Glasgow 1984), 'for flights to the Northern Isles and limited domestic services to the South and all

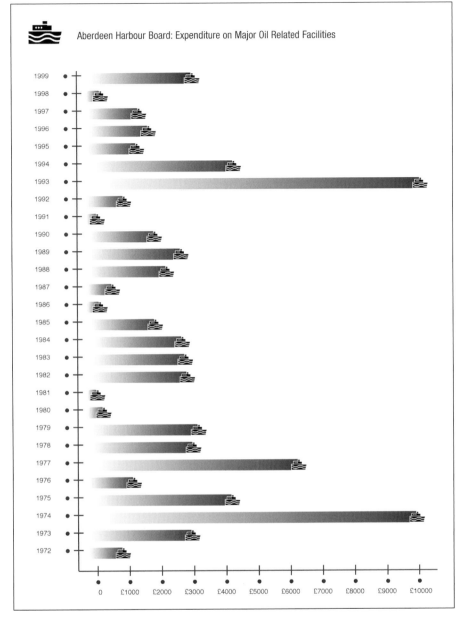

Aberdeen Harbour Board: Expenditure on Major Oil Related Facilities

Plate 132.

(*Boxtree Creative*)

on a proudly recorded throughput of just over 67,000 [passengers].' Like other elements of the North-East economy, there appeared no possibility of future development. Like the harbour, the airport, owned by the Ministry of Aviation, was also in a financially precarious position in the 1960s, losing large amounts of money. When it was suggested local authorities should take over their local air operations, Aberdeen and Aberdeenshire were highly sceptical. The ministry thought it was feasible and warned that if the councils didn't buy the airports they would be closed down. The threat became a municipal election issue, but by then Dyce was £500,000 in the red. Although closure was the last thing the

Plate 133.

Aberdeen Airport in 1974 – and the beginning of the build-up of oil traffic. (*Aberdeen Journals Ltd*)

councils wanted, they resisted the threat strongly and successfully.

The idea didn't go away. In 1969, the Government tried again and the councils still refused. Jim Ferguson observed, 'With the benefit of hindsight and in the light of the airport's current prosperity [the councils] might have done well to pursue the matter.' But by then the oil aircraft of the future, the helicopter, had arrived, and fixed-wing operations also began to increase. Rollingson was among the 153,571 passengers who used Dyce in 1972 in a total of 30,085 aircraft movements. The pattern of growth was incredible: 823,400 people passed through the terminal. Dyce – the tiny, struggling, penurious airport – was being dragooned into the most unexpected but thoroughly welcome position of having to expand. By 1980, when a new air traffic control centre opened, Aberdeen Airport, as it was renamed, had acquired all the trappings of a thriving strategic international air base. At a cost of £20 million, the fixed-wing operation had been switched to the west side with new terminal buildings, enhanced runways and new technology, including much-needed radar. Fifteen significant airlines used the airport and air freight was also booming. An added bonus was the development of an overseas airline holiday market.

With sublime North-East understatement, the region's *Grampian Economic Review* noted in 1990, 'The level of use of Aberdeen Airport is closely related to the fortunes of the oil industry.' One reason lay in the helicopter operations (described in detail in *The Oilmen* (Edinburgh, 2004)) housed alongside the fixed-wing terminal. They too grew enormously through the peak exploration and development years offshore. This heavy dependence on oil was dramatically illustrated during the oil-price crisis of 1986, when the flow of traffic suddenly ceased and 200,000 passengers vanished. The situation remained desperate until 1987, when the figures began to climb again. There was an annual increase of 8 per cent until 1990, when figure reached a record 13 per cent, with 1,940,000 passengers by the end of the year. Even those figures were surpassed in the early 1990s, reaching nearly 2,500,000 by 1996, but passenger numbers again dropped in 1998/99 when the oil industry once more reacted to fluctuations in the world oil price. The reduction was in helicopter traffic, which has continued to drop since. Passenger figures have started to climb back up to the 2.5 million mark and a major expansion programme is planned, including a runway extension to attract long haul flights.

Apart from the oil-enforced crises, the airport has had to survive a number of controversies. The most lengthy and most intriguing could be regarded as the old, independent, 'contermashious' North-East fighting back against progress. It began in 1975 when an attempt to run night mail flights ran into opposition from people living under the flight paths. The rejection was reinforced shortly afterwards by a planning directive from Aberdeen District Council: no flights would be allowed – except for medical emergencies – between 10.30 p.m. and 6.30 a.m. Aberdeen was the only major European airport to have such an early curfew. All through the 1990s the late-landing dispute raged. Against the advice of the airport and the wider business community, the council refused to relent for fear of adverse electoral reaction. Then, in 1998 they agreed to experiment with a limited number of late flights up to 11.30 p.m. A twenty-four-hour service finally came into operation in 2005, with little protest.

Plate 134.

(Boxtree Creative)

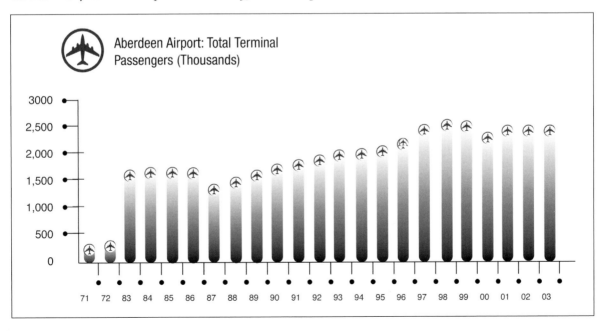

There is another facet to the airport's importance to the region. A survey in 1987 showed the site had attracted 4 industrial estates, where three-quarters of the firms are oil-based, and 5 hotels, providing work for 17,000 people – 13 per cent of Aberdeen's labour force. A further expansion is planned in the form of a £60 million business park. A recent study estimated the airport contributes around £350 million per annum to the local economy.

The learning cycle

With the unpredictable, cyclical nature of the world energy industry, the region, with more than 80 per cent of North Sea business deeply embedded in all levels of its society and economy, has experienced a number of chilling foretastes of life without oil. The first was the early downturn in 1973 forced by the Arab–Israeli War. The two most salutary episodes, however, were the major recessions of 1986–87 and 1998–2000. Both forced transformations in oil company policies and brought hard times for the workforce on- and offshore.

The blast of cold reality in 1986 came just after a euphoric peak year in the UK industry when exploration and production were at their highest in history: the discovery success rate was at its greatest; annual production was up, boosting oil exports; the offshore supplies industry had had its most lucrative year; the fabrication yards had had full order books; in Grampian 51,200 people worked for 800 oil-related companies; and the harbour, airport and heliport were working at record levels. According to a petroleum consultant, 'The North Sea [was] on the brink of a boom that could be sustained through the next decade and into the twenty-first century.'

Fateful words. A year later, an unfortunate combination of external circumstances, including war between Israel and Iran, and a breakdown in the quota system of the controlling global cartel, the Organisation of Petroleum Exporting Countries (OPEC), conspired to send the artificially high world oil price plunging to the depths; 1986 became known as the 'ten dollar oil' year. For a region thirled to the oil and gas business, it was a disaster. Shockwaves spread with alarming speed as the industry reacted in near panic. Oil sales fell by more than half; Shell and BP profits dropped drastically; exploration expenditure was cut and risk investment stopped. The outcome was that annual significant new finds fell from 25 to 14 and the companies began to cull their workforces. Grampian bore the brunt: 10,000 jobs were shed at a rate of 1,000 a month. In the oilmen's Aberdeen enclave, the Bridge of Don, unemployment was worst, at 81 per cent. The impact was widespread: spending on support industries dropped; the flow of oil-company funds back into the industry was down some £3 billion; service companies were hit hard; 40 fewer supply vessels were at sea; the workload in the oil construction yards went down by 60 per cent; drilling companies' commissions dried up and the daily rental rates for drilling rigs fell from $100,000 to $10,000, with 18 redundant structures stacked in the Firth of Forth, the Moray Firth and off Aberdeen. The industry was in deep trouble.

The domino effect continued and for a time net migration returned. First to go were many of the 13,000 migrant workers, taking their spending power with them. Among them were 3,000 Americans, most in the top posts and higher earning brackets. Some departed leaving keys, house and mortgage behind. A phenomenally large number of houses were marooned on the market: 4,000 for sale, increasing at a rate of 100 a week. Almost daily the local newspapers, one of them forced to make staff redundant, chronicled the effects of the recession. The retail trade recorded a drop in spending. Aberdeen's taxi fleet, the vehicle hire firms, the scores of restaurants, bars, clubs, hotels, boarding houses, the airport and its ancillary retail outlets, the heliport and the helicopter companies, the harbour – all were oil business beneficiaries, in some cases dependents. Apart from the harbour, which had to maintain support to the offshore installations, all were suffering and some at the bottom of the supply chain went out of business.

Then, just as suddenly, early in 1987, oil prices doubled and the cycle changed. The industry was on the move again, bidding generously for new North Sea blocks in an encouraging response to the tenth round of licenses. Shell and BP announced plans to develop fields on hold since the crisis, sending a clear signal: the recession was over. Employment recovered but never again would it reach the same heights. Two prescient statements summed up the significance of the crisis. The first was from the House of Commons Energy Select Committee: 'The collapse in price should alert policy makers to prepare [the oil communities] for the time when oil will not be flowing.' The second remark was made twelve years later by Ian Wood: 'The 1986/87 downturn clearly sharpened and enhanced our competitive ability and efficiency and our policy of investing in the downturn is certainly now paying dividends.' So, by the time the second great slump hit the North Sea the industry was leaner and better prepared to deal with a recession that lasted longer than the first.

The scenario of 1998–2000 was, in many ways, different from the others, although it too began with OPEC increasing the supply of oil and forcing a fall in prices. But another threat was hanging over the industry: the possible imposition by the Treasury of a 'windfall' tax on company profits. While the oilmen marshalled their campaign, the oil price continued to slide. When it hit

$13 a barrel, Chancellor Gordon Brown relented and dropped the tax idea. But offshore exploration had already begun to suffer. The companies cut back, shelved development projects, and oil revenues sank to their lowest level since the previous recession. The effect on employment was not so harsh on the Grampian Region as it was in 1986. Nationally some 15,000 of the work force were made redundant, of which 1,500 to 2,000 were based in Aberdeen. Until then the city had been enjoying its lowest unemployment rates for 16 years. The effects on other sectors were also different: there was no sign of crisis in the non-oil service sectors such as hotels; and there was also a lesser impact on another barometer, house prices, which at one point rose 4 times faster than the Scottish average. In contrast there was a slowdown in office property developments with companies reluctant to expand. The worst casualty was again the airport, where fixed-wing and helicopter traffic dropped markedly. And this time the harbour was also hurting from a downturn in offshore support activities.

Finally, in 1999, OPEC relented and the price of oil began to rise again. But even at $25 a barrel the cautious oil companies were reluctant to step up expenditure, and into 2000 the small contractors were still starved of new business. The platforms, however, had been pumping prolifically all through the recession setting a new record in 1999 for production and for the number of oil fields in operation. Then, just as in the previous dip, BP and Shell set the risk business back in motion by announcing huge new spending plans for the North Sea, and other operators followed suit.

The oil price continued to rise, reaching $32 a barrel. The oilmen had learned a salutary lesson: in future they would base their forward planning on a low $11 and a midway $14 a barrel. Another effect was that more effective liaison was established between Government and industry in the form of joint bodies such as the cost reducing initiative CRINE, and then LOGIC and PILOT which were charged with the task of strengthening the UK Continental Shelf as a competitive global force. The downturn also heralded globalisation, as oil companies and their swelling ranks of contractors began to look away from the North Sea to the new oil provinces in the developing countries. They were being joined by local companies expanding their export markets and generating billions of pounds of orders overseas. Like his employers, the Aberdeen oil worker, schooled in the North Sea, also went international, exporting his skills – a course of action already pursued by redundant oil fabrication workers from Scotland's abandoned yards. It is commonplace to see at the international check-in desks at Aberdeen Airport men in the mandatory uniform of the offshore worker, checked shirt, jeans and high boots, clutching a book of airline tickets, ready to commute thousands of miles to follow the work to the next oil field. This from an area where a man from Fraserburgh used to be reluctant to accept a job in Peterhead – 11 miles away. Such is the independence and confidence the industry has imbued in the North-East workforce.

The price

If the two price crashes were the wake-up call for the money men in what had been a heedlessly profligate industry, the world's worst oil disaster had a similar traumatic impact on what – from the earliest days – had been a far from acceptable industry safety realm. The first book in this series, *The Oilmen: The North Sea Tigers*, dealt in some detail with the offshore element of the catastrophe on the Occidental production platform, Piper Alpha, on the evening of 7 July 1988, when 167 men died. But, of course, the terrible events also touched the lives and hearts of people onshore, particularly those assigned to deal with such emergencies.

The images of that dreadful summer night remain indelibly etched on the memories of those who watched safely from the land. The television and newspaper pictures of a holocaust; the realisation of the frailty of man-made structures in the face of the sheer insurmountable force of unleashed natural energy; thousands of tons of steel reduced to a blackened skeleton; the insistent beat of helicopters; the haunted faces; the labours of medical staff; the harrowing accounts of the survivors; the stories of heroism; the stark roll call of the dead pinned on a wall; the grief and the anger of relatives – the world looked on in horror as the North-East wept for its own, from whatever airt they had come.

From an onshore perspective the most important element was the reaction of the emergency services – the rescue teams, the helicopters, the police and the hospitals. At the centre of the whole remarkable operation that night and for some time after was the Accident and Emergency Department at Aberdeen's NHS Foresterhill. The senior consultant in charge, Professor Graham Page, has had to deal with the victims of all the major disasters in the area for more than twenty-five years. He speaks for his colleagues in the emergency service network.

'Oil and oil exploration is, by its very nature, hazardous. Ever since it began we started to plan for a major incident offshore. It is difficult to define where the National Health Service responsibility lies – legally it ends at the low tide mark, but if a ferry overturns on the way to Shetland there is no doubt we would be involved. For many years prior to oil, there have been fishing vessel incidents and medical intervention. Before Piper Alpha, a number of private medical organisations dealt with day-to-day accidents, arranging for patients to come ashore. In addition there is an offshore specialist team, created by UKOOA – a group of hospital consultants who in the event of a major incident are prepared to go out and help. That night I was the consultant in charge here so I didn't go offshore. But a lot of my colleagues did.'

The consultant explained the emergency system that had been in place for many years. 'For an offshore incident the coastguard is in charge until the casualties come over the coastline. Then the police take over. The RAF also play a part with their search and rescue facility and the capability of winching people, which a lot of commercial helicopters do not have. The fundamental planning is constantly updated according to medical advances and from experience of previous accidents. Emergency training exercises on offshore accidents have been mostly paper exercises. In one or two we have actually brought people ashore as pretend casualties. We have also had training involving a North Sea ferry incident. Planning is the same whether you are offshore or onshore but it is always being adapted; as it is at the moment for terrorist incidents. There have been several cases of helicopters ditching and there have always been oil casualties. I suppose as the fishing industry declined the oil industry became more involved.' One of the many responses to the needs of the industry was the development of a corps of doctors trained in diving medicine and prepared to go offshore – Professor Page is one. Some of the expertise existed before oil, however, through the hyperbaric oxygen centre at the hospital.

The accident and emergency consultant said they had never anticipated anything on the scale of Piper Alpha. 'We all knew things could go wrong and result in casualties, you know, blow-outs which they have had since they started drilling for oil.' But Piper was very different. 'I remember getting a phone call to say there had been an explosion half an hour previously, but communications were bad, because contact had gone down. I think the radios on the *Tharos* [the emergency standby vessel] had gone down as well. So our information was coming from the coastguards. There were several explosions, of course, and it became obvious this was, in fact, a very major incident.'

The frontline primary care organisation is Aberdeen Industrial Doctors, who responded quickly, calling out physicians to go offshore. 'I activated the specialist teams – surgeons and anaesthetists – they went to *Tharos*. My job was then to prepare the department for an influx of casualties. As it happened all our plastic surgeons were at a conference in Leicester. So I had to call them back. But we had plenty of time to bring in sufficient staff. We didn't know how many casualties to expect – nobody knew who was alive and who was in the water. That is one of the things you very often don't know about a major incident. Two years before Piper, the Royal Darroch Hotel at Cults blew up and we didn't know how many people were involved. Nobody can tell who is in a hotel at nine o clock in the morning.'

Then the relay of rescue helicopters began to reach Aberdeen and the landing pad at Foresterhill. 'The casualties didn't start coming until six hours after the incident was reported so we were ready. The main injuries were serious burns. Some patients had inhaled smoke but they weren't in dire straits. Others who had inhaled smoke had died on the platform. We had somewhere in the region of eleven serious burns and over the next few days we had several teams of plastic surgeons in Aberdeen excising and grafting the burns. There was one death in the hospital.'

Dealing with the psychological affects was the responsibility of David Alexander from the UA's Department of Mental Health. 'He worked with both the patients and the staff who were involved. You do feel a bit strange after an incident like that. We saw a large number of seriously burned people and I think there was a fair amount of what is called post-traumatic stress and it was dealt with very well by Professional Alexander and his team. But like most people in Aberdeen, the medical profession was shocked by the enormity and the ferocity of the Piper Alpha disaster. I suppose because many of us had never seen an oil blow-out, which wouldn't have been the case with very experienced drillers.'

He continued, 'You can always point to things afterwards and say they could have been done better but we felt the plan had gone reasonably well and we had the right people in the right place at the right time. Without being cocky about it for the future, we had done all right. But you can never be conceited about a major incident. You can never have enough facilities standing by for every occurrence. If an aircraft came down in the centre of Aberdeen on a Saturday afternoon, it might not be easy to deal with. The number of casualties would very rapidly overwhelm the system. One thing about Piper was that it happened at half past ten at night when no routine operations were in progress and doctors were available. If it had happened at nine in the morning and ten or twelve operation lists had started at eight thirty – those people can't be stopped. You can't just jam on the brakes in a hospital.'

Professor Page concluded, 'There was no single person who could say, "I ran Piper Alpha." I think there was good co-ordination that night. We have always worked very well with the coastguard, the police, the fire brigade and the ambulance service. Aberdeen is a city, but in many ways it is just a village community. We all work together.'

The legacies of oil

That community spirit also resulted in the eventual commissioning of the impressive and moving triptych sculpture of oilmen now standing in the beautiful rose gardens at the city's Hazlehead Park. There was already another tangible commemoration of the oil workforce, the small chapel, with its handsome stained-glass windows, in the Town Kirk, the East Church of St Nicholas. John Moorehouse, former director of public affairs for Shell, says he and others in the industry had first discussed setting up a chapel immediately after the industry's worst helicopter crash, the Chinook in Shetland in which forty-five men died, but following Piper Alpha the idea really took shape. John was surprised and gratified the church authorities had immediately and willingly agreed to provide space at the heart of the historic building. 'It is not meant to be a memorial – more of a celebration of the industry and what it has meant to the city. It's not just about the Chinook or Piper Alpha disasters – it's for the whole industry.' That, however, is not how the North-East has chosen to regard the beautiful chapel: it remains a memorial and the focus of all religious ceremonies connected with the industry.

The chapel is one gift to the community from the oil companies. Other contributions representing an attempt at social integration are more esoteric and take many forms: funding for university chairs, scholarships, academic studies and research; donations of money and equipment; patronage of cultural events and charities. The major oil companies also contribute every year to the Oil Industry Community Fund – founded by Sir Maitland Mackie. The money is distributed to worthy causes and some £200,000 has been given away in the past. Many of the big companies such as BP and Shell have also set up special social initiatives encouraging employees to lend their time and expertise to practical community-led projects. Oil executives figure on the list of the area's 'great and the good', serving on public boards, committees and quangos, representing education, industry and enterprise. The internationally famous company logos can be seen in a wide variety of cultural contexts – down to the simple sponsorship of the football strips of hundreds of boys' teams in the area. In so many ways, oil has undoubtedly meshed with the community.

Yet there remains a belief among local people that the industry owes the area more than the kind of Victorian public affairs largesse commonly dispensed by industries in any part of the country. The argument has two parts. The first is that wherever else in the world oil has been found the companies have funded the building of roads, airports, railways and harbours, schools, housing – whatever infrastructure was needed to facilitate the exploitation of the oil fields. Nothing like that had ever been on offer to the

Plate 135.

The beautiful St John's Chapel in the Kirk of St Nicholas, Aberdeen, with its stained glass window depicting oil scenes, created by Sheena McInnes and gifted by the industry in 1990. (*Walter Anderson*)

North-East of Scotland. The region had to pay dearly in the early years to build the infrastructure to accommodate an unimaginably wealthy business. The second part of the argument is that Aberdeen should have followed the example of Shetland and coerced the companies into paying into a permanent fund to compensate for disruption to the community. The common answer from the companies has never changed: our contribution is the wealth, prosperity and stable employment we have brought. It was a sentiment voiced by Herb Nelson, American boss of the Brown and Root fabrication yard, during a 1973 Grampian Television programme. 'We do give thought to the effect on the local community and the simplest effect, of course, being that we bring a large payroll. The fundamental need of a community is money.'

Sir Maitland Mackie insisted the argument that the companies should help to pay for the infrastructure was often put to the industry in the early days. 'They said, "Look, the Government takes God knows what in taxes – let them pay, we pay enough as it is." To hell wi' that. As for Shetland, I suppose you could say we missed out. Ian Clark [the island's chief executive] did really well there. So did Orkney with Flotta. It is easy to be wise after the event, but the companies were prepared to pay them because they were desperate to get into these places.' His municipal counterpart, Lord Kirkhill, agreed that it had been easier for Shetland. 'I was never in favour of doing a Shetland. I suppose you could have done it but it was much more difficult to do in Aberdeen. In any case Aberdeen was better able to absorb oil than Shetland. To my mind the fact we had a huge increase in job opportunities was enough.'

There were just too many of the oil majors, according to former planner Peter Cockhead, now chief executive of the North-East Transport Group (NESTRANS). 'They were able to hide behind each other.' He thought they could have done more with projects such as the Oil Experience, initiated by the Aberdeen Beyond 2000 Group against the day the oilmen departed. The idea, first put forward in 1987, was to create a centre displaying all aspects of the industry, including helicopter flights and simulated deep-sea dives. Like Beyond 2000, the oil centre, intended as a unique tourist attraction, never materialised, although the award-winning Maritime Museum has an imaginative oil section. The 2000 concept was devised by Derek Marnoch, of Aberdeen Chamber of Commerce. 'We lacked leadership to make it happen and we couldn't raise the money so we had to go to the Scottish Development Agency who funded it. Their report came out, but we just couldn't take it forward without leadership. To a certain extent the oil companies became involved. Their view always was: "It's your area. If the council aren't for it why should we be?" They should probably have supported it but they weren't prepared to do it. They said: "That is not what we are here for."'

Epilogue

The astonishing efflorescence of the North Sea oil and gas industry's web of onshore developments round the coasts and islands of Scotland over a thirty-year span, and their remarkable sustainability – sadly not the case for all but one of the turbulent fabrication yards – is the wonder of postwar industrial and commercial history.

The bases, terminals and construction sites were never going to be the countrywide salvation of the declining manufacturing sector, although the vast bounty that flooded from the offshore fields in the 1970s and 1980s eliminated the gap in the UK's balance of payments. Despite the creation of many thousands of new jobs, neither were they sufficient to counter the draining away of well-paid and secure employment as the manufacturing template of the Scottish economy was irrevocably altered.

Yet, far from the doom-laden forecasts of the 'rape and pillage' of vulnerable, underdeveloped and stagnant areas, and the destruction of their unique cultures, in all the areas the industry touched it brought previously unimaginable prosperity and pleasure, skills and opportunities, and hope. Miraculously, in every case, the oilmen arrived at precisely the right moment for the failing economies of most of these communities. As is apparent in the preceding chapters not one oil-related area expressed any regrets at enter-taining the incomers and few would suggest that they had not benefited. Even the great yards, which mostly came with built-in obsolescence and an uncertain finite lifespan, while they developed the steel and concrete giants of the new industrial age, they endowed their workforce and the areas around them with a legacy of new skills and expertise.

The first British oil workers in the early days of exploration were expatriates who had learned their trade in the Middle East and the Gulf of Mexico and brought their knowledge to bear on the North Sea. The new phenomenon has been the Scottish oil commuter who learned the business in the offshore UK field, who is sent forth by companies based in Scotland but still spends his money at home. The most skilled now operate in the upper reaches of the global energy industry.

There have been other boons. While offshore oil has still a way to go, the onshore sector is very much a meritocracy – as many young women with ability can testify. The industry has also instilled self-confidence in the young, encouraging many new entrepreneurs to step out on their own. Morgan Goodlad returned to Shetland and saw his fellow islanders in a new light. Sandy Matheson finds the same change in the psyche of the people on his island of Lewis. John Burns of St Fergus and Mike Budge of Flotta are home-grown entrants who seized their opportunities. Murdo MacIver, who left school in Stornoway at sixteen, acknowledges he wouldn't be where he is – director of a growing service company – if it hadn't been for Lewis Offshore. There are so many other nascent benefits: the industry has breathed new life into higher education; encouraged indigent services to grow and to flourish; and, unexpectedly, brought about a revival in the varied cultures of the oil communities. It is almost as if the new influences have compelled the natives to better appreciate what they have.

Even with the brutal commercial practice of 'downsizing' and encouraged 'natural wastage' there is still sufficient employment to soak up the casualties, as the low unemployment figures for Aberdeen and Aberdeenshire testify. With the vastly inflated oil price, interest has rekindled in both the partially exploited assets in the North Sea and the prospect of finding new ones. Encouragingly many of the majors are strengthening their roots by expanding their presence at the heart of the Scottish oil and gas industry, and there has been a general regrouping of companies, old and new, in an exchange of assets in preparation for a new era. Few people now talk about the wholesale departure of the oilmen in the short term, but rather in multiples of decades, although such views should always be tempered – as previous recessions have shown – with the realisation that the industry carries the blight of unpredictability.

At the time of writing, for example, the industry is apparently struggling to come to terms with a 'windfall' imposition by the chancellor of the exchequer. He has doubled the supplementary tax on oil-company profits, which have soared to record levels from the benefits of an inflated crude oil price hovering at a peak of $70 a barrel; Shell's returns, in 2005 at £12.93 billion, were the highest ever for a British company and BP were not far behind. On the strength of this, the outraged industry, united in concern at the effect of the tax on further investment in the North Sea, is lobbying furiously for a promise the levy will be withdrawn in the event the oil price should fall. The history of the UK province is marked by frequent titanic struggles between the oilmen and the Treasury – the first was in 1974 when the early operators

Plate 136.

Rising above the centre of the city of Aberdeen, the distinctive UK headquarters of the oil operators, Talisman Energy – leader of the ambitious new companies, who may represent the best hope for the longer term future of the North Sea industry.

(*Allan Montgomery*)

warned they would be unable to secure bank loans for development if the Petroleum Revenue Tax was set too high. It was a game of bluff then and it remains to be seen, more than thirty years later, whether or not this is another round of the same game. The answer may be found in an announcement, at the time of writing, that the industry was preparing to invest £1 billion on top of the £10 billion already spent in 2005–06, creating a further 15,000 jobs.

Questions, however, remain and will probably never be answered: why is there still such a minority representation of major Scottish and UK companies and only a few prominent investors – even now? Could the Government have done more to protect and save the oil fabrication yards? Was there ever a time when Aberdeen – like Shetland and Orkney – could have wrung more direct financial concessions from the industry? Gregarious creatures that they are, the so-called 'critical mass' of oil companies was never going anywhere else but the Granite City.

Sir Ian Wood – the brilliant Aberdonian who more than any other seized the moment and the day – furnished what could stand as an epitaph for the North Sea oil and gas industry when he said of his success, 'It's not for my sons, but for their sons. That is the generation which could well be saying, "These guys had a fantastic opportunity. They inherited a potential economy and they had a wonderful golden age. What have they passed on to us?"'